ISBN 978-1-331-61595-8
PIBN 10213309

1 MONTH OF
FREE
READING

at
www.ForgottenBooks.com

By purchasing this book you are
eligible for one month membership to
ForgottenBooks.com, giving you
unlimited access to our entire
collection of over 700,000 titles via
our web site and mobile apps.

To claim your free month visit:

www.forgottenbooks.com/free213309

English
Français
Deutsche
Italiano
Español
Português

www.forgottenbooks.com

Mythology Photography **Fiction**
Fishing Christianity **Art** Cooking
Essays Buddhism Freemasonry
Medicine **Biology** Music **Ancient**
Egypt Evolution Carpentry Physics
Dance Geology **Mathematics** Fitness
Shakespeare **Folklore** Yoga Marketing
Confidence Immortality Biographies
Poetry **Psychology** Witchcraft
Electronics Chemistry History **Law**
Accounting **Philosophy** Anthropology
Alchemy Drama Quantum Mechanics
Atheism Sexual Health **Ancient History**
Entrepreneurship Languages Sport
Paleontology Needlework Islam
Metaphysics Investment Archaeology
Parenting Statistics Criminology
Motivational

THE LIFE

OF

GRISH CHUNDER GHOSE

THE FOUNDER AND FIRST EDITOR

OF

"THE HINDOO PATRIOT" AND "THE BENGALEE,"

BY

ONE WHO KNEW HIM.

EDITED BY

HIS GRANDSON

MANMATHANATH GHOSH, M.A,

CALCUTTA :

R. CAMBRAY & CO.,

6 Hastings Street.

1911.

CALCUTTA :
PRINTED BY D. C. KERR, at the "VALMIKI PRESS," 9, Gopee Mohun Bose's Lane, Bowbazar.

PREFACE.

———o———

WE had originally intended to place before the Public along with this Memoir some specimens of the writings of Grish Chunder Ghose. But the unexpected length of time taken by the printer in passing these pages through the press having caused a great deal of disappointment to some revered friends who personally knew and admired the subject of this Memoir and are therefore naturally anxious to see the work in print in their lifetime, we have been obliged to give up our original plan and to publish this work by itself. The specimens of writings collected by us have in the meanwhile accumulated to such an extent that they are expected to cover some six or eight hundred pages, the printing of which may take up a couple of years. We hope, however, to expedite the work and to present the public with a goodly volume of selected writings in the course of next year. We trust the present work will be received by the Public with such favour as may warm us to our self-imposed labour of love.

96, SHAMBAZAR STREET,
Calcutta, January 1, 1911.

THE EDITOR.

CONTENTS.

Chap.   Page.

I.   Introduction   ...   1

II.   Birth and Parentage   11

III. Boyhood and School-life   24

IV.   Shib Chunder Deb   37

V.   Official Career   65

VI.   Early Journalism—The Bengal Recorder—The Hindoo
      Patriot—The Calcutta Monthly Review   77

VII. Letters   90

VIII. Connection with Literary and Political Associations—
      The British Indian Association—The Dalhousie
      Institute—The Bethune Society   97

IX.   Later Journalism—The Mookerjee's Magazine and
      The Bengalee.   Trip to Benares   ...   106

X.   Troubles at home   114

XI.   Bellore.   The Canning Institute, Howrah   119

XII. Last days—The Bengal Social Science Association—
      The Ooterparah Hitakari Sabha—Lecture on the
      Life of Ramdoolal Dey—Death   ...   133

XIII. Traits of character—Conduct in Private Life—Views
      on Religion and Social Reform   149

XIV. Personal appearance and habits—Style of writing—
      Memorial Meetings—ultimate fate of *the Bengalee*   165

APPENDIX.

A. Grish's Letters   177
B. Memorial Notices, &c.   204
C. Principal Lobb's Letters to Grish   227

—:o:—

LIST OF ILLUSTRATIONS.

GRISH CHUNDER GHOSE,

From an oil-painting,

Frontispiece.

RAI DINA NATH GHOSE BAHADOOR,

From a photo by Bourne and Shepherd,

To face page 25.

SHIB CHUNDER DEB,

From a photo by The Bengal Photographers,

To face page 37.

GRISH CHUNDER GHOSE,

From a Daguerreotype,

To face page 77.

GRISH CHUNDER GHOSE.

KUNTALINE PRESS, CALCUTTA.

THE

LIFE OF GRISH CHUNDER GHOSE.

CHAPTER I.

INTRODUCTION.

DR. JOHNSON once remarked to Sir Joshua Reynolds, " If a man does not make new acquaintance as he advances through life, he will soon find himself left alone. He should keep his friendship *in constant repair.*" This pithy observation of the sage of Lichfield applies with peculiar force to the literary fame of a clever journalist. It is true that all literary fame is more or less mutable. Many a luminary that is classed as a star of the first or second magnitude in the catalogue of one generation, is assigned a much lower magnitude—or perhaps no magnitude at all—in the catalogues of succeeding generations. But the fluctuations of literary reputation are in no case more signally conspicuous than in that of the brilliant and successful journalist; and the reason for this is not far to seek. The scholar or the thinker, who writes for all time and achieves results of a more solid and abiding nature, has not unfrequently to look to posterity for the due recognition of his labours; for, as Landor happily puts it, " No man can measure a great man but upon his bier." The journalist, on the other hand, deals mainly with the burning topics of the day in a brilliant and dashing style ; and as his writings are addressed to his contemporaries, he necessarily looms larger in their eyes than the solitary thinker who dwells more or less apart from his fellows, content with "beholding the bright countenance of Truth in the quiet and still air of delightful studies." It is, however, the old story of the choice offered to Achilles between fame and length of life. The journalist has to pay dearly for his short-lived supremacy over the thinker. However successful he may be in his mission, his splendour is on the wane as soon as his career is closed. His productions, though they may rank as masterpieces of their kind, and be adorned with every literary grace, being generally limited to subjects of a local or temporary interest and being, moreover, scattered through the loose and bulky pages of ephemeral publications, gradually sink into the gulf of oblivion as his admiring contemporaries pass, one by one, into the Great Beyond, until, at last, the journalist himself is numbered with the great but nameless brotherhood of forgotten worthies. Quite otherwise is the fate of a successful author—one, that is to say, who makes his mark in literature. He makes " new acquaintance," not only " as he advances through life " but long after he has ceased to breathe. His fame is thus kept " in constant repair." The author and the journalist have their appointed places and functions in the social organism ; and under ordinary cicumstances, we should no more complain about their unequal fates than we should complain why the cereal that supplies the staff of life, should be trampled under foot as soon as the annual harvest is gathered in, while those " green-robed senators of mighty woods " are allowed to flourish in immortal youth. But there is one aspect of the matter which brings sad thoughts to the mind. There is, at present, scarcely any country in the civilized world in which the press is not a potent factor. Although historically it is an institution of very recent growth, and is, therefore, not inaptly called the fourth estate, it yields to none of its sister estates in point of influence ; and the onward march of modern civilization tends all the more to accentuate this influence and make it paramount. There is, therefore, scarcely any field which possesses greater attraction for a man of light and leading who wishes to devote himself, heart and soul, to the service of his country, than the field of journalism. Thus we find the ranks of journalism in the West largely recruited from the flower of Western culture, and the instances are by no means rare in which a successful journalist also becomes a successful politician and "reads his history in a nation's eyes." Here, in India, how-ever, an intellectual giant who enters the lists of journalism can seldom hope to secure an honoured and conspicuous place in the councils of his country or a share in making its history. He has to sell the birth-right of his genius for a mess of pottage, and after playing the rôle of a journalist during a brief period of meteoric splendour, he is utterly forgotten and consigned to the vile dust like a wayside flower. It is sad to contemplate that men of the intellec-tual calibre of Hurrish Chunder Mookerjee and Grish Chunder Ghose, those two sworn brothers in arms, who fought side by side in their country's cause during the dark days of the Indian Mutiny and the Indigo riots and whose mutual admiration and affection for each other ended only with their lives, were *Keranis* all their days—chained " to that dry drudgery at the desk's dead wood" for what in these days would, for men of their stamp, be considered a poor pittance. There is a note of tragic pathos in this irony of fate which cannot fail to strike the most thoughtless observer, and which doubtless led the scholarly Editor of the now defunct *Mookerjee's Magazine* to describe Grish Chunder, in a laudatory notice of his life which appeared in an early issue of the second series of that highly esteemed periodical, as " A great Indian but a geographical mistake."

The case of Grish Chunder Ghose furnishes indeed a striking illustration of the transitoriness of journalistic fame. Scarcely four decades ago, there was not a cultured household in Bengal or its sister provinces in which the name of the accomplished founder and editor of the *Bengalee* was not familiar as a household word. There was scarcely a public movement with which his name was not promi-nently associated ; for, Grish was not only a clever journalist, but, as the late Principal Lobb well described him at the public meeting held in his honour at the Town Hall of Calcutta on the 16th of November, 1869, he " was a man of high intellectual attainments and gifted with no common oratorical powers." That eminent historian of the *French in India*, the late Colonel G. B. Malleson, who edited the *Calcutta Review* during the period from 1864 to 1869, also bore testimony to Grish's rare gift of speech in the following terms, in a notice which appeared in that Review :—

"The lecturer, Baboo Grish Chunder Ghose, the Editor of one of the best native papers in this part of India, is well-known as a speaker for the brilliancy and fertility of his ideas which he gives utterance to with a fluency which many English speakers might well covet."

Mr. James Wilson, the first Editor of the *Indian Daily News*, who had never been personally acquainted with Grish Chunder, described him, in an obituary notice which appeared in that journal, as "one whose sympathies with, and earnest labours on behalf of, the masses of his countrymen, have been rarely equalled" and paid the following tribute to his character as a journalist :—

"It is no secret that we held him to be at the head of his contemporaries in the Anglo-Bengalee Press. Many of them were content to advocate sectional interests. He had wider sympathies and more noble aims, and we have often read his manly and trenchant articles with undisguised admiration. There was no pettishness or double-dealing in him : and with more men of his stamp, we should not despair of the future of India. It has not been difficult for some time past to trace in the *Bengalee* the master hand conspicuous by its absence. There are many men left amongst his countrymen who are far more pretentious; but we fear there are not many more able or more conscientious than Grish Chunder Ghose. He may well be deplored by his freinds, for it will be long ere they find a successor to fill his place."

Grish Chunder was a staunch and uncompromising champion of the class that wages

"The holy wars that have no truce
' Twixt seed and harvest time."

At a meeting of the Canning Institute, Howrah, held on the 29th of November, 1869, that eminent friend of the Bengal Ryot, the late Revd. James Long, in supporting a resolution to record the meeting's deep sense of the loss sustained by the death of their late Vice-President, Baboo Grish Chunder Ghose, is reported to have said "that he knew the Baboo well, and the great point he admired in him was, his breadth of view, his sympathy for all classes of his countrymen, and more especially the Ryot of Bengal. For him he felt strongly : he knew his debased social condition, and he used his journal, the *Bengalee*, as a medium for bringing the subject to public notice. Any one that read that journal would remember those various pointed and spirit-stirring articles he wrote on the subject, and he thought it would be only a just tribute to the memory of the deceased, were they collected and brought out in the form of a pamphlet. There is unhappily in Bengal a wide gulf between the educated classes and the masses ; between the zemindar and the ryot. Grish Chunder aimed at bridging that gulf, and while the zemindar enjoyed the benefits of the permanent settlement, he wished that permanent settlement should be made with the ryot also. His desire in fact was to elevate the ryot without levelling the zemindar. * * * "

No wonder, then, that the politics of the *Bengalee* often clashed with those of the *Hindoo Patriot*, the avowed organ of the landed aristocracy. In a long obituary notice which appeared in the latter paper, its able editor, the late Rai Kristo Das Pal, while finding fault with the politics of Grish Chunder, had, however, the candour to eulogise his marvellous diction and eloquence in the following strain :—

" Grish Chunder's *forte* lay in descriptive and sensational writing, brilliant, dashing, witty and sometimes humorous, falling on his victims like a sledge-hammer,—or to be more precise—with the force of 84-pounder. During the Mutinies, he chiefly wrote for this paper those scathing and crushing articles against the Volunteers which provoked the vengeance of these mighty sons of Mars upon the devoted head of the Editor. Grish Chunder was never strong in practical politics, but in his own line he was unrivalled. His power of word-painting, of clothing the commonest ideas in gorgeous and glittering costume, radiant with flashes of wit and humour and occasionally of originality, was equally conspicuous in the pages of the *Calcutta Monthly Review* and the *Bengalee*, of which he was the founder and Editor. Latterly, he took to public speaking, and the same qualities which distinguished his writings also distinguished his speeches. As a speaker, he first attracted notice in the Hall of the Dalhousie Institute, when it resounded with the eloquence of Dr. Duff and Sir Mordaunt Wells. He was also a public lecturer ; and his lecture on the life of Ram Doolal Dey, though over-coloured on many points, is a most favourable specimen of his style and spirit."

The late Sir John Budd Phear, Chief Justice of Ceylon, who was eminent no less for his mathematical than for his legal attainments, and who was a Judge of the High Court here, when he was invited to attend the Town Hall meeting in honour of Grish Chunder's memory, remarked as follows, in a letter expressing regret at his inability to attend that meeting :— " I do not feel sure that there has not been manifest among us lately a disposition to render public testimonials too common : but I have certainly known no one whose services more thoroughly deserved recognition at the hands of his countrymen than do those of the late Baboo Grish Chunder Ghose. He was an able, conscientious worker in the cause of social reform, independent in spirit and earnest of purpose. Bengal has too few citizens of this sort and can ill spare one in the prime of life."

That distinguished historian and champion of the aspirations of "New India," Mr. (now Sir Henry) Cotton, in the course of an address delivered by him, when presiding on the occasion of the fifty fourth Distribution of Prizes, held at the Oriental Seminary, early in 1885, named three of the most distinguished alumni of the Seminary, and after speaking of Justice Sambhoo Nath Pundit and Rai Kristo Das Pal, is reported to have spoken as follows of Grish Chunder :—

" A third great name—a great name, because the name of a great man, although possibly to some of those present it might be less familiar than it should be,—was that of the late Baboo Grish Chunder Ghose, who had been a student of this institution, and Mr. Cotton belived, closely connected with it through the greater portion of his life. Although only a subordinate in a Government office, he had been a man of exceptional ability : and had he lived in India at any other time than the present, he would undoubtedly have attained the very highest rank."

It is, however, useless to multiply the tributes, paid to the departed worth of Grish Chunder. A glance at the names, given below, of the noblemen and gentlemen who formed the Grish Memorial Committee, will show at once the esteem in which Grish was held by all classes of the community, European as well as Native ·—

     Raja Kali Krishna Bahadur
      „   Komul Krishna
      „   Narendra Krishna

Raja Rajendra Narain Deb
Hon'ble Justice Dwarka Nath Mitter
Babu Digumber Mitter
  ,,   Peary Chand Mitter
Moulvie Abdool Lateef Khan Bahadur
Kumar Harendra Krishna Bahadur
S Lobb, Esq., M.A.
Major A. E. Osborn
Revd. J. Long
J. B. Roberts, Esq.
James Wilson, Esq.
James Mackenzie, Esq.
Baboo Bijoy Kissen Mookerji
  ,,   Doorga Churn Law
W. C. Bonnerjee, Esq., Barrister-at-Law
Baboo Hurray Kristo Auddy
  ,,   Obhoy Churn Goho
  ,,   Peary Mohun Banerji
  ,,   Digumber Biswas
  ,,   Ram Chunder Mitter
  ,,   Rajendra Lala Mitra
  ,,   Keshub Chunder Sen
  ,,   Tara Prosad Chatterji
  ,,   Anuud Nundun Tagore
  ,,   Cally Churn Shome
  ,,   Kristo Das Pal
  ,,   Kannye Lall Dey
  ,,   Sree Kissen Gangooly
  ,,   Issur Chunder Nundi
  ,,   Romanath Laha
  ,,   Koylas Chunder Bose ⎫ Members & Joint
  ,,   Becharam Chatterjee ⎭ ·Secretaries.

We would refer once again to the article in the *Hindoo Patriot* which noticed the death of Grish Chunder, and quote its opening paragraph which ran as follows :—

" There is a blight upon Bengal. Its best men are falling under the fell scythe of Death like so many blades of grass. Beginning with Raja Issur Chunder Sing, we have, within the last eight years, lost such foremost men, each a host in himself, as Baboo Hurrish Chunder Mookerjee, Baboo Roma Persad Roy, Raja Pertap Chunder Sing, Raja Sir Radha Kant Bahadur, the Hon'ble Sumbhoo Nauth Pundit, Baboo Ram Gopal Ghose, the Hon'ble Prosunno Coomar Tagore, Baboo Huru Chunder Ghose, Raja Sutt Shurn Ghosal, and lastly Baboo Grish Chunder Ghose. Whether in intellectual attainments, legal knowledge, judicial talents, practical ability, social influence, public spirit, princely munificence, or devoted patriotism, the great departed we have named above, were each in his own way equally conspicuous, and it is sad to contemplate how few there are among the rising generation fit to take their place."

Three of the ten names on this illustrious death-roll, *viz.*, those of Hurrish Chunder Mookerjee, Ramgopal Ghose and Grish Chunder Ghose, who died in the years 1861, 1868 and 1869, respectively, were, in the seventies and early eighties, always linked together and cited as the names of three devoted partiots. Those of our readers who had the pleasure of witnessing on the boards of the National Theatre— the first *public* Theatre opened in Calcutta in December, 1872, under native auspices—a performance of that once popular play or masque, the *Bhárat-Mátá*, will recall the thrill which ran through the electrified audience, when *Bharat Mata*, casting a mournful and pitying glance at her lethargic sons, who all lay scattered on the stage like so many dead bodies, invoked the names of her noble and departed sons, Hurrish, Grish and Ram Gopal—" কোথায় হরিশ? কোথায় গিরিশ? কোথায় রামগোপাল? "—in the most piercing and heart-rending accents of anguish and despair.

But the generation that knew Grish *personally*, has, since that time, become well nigh extinct. The generation that knew him *by repute* is also disappearing apace, and we doubt whether the rising generation is acquainted even with his name. We question the wisdom of his Memorial Committee's decision to found a scholarship in his name in the Seminary where he was educated. His memory would have been, we think, perpetuated far more suitably and effectually, had the memorial fund been handed over to the University of Calcutta in view to the institution of a gold medal, bearing his name, to be awarded annually for the best English essay on some suitable subject, to be

selected by the University authorities. A good biography of Grish
Chunder, written by one who enjoyed the privilege of intimate personal acquaintance with him, would, however, have best preserved his
memory. An article in the *Bengalee* of the 28th of September, 1869,
which recorded the death of Grish Chunder, contained the following
paragraph on this head :—

" A biography of Grish Chunder Ghose will be a fitting memorial
of him, and we trust the task will be taken in hand by some one of
his numerous friends, well acquainted with his life. For ourselves and
for the present purpose, we can only give a brief summary."

The article in question was, we believe, penned by the late
Baboo Koylas Chunder Bose, the accomplished Secretary through a
long series of years to the now defunct Bethune Society. As Baboo
Koylas Chunder intimately knew Grish Chunder from his boyhood
and survived him by several years, and as, moreover, he was himself
a man of considerable literary culture and journalistic experience, it
is a matter of deep regret that he did not undertake the task of
writing the biography of his life-long friend, for which no man was so
eminently fitted in every respect. It was at Grish's suggestion that
he delivered an admirable lecture on the life of Ram Gopal Ghose in
the Hall of the Hooghly College.

The late Baboo Sambhoo Chunder Mookerjee, the founder and
Editor of the *Reis and Rayvet*, who was a great admirer of Grish
Chunder, and was personally acquainted with him during the last ten
years of the latter's life, was, we believe, engaged, shortly before his
death in 1894, in writing an account of Grish Chunder's life and
writings, which, however, never saw the light. By rare good fortune,
Sambhoo Chunder himself has found an excellent biographer in
Mr. Skrine, a distinguished Bengal Civilian. Kristo Das Pal has also
been scarcely less fortunate in his biographer, the late Mr. N. N.
Ghose.

But no biography, worth the name, has yet been published, of
Hurrish Chunder Mookerjee, the man who, during his short but eventful career as a journalist, did his country greater service than any other
journalist before him or since. No man was better qualified to write
the biography of Hurrish than his *alter ego*, Grish. The only contribution, however on that interesting subject, which he has left us, is an

unfinished sketch, published in the fifth number of *Mookerjee's Maga-zine* (first series). We distinctly remember having seen the opening chapter of a detailed life of Hurrish which was begun by Grish in his happiest style, but which unfortunately was never completed. The precious fragment was lent by Grish to a cousin of his, who never thought of returning it to him. So the life of Hurrish by Grish even-tually came to be one of the many things to which we apply what Whittier calls " the saddest of all sad words of tongue or pen,"—" It might have been." But it is idle to indulge in such vain regrets. It might have been a very good thing had the biography of Grish Chunder been written by one of his intimate friends, or, at any rate, had many of them been alive now and in a condition to help us. It might have been a very good thing, had we been able to recover any of the manuscripts which he lent to friends who never returned them. It might have also been a very good thing, had we been able to collect more than a very insignificant fraction of his published writ-ings, the rest having been lost beyond redemption with the files of the periodicals in which they appeared. But as no good fairy is likely to come and help us in rescuing from oblivion a noble name which is in imminent danger of perishing for ever, we have ventured to appear before the reading public, with all these imperfections on our head, and humbly hope that our readers will view, with an indulgent eye, our halting efforts to save from the general wreck what little we can, remembering the wise words of Ruskin, " Better a crutch than a lost limb."

CHAPTER II.

———:◡◠:———

BIRTH AND PARENTAGE.

THE subject of this brief memoir was born in the metropolis of British India, on Saturday, the 15th Assar of the Bengalee year, 1236, corresponding to the 27th June of the year of grace, 1829, memorable as the year in which the *Sati* rite was abolished by Lord William Bentinck and the Brahmo Samaj was established by Raja Ram Mohun Roy.

His grand-father, Kasi Nath Ghose, who was a scion of an old and respectable family of *Koolin Kayasthas* which settled long ago at Mansapota, a village in the Nuddea District not very far from Chogdah, a station on the Eastern Bengal State Railway, appears to have been the first member of his family who finally left the old village homestead and settled in Calcutta towards the latter end of the eighteenth century. The following account of Kasi Nath and his ancestors is given in the *Modern History of the Indian Chiefs, Rajas, Zamindars &c.*, Part II, by Babu Loke Nath Ghose :—

" *Kasi Nath Ghose's Family, Simla.*

We trace the history of this old, and no less respectable family, from Sri Krishna Ghose, who was renowned for his proficiency in the Persian language. He was also a good Bengali scholar.

His son Ram Dev Ghose was employed as Baxi or Pay Master in the Krishnagar Raj family. Ram Dev had acquired some wealth, which he left to his only son Ram Lochan Ghose.

Ram Lochan gave a liberal education to his son Kasi Nath Ghose who was one of the most influential members of the then Hindu community of Calcutta.

When Kali Prosad Datta, a descendant of Ram Dulal's patron the well known Madan Mohan Datta, was excommunicated by his friends and relations for his indulgence in forbidden meats and drinks and in forbidden associations, Kasi Nath most warmly co-operated with Ram Dulal Dey to restore Kali Prosad to caste by holding a feast called *Shamannaya,* on which occasion almost all the best *Koolin*

Kayasthas, respectable *Brahmans* and other men of social weight were present. The *Shamannaya* was a complete success and Kali Prosad was restored to caste. In this *Shamannaya*, Ram Dulal had spent two lakhs of Rupees, and his friend Kasi Nath, about Rs. 30,000, for the purpose of rescuing a fellow man from infamy.

Kasi Nath was an assistant Banian to the very respectable firm of Messrs. Fairlie Fergusson & Co., Calcutta. He was highly esteemed and respected by several distinguished European merchants, and had some influence over those native Babus, who, in his time, carried on mercantile business. He had earned much wealth; but his private charities were so numerous that he spent the greater portion of it in this creditable way. *   *   *   *   *   *   *   "

The official *Census Report, 1901, Vol. VII, Part I*, compiled by Mr. A. K. Roy, contains the following brief notice of Kasi Nath Ghose in connection with the lane in Calcutta which still bears his name :—

"*Kashee Ghose's Lane*—Kashee Ghose, son of Ram Deva Ghose, Dewan of the Nadia Raj, was Assistant Banian to Messrs. Fairlie Fergusson & Co., and made a large fortune."

It will be seen that there is a discrepancy between the two accounts quoted above, as regards Ram Dev's relation to Kasi Nath. In Baboo Loke Nath's book, Ram Dev is stated to have been the father of Ram Lochan and grand-father of Kasi Nath, while in Mr. Roy's report he is stated to have been the father of Kasi Nath. According to family tradition, however, Kasi Nath was the son of Ram Lakshman (not Ram Lochan) who was the son of Ram Ram and grand-son of Ram Dev, from whom Kasi Nath was thus the fourth in descent. But we have no desire to lose ourselves in the " misty land of pedigree-manufacturers." Without pretending, therefore, to settle the discrepancies pointed out above, we proceed to state briefly what little we know about Kasi Nath himself.

Kasi Nath died in January, 1849, at about the age of eighty-five, so that the date of his birth may safely be placed somewhere about the year 1763, *i.e.*, a year or two before the acquisition by the English, in 1765, of the Dewani of Bengal, Behar and Orissa. His friend and patron, Ram Doolal Dey, who died at the age of seventy-three on the

1st April, 1825, was, therefore, his senior by some ten years. Nothing definite is known about his early education. But as he was a good accountant and had to keep the vernacular accounts of the gigantic firm in which he was employed, assisted by a large body of mohurirs who worked under his immediate supervision, he must have received a good education according to the standard then in vogue, *i.e.*, in Bengalee and Persian. He must also have picked up, in the course of business, a tolerably fair knowledge of English, as he used to read daily the *Bengal Hurkaru*, without the aid of spectacles, even when he was on the shady side of eighty. That his capacity for business was of no mean order, may well be inferred not only from his success in amassing a fortune of some eight or ten lacs, but also from the fact that so thorough a man of business as Ram Doolal had him for his chief assistant and right-hand man at Fairlie Fergusson & Co's. From an examination of some very old title-deeds relating to Kasi Nath's family dwelling-house in Calcutta, we find that the plot of ground on which the house was originally built, measuring 3¾ cottas, had been purchased by him only for Rs. 120/- in November, 1788 ; which shews that he achieved success in life when he was barely twenty-five years old ; also that land in Calcutta has since then risen to at least thirty times the value it then had. The documents in question also shew that Kasi Nath steadily prospered during a period of at least forty years ; for, we find him making continual additions to the original tenement by acquiring from time to time contiguous lands or buildings, the last acquisition for the purpose appearing to to have been made in December 1826, when a plot of ground measuring 4¼ cottahs, was purchased for Rs. 1100/-

Thus, the modest one-storied dwelling-house, covering scarcely more than three cottahs, gradually assumed palatial proportions, with lofty and spacious halls, roomy parlours, long corridors, extensive courtyards and grand gateways. The house, which, with its appurtenances (including two temples of Shiva and a flower garden attached thereto), finally occupied an area of more than two bighas, has since been partitioned into several houses in Kasi Ghose's Lane, a considerable portion of the original premises having also been sliced off to form a part of the wide street now known as Beadon Street. The soul of Kasi Nath was, however, loftier, and his heart broader, than the halls with which he adorned his residence.

The extract we have already given from the *Modern History of the Indian Chiefs, Rajas, Zamindars, &c.*, describes how Kasi Nath spent about Rs. 30,000/- to rescue a fallen fellow creature from infamy. We quote below an instance of his romantic integrity as related by his gifted grand-son :—

"There were giants indeed in those days! Ram Doolal drew around him—and he had the tact to find them out—native gentlemen endowed with a similar reverence for truth to himself. His chief assistant and right-hand man at Fairlie Fergusson & Co's, Cossynauth Ghose, had once purchased a Government lottery ticket. A prize of 50,000 rupees was declared upon it. Ram Doolal was the first to hear of this prize. He hurried from the lottery office to communicate to his friend the news of his good fortune. As he entered the room in Fairlie Fergusson & Co's office, where Cossynauth, surrounded by native mohurirs, was performing his work, he joyfully announced that Cossynauth's ticket had just won a prize of 50,000 rupees. Congratulating his friend, he asked him how he intended to dispose of this money. That friend coolly replied that the money was not *all* his. Every one in the room stared at this answer. But Cossynauth, fixing his large lustrous eyes upon three of the mohurirs who sat next to him, declared that these had each a fourth share in the prize. The persons pointed out were amazed,—Ram Doolal was confounded. The mohurirs knew nothing about the lottery ticket. Cossynauth had purchased it himself and paid for it; but he had debited the men in his private account-book with a fourth part each of the price of the ticket. The men were his debtors. They knew not until this moment that they were his debtors. Perhaps, if the lottery ticket had carried a blank instead of a prize, the debts would have been cancelled without their ever knowing that they were his debtors. Cossynauth had put in the names of the men in the simple, superstitious belief that if his luck was not sufficient, that of any of these men might possibly secure a prize ; and now that a prize was within his grasp, he disdained to back out of his intention, however secretly formed or kept, though he lost about 40,000 rupees by his romantic folly, as Ram Doolal characterised the affair—Ram Doolal who, good and great as he was himself, could not help feeling awed by the austere integrity of his friend. By such men was Ram Doolal constantly surrounded,—men whose long lives presented one unbroken picture of nobility of thought, worked out by nobility of action. These were our forefathers, and how small and degenerate we look beside them with our ever-lasting tattle of principle and morality, yet perpetual struggle to over-reach our fellows !"

Verily did Kasi Nath's long life present " one unbroken picture of nobility of thought, worked out by nobility of action." At the height of his prosperity his habits were as simple and inexpensive as when, during the last fifteen years or so of his long and noble life, it was his sad fate to outlive his fortune. The sole luxury in which he indulged in his palmiest days was "the luxury of doing good." Though he was pre-eminently the architect of his own fortune, he always looked upon himself as simply holding it in trust for the benefit of the needy and the helpless. His poor relations—however flimsy the grounds on which they might claim kindred with him—always had their claims allowed. He used to take his daily meals in the company of some fifty of such poor relations or no-relations, many of whom he had himself provided with employment at Fairlie Fergusson & Co's. These meals, which were of the simplest description, used to be cooked by his six daughters-in-law, by rotation,—for in those days no respectable Hindu householder cared to partake of " bought food.'' i.e., food prepared by a paid cook,—and were served out alike to the master of the house and to his hangers-on, without distinction or difference. Kasi Nath's private charities were carried out with such secrecy that his left hand scarcely knew what was done by his right hand. Many of his relations had their wants supplied by him in this silent and unostentatious manner. Many of his well-to-do relations and friends were also accommodated by him with loans bearing no interest, when they fell into temporary distress. We would give only one instance out of many of this kind. Hearing one day that the father-in-law of his fourth son had been incarcerated in the debtor's prison at the instance of a creditor whom he owed some eight thousand rupees, he at once discharged the debt and got the unfortunate man released from prison. We blush to relate that when, many years afterwards, Kasi Nath's own fortune fell to a low ebb, and he asked the man whom he had thus befriended, and who was then in affluent circumstances, to pay back the amount he had advanced gratuitously, the ungrateful wretch refused to pay a pice. Although Kasi Nath's personal habits were, as we have already said, very simple and inexpensive, his devoted piety led him to celebrate all the year round the festivals enjoined by the Hindu religion, more especially the *Doorga-poojah* and the *Jhoolan Jattra*, on the most lavish and magnificent scale. Enormous sums were spent on the celebration of the two principal festivals we have named. The offerings made to the gods (*Naivedyas*) consisting of rice, sugar, fruits &c., heaped up in the form of huge cones on brass plates of gigantic dimensions, were distributed amongst a large number of Brahmins. Large quantities of sweetmeats of the choicest descriptions were manufactured in a suite of rooms on the groundfloor of the house specially set apart for the purpose. Besides the feasts given on these occasions, *Jattras* and other musical entertainments were held for the delectation of the assembled guests. But Kasi Nath cared more for the former than for the latter. It is related that on one occassion he was so much annoyed with his sons for having arranged with the famous *Kabi-wallah* Bhola Moira to give a performance on the opening night of the Doorga Poojah for the extravagant sum of seven hundred rupees, that he retired to his bed, in disgust, at an early hour of the night in question. Later on, however, one of his sons prevailed upon him, after a good deal of coaxing, to grace the festive hall with his presence. The *Kabi-wallah*, soon after commenced singing, in his happiest style, an *Agamani* song, *i.e.,* a song describing the annual advent of the goddess Doorga in the home of her father—the Mountain-king Himalaya. Kasi Nath, after fidgeting about for some time with pretended indifference, could not resist this appeal to his deep devotional feeling. He burst into tears and exclaimed in an ecstasy of enthusiasm that this one song alone was well worth the seven hundred rupees! This little incident shews what stuff the man was made of.

Like Ram Doolal, Kasi Nath always rode to office in a palkee, borne on the broad shoulders of six stalwart Rawani Kahars, who used to hew wood, draw water and do all manner of household drudgery when not actually engaged in conveying their master to and from office. One day, the sirdar bearer, Golka by name, came back from office at noon with the mournful intelligence that his master had lost thirty thousand rupees by a certain transaction. This completely upset the sons of Kasi Nath, who were then busily engaged in decorating the house, for the approaching Jhoolan festival, with chandeliers, wall-shades, pictures and the like. They stopped work at once and awaited in doleful silence their father's return from office. In the evening Kasi Nath came home and the first thing that he noticed was the unfinished decorations. He went up to his sons and enquired what made them look so glum. On their explaining the matter to him, he quietly remarked, with a smile, that all commercial speculation had its ups and downs, and that a loss of thirty thousand rupees should not make the difference of a whit in his wonted style of celebrating the Jhoolan festival.

On another occasion, some of his sons called at his office and begged hard of him to be given some employment, as they were ashamed of sitting idle at home while their old father was working so hard for them. Casting upon them a benign look of ineffable affection, Kasi Nath bade them hurry home and never again think of facing the troubles of the work-a-day world. It was with the object, he said, of saving his sons from the toil and turmoil of life, that he himself was working so hard, and Providence had already blest him with a fortune which would enable him to leave at least a lac of rupees to each of his six sons. However much we may condemn the lamentable want of worldly wisdom and forethought betrayed by this touching episode, we cannot help sympathising with the romantic affection which dictated this foolish line of conduct.

His retirement from business, shortly after his friend and patron Ram Doolal's demise, some unexpected and heavy losses that he sustained late in life, his lavish expenditure on Poojahs, and his large charities, all combined to swallow up his accumulated savings, and the evening of his life was begirt with the darkest shades. One by one he had to part with his splendid gardens and other immovable property—those gardens which had at one time enabled him to distribute cart-loads of mangoes and other delicious fruits amongst his neighbours and friends. His valuables also gradually took wing, as the meshes of poverty pressed closer and closer around the broken-down millionaire. The only property that he left behind him at the time of his death, was his palatial residence.

3.

"Before his death," remarks his grand-son Khetter Chunder Ghose in his autobiography, "the old gentleman had the satisfaction of seeing that several of his grand-sons had, by means of their Eng. lish education, entered either Government or Mercantile services, and were likely in a few years to prosper in life and maintain the dignity of the family, together with the religious institutions which he had founded during his own days of good fortune and prosperity. His *mania* for religious ceremonies was, however, so great, and not only *his own mania,* but that of his big sons also, that even the jewels of his daughters-in-law were sometimes pledged to provide for the enor. mously large expenses of the religious festivities, such as the Doorga Poojah, the Jhoolan Jatra, &c., which were celebrated with some *eclat* every year."

Kasi Nath's profound and unaffected piety was in evidence not only in Calcutta, but also in his ancestral village, where he excavated a large tank which was long known as "Kasi-sagar," and built near it a fine temple which he made over to the family of his *Guru* or spiritual guide, together with his share in the ancestral property. The tank, we believe, is still in existence.

Kasi Nath's humility was no less remarkable than his piety. While he was one of the foremost and most influential members of the Hindu community, he was one of the gentlest of men. His friend and patron Ram Doolal had the highest regard for him and always treated him as his equal, sending his sons to Kasi Nath's house (which communicated with his own by a private passage) to receive lessons in Persian from the same Moonshee who taught Kasi Nath's sons. But Kasi Nath had such an exquisitely delicate sense of his obligations to Ram Doolal that he made it a principle not to give the customary *Biday* or tip to servants who brought him presents from Ram Doolal's, lest it should be thought that he considered himself otherwise than as one of Ram Doolal's humblest dependants.

His holy horror of the oppression and cruelty which might be practised upon his tenants by his agents, prevented him from invest- ing his hoarded savings in the purchase of zemindaries, by which means his ultimate ruin might, perhaps, have been averted, or at any rate mitigated. But if prosperity failed to harden his heart, the sweetness of his temper was never soured by age or adversity. In his sear and yellow leaf days he used to roam about his house, panting for breath, but in full possession of all his faculties and with a sweet smile and an ever-ready word of endearment for every one who chanced to cross his path. One of his grand-sons used to relate, long after his death, how, finding old grandpa fidgeting one night for a smoke with his bubble-bubble, he offered to fill his *chillum* for him ; but the dear old gentleman insisted on filling it himself, not even allowing any of the few faithful domestics who stuck to him in adversity to be roused from their sleep, remarking that the poor fellows must not be deprived of their much-needed rest after the day's hard toil.

There is one little episode relating to this period of his life which we cannot resist the temptation of describing here. We have already quoted a passage from the autobiography of one of his grand-sons to show how, even after his good fortune had left him, the principal religious festivals were celebrated with some *eclat* every year. On one of these occasions, a *Jattra* or operatic performance was held, the subject of which was the assumption by the god Krishna of the disguise of a "foreign maid" in order to win back the love of his mistress Radha after a love-quarrel. When, in the course of the play, the lad who personated the part of Krishna sang out that he would stand on one side, dressed like a beggar-maid, "আমি দীন হীন কাঙালের বেশে এক পাশে দাঁড়ায়ে র'ব," our poor old Lear, who had been a passive listener all this while from behind a pillar, was so struck with the strange coincidence between his own plight and that of the god he adored, that he burst into a flood of tears. Who can say what conflicting emotions then struggled in the old man's heart for mastery ? Who can say that the analogy that struck him so powerfully did not bring resignation to his suffering and pious spirit and fill his clouded mind with light? "Out of the suffering cometh the grateful heart."

We close our sketchy and rambling account of Kasi Nath with the remark that even the last scene of his noble life was characteristic of the man. One evening in January 1849, his near relations and friends, who were all gathered round the bed on which he lay in a moribund condition in the biggest room in his house, apprehended that his end was fast approaching and might overtake him before " morn broad-ened on the borders of the dark." As it is the fondly-cherished wish of every orthodox Hindu to draw his last breath on the banks of the sacred river, Babu Promotho Nath Deb, better known as " Latu Babu," asked Kasi Nath, euphemistically, whether he would like to have a look at the holy Ganges. Realising at once the drift of the question put to him, Kasi Nath answered, in a low but clear voice, that his death, though near at hand, was not going to take place till the following day, and that he did not, therefore, wish to be taken to the river-side that evening and thereby put his near and dear ones to the great inconvenience of having to pass a long night at an exposed place in that inclement season. He was accordingly not taken to the river-side till the following morning. That very day he surrendered his soul to his Maker in the sacred stream, but not until his youngest son Gobin—who had been left at home on account of his idiocy, but who had to be sent for at Kasi Nath's pressing request —arrived and poured a handful of water into the mouth of his dying father, who looked his last look at the poor idiot.

Thus lived and died a great and good man who belonged to a type which is now no more to be seen. We have tried, however unsuccessfully, to pourtray the salient features of his character, because his grand-son Grish looked upon him as his " ideal knight" and inherited from him his unswerving rectitude, his unflinching devotion to truth, his intense domesticity, his profound sympathy for the poor and the helpless, his strong affection for his kith and kin, his unaffected humility, his guileless heart, his simplicity of habits, his sweetness of temper, his unselfishness, his love of lavish hospitality, and we are afraid we must add, his easy disposition and want of worldly forethought.

The father of Grish Chunder, Kasi Nath's second son Ramdhone, who did his level best to prop up his falling house and maintain its dignity and who succeeded for a time in his laudable efforts to arrest the hand of decay, presented in many respects a striking personality. His intelligence was far above the average, and it enabled him in some measure to remedy the defects of his early education. He was very fond of reading not only books written in his own vernacular, but also English books and periodicals. He was gentlemanly in his tastes and scrupulously neat and clean in his dress and general habits.

He loved to have every thing about him in apple-pie order. His small sitting room, which also did duty as his bed room, was very tidily, though plainly, furnished. After Kasi Nath's death, if a visitor of distinction happened to call at the house, he was invariably shewn into Ramdhone's parlour ; for, the courtly and polished manners of Ramdhone, his fine address, his shrewd sagacity and thorough knowledge of men and manners, his ready wit and sound sense eminently fitted him to do the honours of the house. It is a pity that he had never been bred to any business ; for, his strong common sense and rare tactfulness would have ensured him success in any line of business. Grish Chunder inherited from his father his strong common sense, ready wit and easy deportment in society. Ramdhone died at the age of sixty-seven in June 1867.

"A sweeter woman ne'er drew breath" than Grish Chunder's mother, who was a daughter of Atmaram Dutt, a scion of the well-known Dutt family of Hatkhola in Calcutta. Grish inherited from her, in full measure, an almost inexhaustible stock of patience, a most winsome amiability, and unsullied purity of character. The good lady died at the age of seventy on the 31st December, 1872.

Grish was the youngest of three brothers who were happily described by the late Rai Kristo Das Pal as a " literary triumvirate ;" for, they were all remarkable for their intellectual gifts and devotion to letters. The eldest, Khetter Chunder, who was born in January, 1824, was older than Grish by about six years. In point of scholarship he was superior to his younger brothers. He was the *Dux* or Captain of the Oriental Seminary in the days when that seminary successfully competed with its formidable rival, the Hindoo College, which then had for its Principal no less a man than Captain Richardson, the celebrated " D. L. R.," whose reading of Shakespeare evoked the unbounded admiration of so distinguished a critic as Lord Macaulay. As an instance in point, we quote the following from Khetter Chunder's autobiography :—" It was whilst in that school and in the seventeenth year of my age that I carried away a prize of five gold mohurs, which, together with three other prizes, was given by Babu Ram Gopal Ghose for proficiency in certain branches of learning, such as Indian History, Moral and Mental Philosophy, Essay-writing and Mathematics. It was a student of Dr. Duff's school who succeeded in carrying away a prize in the last mentioned branch, whilst I myself and a fellow student of mine, Bhobany Prosad Dutt, a member of the rich Dutt family of Nimtollah in Calcutta, carried away the other prizes, the young lads of the Hindu College having failed to pass in any of the branches for which they competed."

But Khetter Chunder's love of reading—which he retained throughout his long life—prevented him from undertaking any serious literary work, beyond taking at times an animated part in the debates of the Bethune Society and the Dalhousie Institute, or occassionally contributing to the columns of the *Bengal Recorder* and the *Hindoo Patriot* while those papers were edited by his brothers Sree Nath and Grish, respectively. He started in life as a school-master, but soon exchanged the school-master's ferule for the counter of a merchant's clerk. He ultimately entered the service of Government in June, 1853, as a clerk on Rs. 75 *p. m.* in the late Military Auditor General's office, where his brother Grish was then employed and had some influence. After attaining a maximum pay of Rs. 400 *p. m.*, he retired from the service in June, 1879, on a superannuation pension of about Rs. 200 *p. m.*, which he had enjoyed for nearly twenty-four years when he died in his eightieth year on the 4th March, 1903.

Sree Nath, who was older than Grish by a little over two years, was also educated at the Oriental Seminary, where, by his intelligence and assiduity, he became the favourite of his teachers and of the proprietor of the Seminary alike, and was awarded two gold medals for general proficiency.

After leaving school, he obtained employment as a clerk on Rs. 16 *p. m.* under captain Boothby, a ship-surveyor. His pay was subsequently increased to Rs. 32 *p. m.* ; but seeing no prospect of further increase, he resigned his post. He now started a weekly paper which he named the *Bengal Recorder*, and edited it, with the help of his brothers, from 1850 to 1852. We give this period, as we find it specified in a leading article in the *Reis and Rayyet* of the 14th March, 1903. We notice, however, that in the account given of Babu Haris Chandra Mukerji in Mr. Buckland's *Bengal under the Lieutenant Governors*, Vol. II, it is stated that "when the *Bengal Recorder* was brought out in 1849, he contributed several articles to it." In the absence of any files of the *Recorder*, we are unable to decide whether the paper was brought out in 1849 or 1850. We shall see later on how that paper became the stepping-stone to Sree Nath's admission to Government service and eventual appointment as a Deputy Collector in 1854. He was subsequently appointed Personal Assistant to the Commissioner of ˈRevenue Circuit, Presidency Division, and was in receipt of Rs. 600 *p. m.* in that capacity when he was appointed Vice-Chairman of the Corporation of Calcatta in July, 1875, on a salary of Rs. 1000 *p. m.* Failing health compelled him, however, a few years later, to vacate that appointment and retire on a special pension of Rs. 4000 a year in 1880. Nor did he long enjoy his well-earned pension ; he died at the age of sixty on the 29th September, 1886. As Sree Nath and Grish were nearly equal in age and had kindred tastes and pursuits, a close intimacy sprang up between the two brothers in their infancy which remained unaltered by marriage, long separation, or any other disturbing element short of death. The mutual good understanding and affection which existed between their wives knit the bonds of fraternal affection all the more firmly, till the two brothers became like two " consonant chords that shiver to one note."

Having given some account of Grish's grand-father, father, mother and brothers,—he never had a sister to share his affection—we should like to say a word or two about his uncle—Kasi Nath's eldest son Hurrish—before we proceed to describe his own happy childhood. Hurrish was a veritable specimen of the " ne'er-do-weel" type of men. He could never persuade himself to take a serious view of life or realise its manifold duties and responsibilities. He possessed, how-ever, an infinite fund of humour and affection, and managed to rollick through his part in life—which was an unusually long one—in the right happy-go-lucky style. Commiserating his childless condition, Kasi Nath induced Ramdhone to allow his youngest son to be adopted by Hurrish. Although Ramdhone's jealousy would never allow Grish to address his uncle by any other title, he always address-ed his aunt as his "eldest mother," and she proved to him indeed a second mother. Grish thus enjoyed the privilege of making a dual use of that sweetest of all monosyllables and the first that is ever lisped by infant lips—" Ma."

CHAPTER III.

BOYHOOD AND SCHOOL-LIFE.

Petted by his uncle and aunty, Grish Chunder passed a very happy childhood, though he had not been born with a silver spoon in his mouth and though the reduced circumstances of his grand-father did not allow of his being nursed in the lap of luxury. As a child he was remarkable for the same sweet temper and winning ways which distinguished him in after-life. His chief amusement seems to have consisted in making idols of clay and celebrating their worship some-what after the manner of his grand-father, though, of course, on a liliputian scale. His brother, Sree Nath, who invariably officiated as priest on these occasions, used to partake of the sweets and fruits offered to the gods, by virtue of his holy office. Grish had a Fidus Achates or faithful henchman in the person of his cousin Kali-prosonno Bose, the only son of Kasi Nath's widowed daughter. Kali Prosonno always followed Grish like his shadow, but would sometimes leave him in a pique and try to ingratiate himself with Sree Nath. As, however, Sree Nath was Grish's permanent ally and was bound by treaty not to enter into an alliance with a power at war with Grish, Grish would peremptorily ask Sree Nath not to have any thing to do with the offender. Poor Prosonno had, therefore, to sneak back to Grish and make it up with him as best he could. Cousin Dina Nath, the eldest son of Kasi Nath's fifth son Bissumbhur, was also one of Grish's early playmates. He was younger than Grish by some two or three years. The following anecdote shows how quick-witted Grish was even at an early age. Dina Nath, being junior to Grish, was not entitled to call him by name, much less to call him names, as he once felt tempted to do on falling out with Grish. He accord-ingly hit upon an ingenious device. He began repeating the follow-ing lines from a Bengali translation of Chanakya's famous maxims '— " দশ হাত দূরে রাখি যাইবে শৃঙ্গীরে ।'' The meaning of the line is :—Keep horned cattle at ten cubits' length, i.e. give them a wide berth. Now, Dina Nath, just to spite his cousin, laid particular stress on the

RAI DINA NATH GHOSE BAHADOOR.

Kuntaline Press, Calcutta.

syllable "*Giré*" of the word "*Sringiré*" which means *horned*, "*Giré*" being a common corruption of the name "Grish." On Grish's pro‑ testing against the abusive epithet, Dina Nath coolly replied that he was simply conning his lesson. Without a moment's hesitation, Grish paid him back in his own coin by improvising the following line :—" সোমবার দিনে বাঁদর নাচিবে ।"—The meaning of the line is :— On Monday there will be a monkey-dance. Now the word "*Diné*," which means *on a day*, is a common corruption of the name "Dina" and by adding to it the word "*Bándor*" which means *monkey*, Grish not only corrupted the name of his cousin, but also applied to him the abusive epithet " monkey."

Such were the wit-combats which took place in their early years between the two cousins, who retained a warm affection for each other in riper years and who both rose to eminence in their respective walks of life. Dina Nath joined the Finance Department of the Government of India as a very poorly-paid clerk, but gradually rose to be the Registrar of that Department on a salary of Rs. 700 *p.m.* He was made a Rai Bahadur and granted a special pension of Rs. 350 *p m.* which he enjoyed till his death in August, 1891. He was an intimate friend of that mirror of courtesy—the late lamented Maharaja Sir Jotindra Mohan Tagore— at one of whose evening‑ parties he had the honour of being introduced to Lord Northbrook by the late Mr. R. B. Chapman, C. S I., the then Financial Secretary to the Government of India, as the Compiler of the *Civil Leave Code*. But we must end this digression ; for, the school-bell is ringing lustily, and Grish, " with his shining morning face, is cree‑ ping like snail unwillingly to school."

Before narrating, however, the school-life of Grish Chunder, it would be as well to sketch very briefly the history of his *alma mater*. The Oriental Seminary was founded by Babu Gour Mohan Addy on the 1st March, 1829, only a few months before the birth of Grish Chunder, whose grand-father, Kasi Nath, was prominent among the leading Hindu gentlemen who lent the infant institution their powerful moral support, until it developed, in the course of a few years, into one of the foremost institutions in Calcutta, where the highest or Collegiate standard of English education was imparted— a standard which the Seminary continued to maintain down to 1862.

The phenomenal success of the institution was due not only to the fact that it supplied a pressing want, by bringing within the reach of men of moderate means the opportunity of giving their sons the benefit of a sound English education, unalloyed by Missionary influences, but also to the fact that its enterprising and self-taught founder, though a man of no great attainments himself, had the rare tact to secure for his Seminary the services of competent but low-paid European teachers of somewhat tarnished reputation, who taught the higher classes, whilst the intermediate classes were placed in charge of experienced native teachers. The lower forms were placed under the care of European or Eurasian teachers, in order to give little boys, just learning to spell and pronounce English words, the benefit of correct English accentuation and pronunciation. Babu Gour Mohun used to watch with a more than fatherly interest the progress made by his boys, both in and out of school hours, and sedulously kept himself in touch with their guardians. He also spared no efforts to induce high officials and other distinguished personages to visit his Seminary or to take part in its public examinations, which were held at the Town Hall. Men of the highest eminence—such as Sir Edward Ryan, Chief Justice of the late Supreme Court, or the Hon'ble Mr. Amos, Law Member of the Supreme Council and at one time Tutor to Queen Victoria in Constitutional Law, or the Venerable Archdeacon Dealtry—took part in such examinations. Khetter Chunder used to show us, with becoming pride, a beautiful and massive silver standish which had been presented to him, as the head boy of the Oriental Seminary, by no less a personage than the Governor-General of India, Lord Auckland, on the occasion of his visit to the Seminary in the year in which Khetter completed his scholastic career.

The following extract from Khetter Chunder's Autobiography gives some interesting glimpses of Babu Gour Mohan and his Seminary :—

"At first I was placed in an English school which was opened by some European gentlemen in our own neighbourhood in Manicktolah Street at Simla, a school which existed for a few months only. I was afterwards transferred to a school at a small distance from our house, which was established by a native gentleman, named

Babu Gour Mohun Auddy. It was called the Oriental Seminary; and is still in existence at Gurranhatta on the Chitpore Road, though of course, it no longer imparts that high English classical education to its students, which, at the time of its founder, made it one of the most famous institutions in Calcutta, rivalling the Hindu College, now the Presidency College at Puttaldanga. When I entered that institution, I was a little boy of some ten years of age only, and successfully prosecuted my studies for some six or seven years under European teachers, whom the Proprietor had the good sense to employ on small salaries, the highest of which did not exceed Rs. 100 per month. In those days it was not difficult to find European teachers on small salaries; and as the owner of the school was careful to select such men only as those who, although very clever, were somewhat in disgrace among their own countrymen on account of habits of intemperance, &c., he was able to employ them on very moderate pay only. Such a man he found in Mr. Herman Geoffroy, a very clever man, master of some six or seven European languages, who came out to India originally as a barrister, but who, on account of his intemperate habits, never succeeded in the legal profession. I and my class-students had the advantage of profiting by his tuition during some three or four years. Even in his drunken moments, that gentleman, by his learned quotations from English authors, contributed very much to our progress in English Literature. I was, when very young, at the head of the first class, and the prizes which I carried away consisted of many valuable books given at the annual examinations of our school. Babu Gour Mohun Auddy, the Proprietor of the school, was very fond of me—so much so—that when the reduced circumstances of my grand-father did not enable him to pay the school-fees on account of me and my brothers, he, Babu Gour Mohun, was good enough to permit us to attend his school *gratis* and profit by the instructions obtained therein. One day I remember the Babu to have spoken rather harshly to one of my fellow pupils, who had failed to make a punctual payment of his monthly school-fees, and I, as a very sensitive lad, took his reprimand, though not directed towards me, so much to heart, that on returning home, I spoke about it to my father and expressed a resolution not to attend the school any longer, unless my school-fees were paid. My father told me that as Babu Gour Mohun had not asked me for my school-fees,

I should attend his school as usual ; but I was quite obstinate about the matter and absented myself on the next day from the school. In the evening, after closing the school, who should visit my father, but Babu Gour Mohun himself, who asked me the reason why I had not attended school as usual. On my explaining the reason of my absence, he was good enough to assure me that he considered it a great honour to his school, that clever boys like myself were pupils of his institution, and that he never expected to receive any school-fees from me, who could read *gratis* as long as I liked. He further told me that the reason why he had spoken so harshly to a fellow student of mine for not paying his school-fees in due time, was be-cause he was the son of a rich man who should have been more punctual in making his payments than he chose to be. These kind words very much soothed my feelings, and I attended the school from the next day, to the satisfaction of my father and Babu Gour Mohun, the latter having always been very kind in his behaviour to me during the time he took charge of my tuition. I need not say how grateful I always was to my Bengali master. Whatever English I learned, was owing to him and the clever teacher, the above men-tioned European gentleman, whom he employed as his Head Master. Besides the instructions which I and my fellow pupils received during the usual school hours, Babu Gour Mohun, for our further advance-ment in the knowledge of English, established a reading club, which was held in the evening and in which we read many other books than those which formed the curriculum of our studies during the school hours. In short, Babu Gour Mohun was more than a father to me and on account of my extreme boyhood he was good enough to escort me home every night from the reading club ; and during the cold season, when on account my poor circumstances I could not afford to put on warm clothing, he invariably took care to cover my head with his own shawl, for fear I should catch cold, and leave me at the gate of our palatial house. As I was very nervous and afraid of ghosts, he used to bawl out from the gate to assure himself by enquiry, that I had reached the inner department of my house. After I and some of my fellow students had made sufficient progress in our studies, we used to hold a debating club every week, our Head Master, Mr. Herman Geoffroy, acting as our President. As I was a very eloquent speaker and considered to have been endowed by nature with the gift of the gab, Mr. Geoffroy always complimented me upon my oratorical powers, calling me the Demosthenes of the club and calling another boy, the late Babu Shumbhoo Nath Pundit, who was somewhat older than I was in years, but my junior in the class, as Phocion, whose arguments were much stronger but whose powers of eloquence were somewhat inferior to mine. That gentleman prognosticated that both Shumbhoo Nath and myself were destined, after leaving school, to figure in the world. With reference to my class fellow, Shumbhoo Nath Pundit, the prediction was verified ; as, after leaving scdool, that young man, by dint of a hard study of Law, rose from a subordinate position as a Munshi in the late Sudder Dewany Adalut, to be a Judge of the Calcutta High Court on a salary of Rs. 50,000 per annum, a position which he filled with great honour for a few years only, an untimely death having unfortunately put an end to his glorious career ; as for my part, the pressing calls of poverty compelled me, after leaving school at the age of seventeen, to accept, for a few months only, the situation of a teacher in a Government School at Jessore on Rs. 50 per month, and afterwards, on my resigning that post at the urgent request of my father, I accepted the situation of a writer in a Mercantile office. *   *   *"

Babu Gour Mohan Auddy was born on the 20th January 1805, memorable as the year in which Nelson won his last victory and died a hero's death. Gour Mohun always dreaded a journey by water, and curiously enough, the only river journey that he ever undertook in his life, in quest of a European teacher for his Seminary, proved fatal. His boat was caught in a gale, while he was returning from Serampore to Calcutta, and he was drowned in the Hooghly off Goosery on the 23rd February 1845. So perished, in the prime of life, one who, though he was of humble parentage, limited means and mediocre attainments, did more for the spread of English education amongst his fellow countrymen in Bengal than perhaps any other Indian who could be named. As a Pioneer of English education in Bengal, he is worthy of having his name associated with the ever-memorable names of David Hare and Alexander Duff. A memorial tablet has only recently been erected in the Seminary of which he was the founder. It was unveiled on the 10th March 1905 by the late Lieutenant-Governor of Bengal, Sir Andrew Fraser.

If a tree is judged by its fruits, the worth of the institution found.
ed by Gour Mohan is amply attested by the many distinguished
names which adorn its rolls.   Four of these names, viz, those of
Shumbhoo Nath Pundit, Akshay Kumar Dutt, Kristo Das Pal and
Grish Chunder Ghose, were singled out by our distinguished country.
man, the late lamented Mr. Romesh Chunder Dutt, and referred to in
the course of his presidential address at the Anniversary of the
Oriental Seminary held on the 14th February 1903.   With regard to
the two great journalists last named, Mr. Dutt remarked that they had
"for many years voiced the aspirations of their country with great
moderation and judgment."

The extract we have already given from the autobiography of
Khetter Chunder Ghose, presents to us the remarkable personality of
Mr. Herman Geoffroy.   His name shows that he was of French
extraction, though he belonged to the English Bar.   He probably
came out to India in the early thirties to practise as an advocate in
the late Supreme Court; for, in 1834 we find him employed as Law
Lecturer at the Hindu College.   But his addiction to the insidious cup
ruined for ever his prospects of forensic success.   As the readiest.
made shoes are cutdown boots, so it not unfrequently happens that a
briefless barrister is most readily converted into a clever teacher.
Mr. Geoffroy was accordingly offered by Gour Mohan the Head
Mastership of his newly established Seminary on a salary of Rs. 100
per mensem, with free quarters—an offer which his pitiable plight
made him accept with alacrity.   Mr. Geoffroy's linguistic attainments
were exceptionally high.   He possessed a thorough knowledge not
only of Greek and Latin, but also of most modern European langu.
ages, including Spanish, Portuguese and even Romaic or Modern
Greek, for he could repeat *verbatim* the Romaic original of Byron's
well known song entitled "Maid of Athens."   French, of course, he
could speak with the fluency of a native and with the accent of one
to the manner born.   He also possessed the remarkable power which,
we are credibly informed, was also possessed by the late Justice
Dwarka Nath Mitter, of translating any French book that he might be
reading, into English *instanter*, so that no body could suspect that he
was not reading aloud from an English book.   All the three brothers
Ghose learnt French from their Head Master and retained a more or

less accurate knowledge of the language throughout their lives. Grish's small library comprised a beautiful edition of Molière's Plays, in six volumes, and the works of Voltaire in original. In a letter which was published in the *Bengalee* of the 23rd October 1869, Colonel Malleson, who was himself a ripe French scholar, bore the following testimony to Grish Chunder's knowledge of the French language :—

"It may not be generally known that, unaided save by a grammar and a dictionary, he had mastered all the intricacies of the French language; and although, from the want of opportunity of conversation, he could not speak nor even pronounce it, there was not a book in that language which he was unable to read." But of the three brothers, Khetter Chunder was by far the best French scholar. We may add that his eldest son, Babu Chandi Das Ghose, the popular Police Magistrate of Sealdah, has inherited his father's taste for French literature. If Mr. Geoffroy was ruined by drink, he was, like Milton's Satan, "not less than an archangel ruined" and "his form had not lost all her original brightness." Even in his drunken moments he could quote, with perfect accuracy, passage after passage from the ancient classics and stanza after stanza from "Childe Harold's Pilgrimage." What then must have been the "original brightness" of his mind ! It is sad to contemplate that a man of such rare culture should have been so greatly demoralized and degraded by drink that Gour Mohun was often obliged to withhold payment of his salary in cash and to arrange for his meals, &c. He used to live on the school premises with a big dog for his sole companion. Yet he appears to have felt a genuine affection for his dusky pupils and to have taken great interest in teaching their "young ideas how to shoot." He taught them Elocution and created in them a taste for the English Drama. The standard books on these two subjects, respectively, in the early part of the nineteenth century, were *Enfield's Speaker* and the *Modern British Drama* (in five bulky volumes.) Shelley and Byron were once familiar with them, and Mr. Geoffroy did his best to make his Indian pupils equally so.

There was a good deal of rivalry between Mr. Geoffroy and the then Principal of the Hindu College, Captain Richardson, both of them having made the art of elocution their special study. Captain Richardson used to sneer at Mr. Geoffroy's French extraction and

to characterize his style of elocution as French. Sree Nath used to
relate how, on one occasion, he was examined in English Poetry by
Captain Richardson, and how, after hearing Sree Nath read out a
passage from Pope's *Essay on Criticism*, Captain Richardson asked
him with a sneer, " Were you born in France, boy?" It would be the
height of presumption on our part if we were to make the slightest
attempt to pronounce an opinion as to the comparative merits, as
elocutionists, of Herman Geoffroy and Captain Richardson, neither of
whom we ever had an opportunity of hearing. But those who, like
us, ever had the privilege of listening to readings from Shakespeare
by the brothers Ghose, never hesitated to acknowledge that their
preceptor, Herman Geoffroy, was no ordinary adept in the art of
elocution. Grish Chunder always used to ascribe his success as an
orator to his early training in the art of elocution, and his mastery
over the English language to his early study of the *Modern British
Drama*.

Several events happened during the infancy of Grish Chunder
which materially favoured his future career as a journalist, viz, the
establishment of the Oriental Seminary in the very year of his birth
and the appointment to its Head-mastership, a few years later, of so
accomplished a scholar as Herman Geoffroy ; the acceptance by Lord
William Bentinck, early in 1835, of Macaulay's famous minute recom-
mending that Western culture should be imparted to the people of
India through the medium of the English language ; and the liberation
of the Press in India, later on in the same year; by Lord Metcalfe
during the short time he acted as Governor-General of India.

We cannot do better than narrate the school-life of Grish
Chunder in the words of his school-fellow, the late Babu Koylas
Chunder Bose, the writer of the article in the *Bengalee* of the 25th
September 1869 from which we have already given an extract. :—

" In his childhood he was as quick and inoffensive as in his riper
years. He was sent to school by his parents at the age of nine, and
he completed his school career even at sixteen. The Oriental Seminary was his *alma mater*. When in the higher classes, he was a
great favourite of the proprietor of the school, Babu Gour Mohun
Auddy, and of the Head Master, Mr. Herman Geoffroy, a teacher of
great ability and classical learning. Mr. Geoffroy liked him much for

his English composition and would always give him subjects for practice in English poetry. Once he wrote some excellent verses, the subject being given to him from a classical poet. We even now remember the first two lines of one of these pieces :—

> 'Once on a time in a rosy bower,
> Young Cupid plucked a blooming flower.'

For Mathematics he had scarcely any taste and was therefore never at the head of his class. At the annual distribution of prizes, which then came on with great eclat at the Town Hall, he either got the second or the third prize."

In connection with the reason given above, why Grish Chunder was never at the head of his class, viz, his backwardness in Mathematics, it may be mentioned that his brother Sree Nath used to say that Grish was more fond of play than study, and that after idling away the better portion of the year, he would apply himself to his studies in right earnest as the annual examination drew near, when the natural quickness of his parts enabled him to make up for lost time to such an extent that he generally obtained the second prize. We have seen only one of such prizes—it was a splendid set of the *Encyclopædia Americana*, then newly published in thirteen volumes, which was awarded to Grish as the second prize at the annual examination of the second class. Talking of prizes, we once heard from Grish himself the following characteristic anecdote of his boyhood At the close of the annual examination of a junior class to which Grish then belonged, he happened to remark to a classfellow, in a fit of boyish despondency, that he feared he had no chance of winning a prize that session. The classfellow in question, who was not over-famous for his generosity in his riper years, thereupon asked Grish whether he would let him have his prize in case he got one. Grish, in all simplicity, agreed to the proposal, little dreaming at the time that he would get a prize and that when the prize-day came the boy-Shylock would exact fulfilment of a promise so thoughtlessly made, and ruthlessly snatch away from his grasp a beautiful copy of the *Children of the Abbey*—a novel by Regina Maria Roche, which was very popular in the forties and which still maintains a certain degree of popularity.

5.

If Grish had no taste for Mathematics, it does not appear that his taste for Metaphysics was any greater. A Mr. Pascal, who used to teach Metaphysics at the Seminary, finding it a hopeless task to make Grish understand Locke's *Essay on the Human Understanding*, spoke of him as follows to his brother Sree Nath :—

" I say, Sree Nath, that fellow Grish—your brother—big, hulking fellow—has got a large head, but no brains ! " And this was the estimate formed by Mr. Pascal—who was no relation, we suspect, of the famous author of the *Provincial Letters*—of the intellectual gifts of a boy who afterwards became one of the most intellectual of journalists and whose journal formed the chief medium through which the luminous philosophy of Auguste Comte, "the Aristotle of the Nineteenth Century," was popularized in this country. Our readers will call to mind the opinion expressed by the mother of David Hume regarding the mental powers of her gifted son when he was a boy—" Our Davie's a fine good natured crater but uncommon wake-minded."

An obituary notice of Grish Chunder which appeared in the *Reflector*, a newspaper published at Allahabad, contained the following statement :—

"As an Anglo-Bengalee journalist, Baboo Grish Chunder was, decidedly the foremost man of his time. Such was his innate love of journalism and his mental activity, that while yet a student, he assisted by a galaxy of brothers and cousins (who were also his school-mates), established, what may be called, a system of Manuscript Newspapers in the Seminary. These contained essays and dissertations on literary subjects and other important subjects of the day, and were written out by himself and his fellow students and circulated amongst his friends in his *Alma Mater* '

The above must have been written by one of Grish Chunder's contemporaries at school, and is, in the main, correct. We remember, however, to have heard from Sree Nath that although Grish was a leading contributor to the manuscript journal in question, Koylas Chunder Bose was its editor, in so far that he used to collect and arrange the several contributions and copy them out in his fine, clerkly hand for circulation in the Seminary.

Before concluding our account of the scholastic career of Grish Chunder, we wish to say that although, like most men of an imaginative turn of mind, he had no particular bias for mathematics, it must not, for a moment, be supposed that he had a distaste for the science to any thing like the degree which made that most lovable of all English men of letters, Oliver Goldsmith, declare that "Mathematics is a science to which the meanest intellect is equal," or which made even so sober a thinker as Sir William Hamilton wage incessant war against mathematical studies, as a mental exercise, and quote with approval Warburton's dictum—"It is a thing notorious that the oldest mathematician in England is the worst reasoner in it." It would be as well to mention one or two facts which support our view. We shall see presently that Grish was married while he was still at school. We have heard from Grish himself that shortly after his marriage his father-in-law presented him with a silver inkstand, which he disposed of for five rupees and bought with the money a copy of *Chambers's Conic Sections and Solid Geometry*. This clearly shows that he preferred a mathematical treatise to a trumpery inkstand made of silver. Grish used to take great interest in the Beloor Anglo-Vernacular School of which he was the Secretary. On one occasion we found him examining the boys of one of the upper classes—we forget which—in the Elements of Euclid. Need we add that only a year or two before his death we found him one evening studying either *Cape's Mathematics* or the *Sandhurst College Text-book of Algebra*—we forget which—to brush up his knowledge of Indeterminate Equations? Though he was not an expert himself, he had a high regard for mathematical experts. But we have said more than enough on this subject and hasten to deal with the more interesting topic of Grish's marriage.

In accordance with the custom which then universally prevailed, Grish was married at the early age of fifteen, while he was still at school, to the eldest daughter of the late Babu Shib Chunder Deb of Konnagar, a populous town situated within the limits of the Serampore Municipality, about nine miles from Calcutta. The bride was a pretty litte girl, only nine years old. Her father was then employed as a Deputy Collector in Balasore—an appointment which in those early days was considered a highly honourable one and of much greater weight and consequence than are now attached to the post. An alliance with such a man, in the then reduced circumstances of Kasi Nath's family, was considered by the relations and friends of Grish Chunder as a most eligible one. Babu Shib Chunder Deb, who was a distinguished alumnus of the Hindu College, was, on the other hand, so highly pleased with the way in which Grish Chunder had acquitted himself on being tested as to his knowledge of English by the late Babu Grish Chunder Deb, Head Master of the Hare School, that he was glad to have him for his son-in-law, overlooking the poverty, for the sake of the prestige, of the family. The marriage of Grish Chunder proved indeed a very happy one. It not only gave him for his partner in life "a perfect woman, nobly planned," but also brought him into intimate relations with a truly great and good man, who proved a second father to him and exercised over him a deep and abiding influence. To understand this influence it is essentially necessary that we should give a short sketch of the life of Babu Shib Chunder Deb. In doing so we shall freely avail ourselves of a brief *Autobiography* written by him in July, 1888, and published, shortly after his death, in the *Indian Messenger* of the 23rd November 1890

SHIB CHUNDER DEB.

KUNTALINE PRESS, CALCUTTA.

CHAPTER IV

SHIB CHUNDER DEB.

Babu Shib Chunder Deb was born at Konnagar on the 20th July 1811. He was the youngest son of Babu Brajakisor Deb, who, in the course of his long service with the army as a sircar on Rs. 10 *per mensem*, managed to acquire a fair knowledge of English and considerable wealth, which enabled him to build a large house at Konnagar where he used to celebrate the Poojahs in a becoming style after his retirement from the service in his old age on a pension of only Rs. 5 *per mensem*. He also owned several bungalows in the cantonment of Barrackpore which in those days fetched good rents, besides extensive lands and gardens at Konnagar, Rishra and other places. Brajakisor died in 1846 at the advanced age of ninety-five and his character and habits are thus described by his son :—"He was courageous, energetic and strict in his conduct. His habits were temperate and regular. He used to take his meals and do other daily business at fixed hours, from which he seldom deviated. To be punctual in these matters, he always kept a watch by his side."

Shib Chunder gives the following interesting account of his own early education :—

"I was never sent to any school for vernacular education, as there was no such institution in the village at the time, but was taught by a *Guru Mahasay*, employed by my father, in Bengali reading, writing and arithmetic of the commonest description.

When I was about ten years old, I began to learn at home a little of English from my late cousin Babu Madan Mohan Mitra. This part of my education consisted of spelling and reading lessons and the meaning of words learnt by heart.

At eleven I lost my mother, and spent my time idly for two years after that event. But when I heard that good English schools had been established at Calcutta, I felt a great desire to study in one of them. Although my father was very fond of me, yet I had not courage enough to speak to him on the subject, as he was naturally of a hot temper. In this difficulty I requested my cousin Babu Uma Charan Deb to draw up an application for me (in English), addressed to my father, soliciting him to send me to some school at Calcutta. The petition being ready, and finding my father asleep at noonday, I put it on his writing box, which was always kept by his side. When he awoke, he read the application, and having sent for me, expressed his willingness to comply with my request.

I was sent to Calcutta in November 1824, when I was thirteen years old. I lived in the house of a relative, the late Babu Ramnarayan Ghosh of Hatkhola, and attended a private school kept there by one Mr. Read, for a period of about eight months. Not being satisfied with the instructions I received there, I begged of my father to send me to the Hindu College, which he consented to do. Accordingly I was admitted into the seventh class of that institution as a Pay Scholar on the 1st August 1825, when I was fourteen years old."

Babu Ramnarayan Ghosh, the relative at whose house Shib Chunder used to put up while he was a student in Calcutta, was the husband of Brajakisor's niece (brother's daughter). Brajakisor could not, with propriety, offer money to his niece for boarding her cousin, but he used to send her every now and then presents in kind. Shib Chunder was ever afterwards very grateful to his cousin, who was his senior by several years ; but as his habits were very simple, he was no trouble to her. There was, however, one inconvenience which he keenly felt. He had no room to himself for study, and had to carry on his studies in the same room in which certain young inmates of the house used to play at cards or otherwise amuse themselves. These young sparks did not like the studious habits of the shy new-comer from the country and tried to wean him from such habits by blowing out his light or otherwise disturbing him in his studies. But the long-suffering patience and gentleness of Shib Chunder prevailed at last and his tormentors ceased to annoy him. One of these young men had occasion, many years afterwards, to wait upon Shib Chunder at the palatial house he had built at Konnagar. While he was being shown over the house, the poor fellow could not help recalling his past conduct towards Shib Chunder, for which he expressed his sincere contrition and observed that had he been in his boyhood as diligent a student as Shib Chunder was, he could have built for himself as fine a house.

The Hindu College was originally a private institution, managed by a Committee, composed of eight European and twenty native gentlemen. It was opened on Monday the 20th January, 1817, at Gorachand Byasak's house in Gurranhatta—the house on the Upper Chitpore Road now occupied by the Oriental Seminary. The College was afterwards removed to Roop Churn Roy's house in Chitpore, and thence to Feringhi Kamal Bose's house in Jorasanko. In 1819 the institution felt a financial pinch which continued to increase from year to year, until in 1823, the managers found it necessary to apply to Government for pecuniary help and for a suitable building. A similar application was made in 1824 to the General Committee of Public Instruction. Government thereupon resolved to aid the College by founding a professorship of experimental philosophy and by supplying the cost of school accommodation. Arrangements were finally made for the construction of one building for the Sanskrit and Hindu Colleges. Government gave Rs. 1,24,000; and " Mr. David Hare gave up for the benefit of the College the piece of land he owned on the north side of the College Square." The foundation-stone of the College building was laid on the 25th February, 1824, and the building was completed in January, 1825. By the failure of Joseph Barretto & Sons, the Hindu College lost all its funded property and was obliged to apply again for pecuniary help from Government. Government agreed to help the College provided the Committee of Public Instruction were allowed to exercise some control over the management. After some correspondence it was settled that the General Committee of Public Instruction would exercise supervising control only in respect of the grants that might be made by Government from time to time, such control being exercised on behalf of the Committee by Dr. H. H. Wilson, who was accordingly elected by the Managing Committee as an ex-officio member and Vice President. Mr. Hare was also made an honorary member. Such was the constitution of the Hindu College during the time Shib Chunder studied there.

In his Autobiography he states—

" I studied in the Hindu College for six years and five months, of which the latter two years I was in the first class, and held a scholarship of Rs. 16 a month. Having obtained a Certificate of Proficiency, I quitted the College on the 20th December, 1831."

From this we infer that he studied in the first class during the years 1830 and 1831, in the second class in 1829, in the third class in 1828 and in the fourth class in 1827. We know that he studied in the seventh class for five months only, viz. from August to December 1825. We therefore conclude that he was promoted from that class at once to the fifth class and that he studied in the latter class in 1826.

In the reminiscences of David Hare communicated by Shib Chunder to the late Babu Peary Chand Mittra and published in the latter's invaluable *Biographical Sketch of David Hare,* the following passage occurs, shewing how early he had attracted the notice of that great philanthropist and educationist :—

" When I was a student of the 4th class, Hindu College, and while sitting in the class one day, Mr. Hare came and presented me with a copy of Tara Chand Chakraburti's English and Bengali Dictionary (a work just then published). This circumstance quite surprised me, as I was a pay scholar of the College, and had but slight acquaintance with him at the time. On my asking him the reason of his making the present to me, he said that he was much pleased with the manner in which I had acquitted myself at an examination of the class held a few days previously by some gentleman, and that he gave me the book as a token of his gratification. From that time he took great interest in my welfare. It was at his suggestion that I applied for a scholarship, and obtained it after passing the necessary examination."

In 1827, Mr. Henry Louis Vivian Derozio was appointed an Assistant Master in the Senior Department of the Hindu College, while he was scarcely out of his teens. This remarkable individual, who was an East Indian by birth and education, whose complexion was as dark as that of any native of India, who not only looked like a boy in stature and in the genial expression of his round and chubby face but also retained a boyish buoyancy of spirits and simplicity of character to the last, whose long, dark hair was always parted in the middle, and whose large, lustrous eyes unmistakably betrayed his genius, was destined to play a momentous part in the history of the Hindu College during the brief period of four years over which his connection with that institution extended. He was born on the 10th April 1809 and died on the 23rd December 1831. But during his short span of life he published a poem—the *Fakir of Jungheera* written in his teens—which showed that he possessed poetical powers of no mean order which only required riper years to chasten and mature. He also published objections to the Critical Philosophy of Kant which were pronounced by a competent critic to be perfectly original. Above all, he gave an impetus to the moral and intellectual development of the advanced students of the Hindu College which lasted all their lives. He roused in them a spirit of free enquiry which leavened all their thoughts and imbued them with a courage of conviction which made them fearless of consequences in the pursuit and realization of truth. It is worthy of remark that this spirit had been imbibed by Derozio himself from his teacher, David Drummond, who was a most remarkable man and an avowed disciple of David Hume. It is related of Derozio that he was so very indifferent to systematic teaching that on one occasion, when he took his monthly progress report to the Head Master, Mr. D'Anseleme, the sight of the report so much exasperated the latter that he raised his hand to strike Derozio who averted it by receding. But he was no routine teacher ; he had a far higher conception of the duties of his calling. Instead of cramming the minds of his pupils with ill-digested knowledge, he taught them how to think and " worship truth's omnipotence." His own verses beautifully express how he watched their intellectual development :—

> " Expanding like the petals of young flowers,
> I watch the gentle opening of your minds,
> And the sweet loosening of the spell that binds
> Your intellectual energies and powers."

" It was not alone in the class-rooms and during the hours of teaching," observes his biographer, Mr. Thomas Edwards, " that the

6.

genial manner, the buoyant spirit, the ready humour, the wide
reading, the readiness to impart knowledge, and the patience and
courtesy of Derozio won the hearts and the high reverence of his
pupils. In the intervals of teaching he was ever ready in conversation to aid his pupils in their studies, to draw them out to give free
and full expression to their opinions, on topics naturally arising
from the course of their work in the class-rooms ; and before the
hour at which the usual work of his classes began, and sometimes
after the hour for closing the day's duties, Derozio, in addition to
the work of the class, in order to broaden and deepen the knowledge
of his pupils in the thought and literature of England, gave readings
in English-literature to as many students of the Hindu College as
cared to take advantage of his self-imposed work. In consort with
his pupils, he established the *Academic Association*, which met in a
garden-house belonging to the Singh family in Manicktollah, where
night after night, under the presidency of Derozio, and with
Omachurn Bose as Secretary, the lads of the Hindu College read
their papers, discussed, debated and wrangled ; and acquired for
themselves the facility of expressing their thoughts in words and the
power of ready reply and argument. To these meetings there
frequently came the unassuming, large-hearted philanthropist, David
Hare, in 'white jacket' and old-fashioned gaiters' or 'blue coat,'
with large brass buttons, the dress-coat of his youth ; and occasionally Sir Edward Ryan and Colonel Benson, Private Secretary to Lord
William Bentinck; Colonel Beatson, afterwards Adjutant General,
and Dr. Mills, the Principal of Bishop's College, visited the meetings.
Poetry and Philosophy were the chief themes discussed. Derozio's
attainments in Philosophy were as wide and varied as his acquaintance
with the poets and dramatists.".

In his famous *Essay on Culture and Anarchy*, Mathew Arnold
defined Culture to be "a pursuit of our total perfection by means
of getting to know, on all the matters which most concern us, the
best which has been thought and said in the world; and, through this
knowledge, turning a stream of fresh and free thought upon our
stock notions and habits, which we now follow staunchly but mechanically, vainly imagining that there is a virtue in following them

staunchly which makes up for the mischief of following them mechanically." It is a noteworthy fact that more than forty years before the publication of Matthew Arnold's book, a young East Indian teacher had tried to impart precisely this kind of culture to his Hindu pupils by "turning a stream of fresh and free thought upon their stock notions and habits."

But as Heine says somewhere, "wherever a free soul has spoken, there is sure to be a Golgotha." The Philistines were soon up in arms against Derozio whose teachings, they apprehended, were unsettling the faith of the boys in the Hindu religion. Nor was the apprehension altogether groundless. "The junior students", says Babu Peary Chand Mittra, in his *Biographical Sketch of David Hare*, "caught from the senior students the infection of ridiculing the Hindu religion, and where they were required to utter *mantras* or prayers, they repeated lines from the Iliad. There were some who flung the Brahmanical thread instead of putting it on. The horror of the orthodox families was intensified—withdrawals of pupils took place."

At last the Managing Committee resolved to remove Derozio, who accordingly sent in his resignation on the 25th April, 1831, at the suggestion of Dr. Wilson ; but contrary to Dr. Wilson's advice, he distinctly stated that he tendered his resignation in order to save himself the mortification of receiving formal notice of his dismissal.

Even after his dismissal from the College, many of Derozio's pupils regularly visited him at his house, and some of them tenderly nursed him when he was stricken down by cholera, and when all was over with him, followed him to his last resting place in the South Park Street Cemetery.

"The pupils who constantly sought for Derozio's Company," says Babu Peary Chand Mittra, who was himself one of the number, "were Krishna Mohun Banerjee, Russic Krishna Mullick, Duckhina Runjun Mookerjee, Ram Gopaul Ghose, Madhub Chunder Mullick, Ramtonoo Lahiree, Mohesh Chunder Ghose, Shib Chunder Deb, Huru Chunder Ghose, Radhanath Sickdar, Gobind Chunder Bysack, Amrita Lall Mittra and others, who may be called the 'Young

Calcutta.' The first four for some time acted as firebrands. Time moderated their impulsiveness. The uppermost thought was to expose Hinduism, and to renounce it." After describing the different ways in which Derozio influenced the character of each of the young men named above, who all rose to eminence in their riper years, Babu Peary Chand pays the following well-merited tribute to Shib Chunder :—

"There is one name which deserves special mention. Shib Chunder Deb was a quiet and unpretending scholar. Those who know the good he has done to Konnagar, where he lives, by the establishment of the English, Bengali and Female Schools, a Library and Samaj, will be able to form an idea what the strength of a man is when he is rightly trained."

Shib Chunder was one of Derozio's favourite pupils and bore his stamp and impress to the end of his long life. He treasured up with care a splendid set of Dugald Stewart's Philosophical Works, which he had won by writing a prize essay on some philosophical subject set by Derozio—or D'rozio, as he invariably pronounced the name. Dugald Stewart is not made much of, as a philosopher, in our day ; but in those days he enjoyed an extraordinary reputation as such, and so charming was his delivery that students from the most distant lands flocked to hear his lectures. Shib Chunder used to describe to us, in his old age, what a treat it was to hear Derozio recite the poetry of Lord Byron, which had not then lost any of its glamour, the noble bard having died only in 1824. So great indeed was the enthusiasm with which he always spoke of the young preceptor of his joyous prime, that we could not help exclaiming with the Poet of Nature—

> "Bliss was it in that dawn to be *alive*,
> And to be *young* was very heaven."

While at College, Shib Chunder was noted for his proficiency in the higher Mathematics, which included the Differential Calculus or, as it was then called, Fluxions. He was a favourite of the Professor of Mathematics, Dr. Tytler—a son of the eminent historian Patrick Fraser Tytler. Of Dr. Tytler, whom Captain Richardson succeeded as Principal of the Hindu College in January, 1836, Shib

Chunder used to say that he was so studious that he often had two bulky volumes under his arms when resorting to the water-closet.

On leaving College, Shib Chunder entered Government service as a Computer in the Great Trigonometrical Survey on a salary of Rs 30 *per mensem* (which was subsequently raised to Rs 40', along with his friend, the late Babu Radha Nath Sikdar, who was a man of such rare mathematical attainments and whose services were so highly appreciated by the head of the Department, Colonel Everest, that he afterwards rose to a high position in the Department. Shib Chunder did not, however, remain long in the Survey Department, as he was appointed, on the 20th February 1838, a Deputy Collector in Balasore on the nomination of the Board of Revenue, he having previously passed an examination in Surveying which qualified him for employment in the subordinate branch of the Revenue Survey Department.

In Balasore he was employed, with great credit, on Settlement and Resumption duties, for upwards of six years, and was promoted from the third to the second grade on the 9th January, 1844.

In May, 1844, he was transferred to Midnapur, and on the 15th February, 1849, he was promoted to the first grade. In January, 1850, he was transferred to the 24 Pergunnahs.

Originally there were only three grades of Deputy Collectors, the lowest carrying a salary of Rs 250, and the salaries of the two higher grades being Rs. 350 and Rs. 450, respectively. The officers were promoted after a term of five years' service in each grade. In 1853, the Board of Revenue re-classified these officers into five classes, according to merit, and the salary fixed for the first class was Rs. 700, that for the second class Rs. 600 and so on, the last grade carrying a salary of Rs. 200. By this re-classification, Shib Chunder was placed in the second class on the 6th March 1854, and his salary was gradually raised from Rs 450 to Rs. 600. About this time he was employed in obtaining lands for a new canal from Baliaghata to the Hooghly river at Chitpore.

On the 29th November, 1858, his services were placed at the disposal of the Railway Commissioner, Mr. W. Ainslie, for the acquisition of lands required for the Eastern Bengal Railway. At the conclusion of this work in March, 1860, he availed himself of three months' privilege leave and took a trip, with his friend the late Babu Peary Chand Mittra, to the Upper Provinces for the benefit of his health.

On the expiration of his leave, he rejoined the 24 Pergunnahs Collectorate, was promoted to the first class of Subordinate Executive officers on the 10th December, 1859, and was appointed a Deputy Magistrate with the powers of a Covenanted Assistant to a Magistrate on the 24th March, 1860.

On the 19th September 1860, he was appointed Deputy Collector of Calcutta in addition to his appointment in the 24 Pergunnahs; so that he held his office at Alipore and Calcutta on alternate days.

Owing to failing health, he retired from the service on the 1st January, 1863, on a pension of about Rs. 4,000 *per annum*, the maximum pension then allowed by rule.

In noticing his retirement, the late Rai Kristo Das Pal characterized his services as follows, in the *Hindoo Patriot* of the 8th December, 1862 :—

"The Baboo was a highly intelligent and efficient officer. As a revenue official, his knowledge of the fiscal laws of the country was very great ; while his familiar acquaintance with English added not a little to his usefulness in the estimation of his superiors. The Deputy Collectors as a class are by no means in good odour with the people on account of their over-zealous proceedings in the interest of Government to the manifest detriment of justice to the people; but Baboo Shib Chunder Deb was an honourable exception to the rule. His high conscientiousness, added to the urbanity of his manners, won for him golden opinions from all parties who had to appear before him, whether gainers or losers. We have before had occasion to allude to the labors of Baboo Shib Chunder in the cause of the amelioration of the condition of his countrymen. Konnaghur owes its excellent English school to his exertions. Unassuming and quiet, he has done a vast deal of good to his country by stealth. Relieved of the cares and troubles of office, we hope and trust he may long pursue the career of usefulness for the improvement of his countrymen."

Here we close our meagre outline of Shib Chunder's meritorious and varied official career. Let him now tell us, in his own modest and unassuming way, what he did for the improvement of his native village of Konnagar, which, in his boyhood, was, like most other villages of that day, overrun with dense jungle, destitute of any good roads or postal or rail communications, without any sanitary arrangements and worst of all, without any educational or medical institutions, but which, at the time of his death, was one of the most prosperous towns of its kind in this part of the country, well-equipped with all the appliances and facilities of modern civilization :—

"On my being transferred as Deputy Collector from Midnapur to the 24-Pergunnahs in January 1850, I resided at Khidirpur or Alipore, visiting my family at Konnagore every Saturday and returning to Alipore on Monday. At this time I felt a great desire to do something for improving the condition of my native village, Konnagore. With this view I called a public meeting of the inhabitants of the place on the 29th Ashar, 1259 B. S. (July 1852), the result of which was the establishment of an association called the 'Konnagore Hitaishini Sabha' (Benevolent Society), the objects of which were as follows :—

1. To do whatever will tend to promote the beauty of the place and the good of the community.

2. To reform all indecent and immoral customs which prevail in the village, without interfering with the religion and castes of the people.

3. To give relief to persons in distress brought on by misfortunes, or unforeseen events.

4. To adjust all disputes amicably, provided both the parties concerned apply to the Sabha for arbitration.

The society existed for a period of three years, at the end of which it was dissolved in July, 1855, for want of adequate support from the inhabitants of the place.

During the above period the Sabha made necessary repairs to the roads, constructed culverts where urgently required, gave relief to indigent persons and granted aid for building school-houses, &c.

The establishment of an English school at Konnagar oeing suggested by the above society, I granted a piece of land for the site of the school-house, which was built by subscription, and the school was opened on the 1st May, 1854. It was at first a private institution, but it obtained a grant-in-aid from Government on the 8th November, 1855. The school is now one of the best Aided English schools in Bengal.

Under the system of vernacular education introduced by Lord Hardinge, a Government Vernacular School had been established here, but it was abolished on the 1st May, 1856. However, through the exertions of myself and my friends, a vernacular school was established under the Government grant-in-aid system on the 14th June, 1858, which is still in existence and is considered one of the best schools of the kind.

Being convinced that education would be promoted by the establishment of a Public Library, I raised an adequate sum by private subscriptions and built for the purpose two rooms in the upper story of the English school-house. The Library was opened to the public on the 1st April, 1858. It has a good collection of English, Vernacular and Oriental classic works. Its current expenses are met by monthly subscriptions paid by the readers and other supporters of the Library.

When I was a student in the Hindu College, I became convinced of the importance of Female Education. Accordingly I felt a great desire to teach my wife reading and writing in Bengali and did everything in my power to accomplish that object. In time I employed a Pandit to teach my daughters, one of whom was sent to the Calcutta Bethune School.

With the view of having a Girls' school established at Konnagar, I submitted a proposal to Government in 1858, in which I agreed to pay Rs. 500 for the erection of a school-house, provided an equal sum was granted by Government for the purpose. Besides, I guaranteed the payment of Rs. 15 per month from local sources and solicited a monthly grant of Rs. 45 from Government. This application, after long correspondence, was disallowed. But without further waiting for any aid from Government, I at once opened a Girls' school at my own house on the 12th April, 1860, appointing a Pandit for the instruction of pupils. A monthly grant-in-aid was afterwards obtained from Government. The school was then removed to a house built on a piece of ground belonging to me at my own expense. This school has been well managed; from it a number of girls annually pass the Vernacular Girls' Scholarship Examination and obtain scholarships.

When the East Indian Railway was opened to the public in 1854, no provision was made for stopping the trains at Konnagar. Consequently, to avail themselves of the Railway, the inhabitants of this locality had to go either to the Bali or the Serampur station, a distance of three miles on either side. To remove this inconvenience, I applied to the Railway authorities for the establishment of a station at Konnagar, which, after much pressure, was allowed an 1856.

There was another want much felt by the people of Konnagar. There was no post-office in the village, so they had to proceed to Bali or Serampur to post their letters. To supply this want, I sent an application in 1858 to the Postmaster-General, soliciting him to open a post-office at Konnagar as a tentative measure for three months, and guaranteeing the payment of any excess of expenditure over receipts in postage, which might occur during the period of trial. Accordingly, a post-office was opened here in that year, which has become a permanent institution.

The establishment of a Charitable Dispensary at Konnagar was another desideratum. Endeavours were made by the late Hitaishini Sabha for the accomplishment of that object, but without success.

Having great faith in the system of Homœopathy, I called a public meeting, in 1868, of the inhabitants of the place, with the view of establishing a Charitable Homœopathic Dispensary, which, according to the resolutions passed at that meeting, was opened on the 1st September of that year; but it was closed in December, 1869, for want of support from the people. It is however satisfactory to state that Homœopathic medicines have since been gratuitously distributed to the sick applying for them, at the expense of the Konnagar Brahmo Samaj.

7

Epidemic fever having broken out in Konnagar in 1875, causing great mortality among the people, a Charitable Dispensary in connection with Government was established at the place through the exertions of myself and my friends. It was located in a pucca house lent by me for its use and was supported partly by private subscriptions and partly by Government. The Dispensary was abolished by Government in 1881. In December, 1883, a Charitable Homœopathic Dispensary was opened at my house at the expense of my wife, which is still in existence."

Comment is superfluous on the above simple, but noble record of Shib Chunder's systematic and well-directed efforts to ameliorate the condition of his native village. It speaks for itself. There is a saying that God made the country and man made the city. It would not be too much to say that Shib Chunder made Konnagar what it now is. If every village in Bengal produced a man of his stamp, the entire aspect of the country would be changed for the better in no time. Unfortunately, however, for our country, it can boast of few citizens of his stamp—men who "do noble deeds, not dream them all day long," men who "do good by stealth and blush to find it fame." Shib Chunder hated all fuss and display. He did not like to have his actions bruited about by the blare of trumpets. His innate modesty always made him keep himself studiously in the background, unless he found it absolutely necessary to come forward for the public good. Evidence of such modesty is not wanting in his brief record of the world of good he achieved for Konnagar. He says, for instance, that the Konnagar English school-house was built "by subscription" on land granted by him, but does not tell us that the bulk of the amount of subscriptions realized came from his own purse; had it been otherwise, the project would have, doubtless, fallen through, like the Hitaishini Sabha, "for want of adequate support from the inhabitants of the place." The same remark also applies to his statement that he "raised an adequate sum by private subscriptions" and built, for the purpose of establishing a Public Library, two rooms on the upper floor of the English school-house. In this case, he has further refrained from letting us know that he gave away his own valuable private library, to form the nucleus of the Public Library.

Shib Chunder was also untiring in his efforts to improve the roads and sanitation of Konnagar during his long term of office as a Municipal Commissioner of Serampore—an office to which he was appointed by Government in 1865 and which he was compelled by ill health to resign in March, 1878. Old as he was, and of a naturally delicate constitution, he never spared himself the physical strain imposed by his long and frequent journeys to Serampore, to attend the Commissioners' meetings, at which he had every opportunity of coming in close personal contact with the Covenanted Subdivisional Officer of Serampore, who generally presided at such meetings as *ex-officio* Chairman of the Municipality. Shib Chunder fully utilized these opportunities and induced successive Subdivisiona, officers to take a warm interest in the educational institutions of Konnagar and to preside at the annual distributions of prizes. Even the scholarly editor of the *Friend of India*, Dr. George Smith, who was not generally given credit for an excess of sympathy for the natives of India, had such a high regard for Shib Chunder that he presided on such occasions more than once, accompanied by his amiable wife. So highly pleased was he with what he saw of them, that he described the schools of Konnagar as " an almost perfect educational system." The late Mr. Henry Woodrow, Director of Public Instruction, Bengal, who, while he was an Inspector of Schools, often presided on such occasions, also took every opportunity of expressing his high appreciation of the value of the schools founded by Shib Chunder and of the philanthropy and public spirit of their founder. That blessed martyr to the cause of the down-trodden indigo-cultivator, the late Reverend Mr. James Long, was also a frequent guest.

Government recognized the worth of Shib Chunder by granting him a Certificate of Honour, on the occasion of the assumption, by our late gracious Queen, of the title of "Empress of India" on the 1st January, 1877. But his real worth is recorded in a book "by seraphs writ with beams of heavenly light."

We would now say a word or two about Shib Chunder's literary work. Realising at an early period of his life the sad dearth which then existed of good books in his own vernacular, he, in conjunction with his intimate friend and fellow-student, the late Babu Hari Mohan Sen, who afterwards became Dewan of the Native State of Jaipur,

wrote and published, while still at College, a good Bengali translation
of a portion of the Arabian Nights' Entertainments. But his chief
contribution to Bengali literature, and that by which he is best known,
is a treatise (শিশুপালন) on the Treatment of Infants, which he
· compiled from the works of Andrew Combe and others on the
subject, and the first and second parts of which were published in 1857
and 1862, respectively. Both the parts were favourably noticed by
the *Hindoo Patriot*, the leading native journal of the day; but we
can only give the following brief extract from its review of Part II ·—
"The author is a quiet, unobtrusive gentleman, who does good by
stealth, scarcely letting his left hand know what his right hand does.
He takes a particular interest in infant education, and the thoughts
and precepts which he has collected in this treatise are indeed of the
most important character. The book is written in easy familiar style,
full of matter and will form an unexceptionable guide to infant
treatment." This treatise long supplied a pressing want and enjoyed
a well-deserved popularity. The late Rai Dina Bandhu Mitra
in his সুরধুনী কাব্য, a poem describing the course of the Ganges and
the different cities situated on its banks, made a graceful allusion to
Shib Chunder as the "Father of Infant Treatment" ("শিশুপালনের পিতা").
Shib Chunder also published, in 1867, a Bengali treatise (অধ্যাত্মবিজ্ঞান)
on Spiritualism, in which he was a firm believer, though personally he
never had any supernatural experiences. Shib Chunder does not
appear to have ever undertaken any literary work in English.

It was while studying in the fourth class of the Hindu College that
the religious discussions held under the guidance of his tutor Derozio
unsettled Shib Chunder's faith in the Hindu religion and he became a
believer in one God. But it was not till 1844, when he was transferred as Deputy Collector from Balasore to Midnapur, that he first
became acquainted with the doctrines of Brahmoism by happening to
read an issue of the then newly started *Tatvabodhini Patrika*. He
immediately became a subscriber to that paper and commenced
worshipping God in the manner therein indicated.

In 1846, he established a Brahmo Samaj at Midnapur, which
continued to exist till his transfer to the 24 Pergunnahs in January,
1850. Some time after the latter event, he formally embraced the
Brahma Dharma and became a member of the Adi Brahmo Samaj at
Jorasanko.

Shortly after his retirement from the service, he established on the 28th May, 1863, a Brahmo Samaj at his residence at Konnagar, the services of which were, during the first six or seven years of its existence, held every fortnight, and therafter weekly. The Samaj was originally founded under the auspices of the Adi Brahmo Samaj, and the late Maharshi Debendra Nath Tagore, who was a personal friend of Shib Chunder's, conducted the inaugural service. But after the secession of the late Babu Keshub Chunder Sen and his friends and the establishment by them of the Brahmo Samaj of India, the Konnagar Brahmo Samaj showed a leaning towards that Samaj, although in all matters it maintained perfect independence and at its anniversary festivals the leaders of both the Samajes conducted divine service alternately.

To provide the Konnagar Brahmo Samaj with a prayer-hall of its own, Shib Chunder granted a piece of land owned by him on the riverside and built thereon a commodious and well-ventilated hall, with an upper gallery for females, at a cost of upwards of three thousand rupees, raised by subscription. A material portion of the amount was contributed by Shib Chunder himself, and by his friend, the late Maharshi Debendra Nath Tagore, who, with his characteristic generosity and munificence, sent, *unsolicited*, a cheque for the amount by which the subscriptions realized had fallen short of the expenditure incurred, on his accidentally coming to hear of the deficit. Some houses were also built for the residence of ministers or missionaries; but these became gradually dilapidated by long disuse and have since been dismantled. The prayer-hall or *mandir*, which was consecrated on the 8th March 1879 and shortly afterwards made over to trustees appointed under a duly executed trust-deed, has, however, been kept in good repair, due provision having been made in Shib Chunder's Will for maintaining the *mandir* in a habitable condition, as also for meeting the expenses of the anniversary festival.

To complete our account of the religious side of Shib Chunder's many-sided life, it is necessary to make some reference to the prominent part played by him in the establishment and consolidation of the Sadharan Brahmo Samaj. The limits and scope of the present work preclude us, however, from dwelling at any length upon this subject, which properly forms a chapter—and a most important

chapter, too,—in the history of the Brahmo Samaj in India. We have
no desire to trench upon Church History by attempting to describe the
various causes which led to that schism in the church of the late
Babu Keshub Chunder Sen which culminated in the establishment of
the Sadharan Brahmo Samaj on the 15th May, 1878, or the circumstances under which so unobtrusive a man as Shib Chunder, who did
not possess the gift of speech, so generally required of a great party-
leader, was unanimously elected by the originators of the new movement to be their leader. But they were, doubtless, guided in their
choice of a tower of strength in the hour of peril, by the lofty and
stainless character of Shib Chunder, his life-long and single-hearted
devotion to the cause of Brahmo Theism, his patriarchal figure, his
enthusiastic and unswerving allegiance to truth, and above all, his
calm and dispassionate judgment. And how amply was the wisdom
of their choice vindicated by the way in which the old pilot weathered
the storm and brought the vessel safe into port ! For five successive
years Shib Chunder held the office of President of the new Samaj
and when he retired from that office he had the supreme satisfaction
of seeing that the infant Hercules had, under his judicious care,
thriven well in thews and sinews.

Having given some account of Shib Chunder's collegiate, official
public, literary, and religious life, we shall now endeavour to des_
cribe, as briefly as possible, his general character and conduct in private
life, premising at the outset that it is not in our power to give—

"That best portion of a good man's life,
His little, nameless, unremembered acts
Of kindness and of love."

There is one unique circumstance which has struck us more
forcibly the more closely we have studied the life of this remarkable
man, who died in the eightieth year of his age on the 12th November
1890, viz. that at no period of his unusually long life did he ever
deviate by a hair's breadth from the "straight and narrow path" he
had chalked out for himself in early boyhood. The book of his life
was, from cover to cover, one unbroken record of noble aspirations
nobly fulfilled—"progressive virtue and approving heaven." We have
heard from the veracious lips of his only sister, who was his senior by

several years and who predeceased him by many years, that even in his childhood he never played a childish prank. Successive witnesses have borne testimony to his uniformly pure and blameless life. Even in the heyday of youth, he was remarkable for the austere purity of his character—

> "Chaste as the icicle,
> That's curded by the frost from purest snow,
> And hangs on Dian's temple."

We have known many good men—very good men, too,—who stumbled at one time or other in their lives and then mended their pace ; but we are awe-struck as we gaze at this octogenarian who never made a false step in his life, whose book of life remained as spotless at its close as when it came fresh from the hands of its Maker, and was never disfigured by a single blot or moral blemish or "erratum," as Franklin quaintly calls it.

We have already seen how even in his extreme boyhood he rose above his environment and timidly asked his father to send him to Calcutta for education. We have also seen with what assiduity and ardour he prosecuted his studies in his youth ; how creditably he discharged in the prime of manhood the duties of the honourable positions he successively held in the public service ; and how after retirement from the service in green old age, he disdained to spend his retired leisure in ignoble ease, but preferred to work incessantly for the physical, intellectual, moral and spiritual well-being of his fellow-citizens. Let us now hear from his own lips how he was rewarded by his fellow-citizens :—"Owing to my religious beliefs, and specially to my son's marriage under Act III of 1872, the ortho- dox Hindus of Konnagar have excommunicated me from their society, and not only that, they do not scruple to insult and persecute me whenever they find an opportunity of doing so. But I am not at all sorry for this treatment, as I anticipated it, and was quite prepared to meet it. May God grant them light to see their error and mend their conduct."

Now, was not such a life "one grand, sweet song "?

The key-note of Shib Chunder's noble life is to be found in his utter want of self-aggrandisement ; in all that he did he was actuated

by an ever-present sense of his own insignificance ; he always considered himself merely as an humble instrument in the hands, and under
the eye, of his Great Task-Master. Is it to be wondered then that
his humility was so great that he never hesitated to learn wisdom even
from a child and never felt so uncomfortable as when he heard his
own praise ? He never indulged in uncharitable remarks himself, nor
did he ever encourage or allow others to make such remarks in his
hearing ; he had a happy knack of putting the best construction upon
the worst actions or words of other people. His habitual love of
truth never made him disregard the feelings of others and indulge
in blunt speeches. He never lost his temper in the heat of a
discussion, but always tried to convince his adversary "with gentle
yet prevailing force."

"Prune thou thy words," says Cardinal Newman. Shib Chunder
acted on this golden maxim all his life. He never wasted his time in
idle talk and he never indulged in gushy sentimentalism. His feelings were "too deep for tears," and his sentiment always found
expression in deeds, not in words. Although his susceptible and tender heart overflowed with the milk of human kindness, we do not remember having ever seen his "water-works at play," to use a favourite
expression of Thackeray's. His marvellous self-command made him
"a stoic of the woods—a man without a tear." The heaviest affliction
with which he was ever visited in this vale of tears was the untimely
death of his darling son-in-law, Grish Chunder, at Beloor ; yet, on
his arrival there from Konnagar almost immediately after the sad
occurrence, he did not shed one drop of tear. He found Grish's
helpless widow left quite alone and friendless—for Grish's aged mother
and his brother, Sreenath, had already started on their way back to
Calcutta. There was not sufficient money left in the house to meet
even the expenses of cremating the dead body. Shib Chunder made
all necessary arrangements, and commenced taking an inventory of
the effects of the deceased, not neglecting even the most pitiful bit of
lumber. Many years afterwards, he rendered a strict account of them
to Grish's children. The Searcher of Hearts alone could see what
was passing all the while through the old man's heart. A friend and
neighbour, who happened to meet him that very day on his return to

Konnagar, found him, not in tears, but only murmuring to himself the words of a favourite hymn—

" তুমি হে ভরসা মম অকূল পাথারে,
আর কেহ নাহি যে বিপদভয় বারে,
এ আঁধারে যে তারে । "

"Thou art, O Lord, my only hope and stay in this limitless waste of waters. No one else can avert the dread of danger or save me amidst the encircling gloom." But although no scar was outwardly visible, we must not conclude that he never felt the wound. Long after this, when Grish's widow and orphans had been established once more in their old homestead in Calcutta, Shib Chunder confessed to his wife, on her taxing him with unkindness towards his eldest daughter in not visiting her as often as he visited his other daughters in Calcutta, that he could never cross the threshold of Grish's house without feeling his heart rent in twain. There you see Achilles' heel uncovered for once !

To all grumblers, Shib Chunder had but one advice to give—"Have patience." His fortitude was signally displayed on two occasions on which he had to place himself under the surgeon's knife to get rid of a carbuncle. On either occasion, the operation was a most painful one, but he bore it almost without a groan. His presence of mind was no less remarkable than his fortitude. On one occasion, seeing one of his servants about to jump into a tank to rescue a grandson of his from a watery grave, he peremptorily forbade the man's doing so, but ordered him to hold a long bamboo by one end and let the drowning youth catch hold of the other end and be thus pulled ashore. But for this wise precaution, two lives would have been lost that day. Shib Chunder never indulged in the loud laugh that "bespeaks a vacant mind," but he was habitually cheerful, and a genial smile always lit up his features. He did not look upon moroseness as constituting one of the cardinal virtues ; and he was, at times, inclined even to be facetious. He was fond of all innocent fun or frolic, and his fine sense of humour made him heartily enjoy books like Colman's *Broad Grins*. Asceticism formed no part of his creed, and he always loved to see happy faces around him. He was passionately fond of good music of both kinds—vocal and instrumental—though he generally preferred the former. It was through his exertions that a music school was opened and maintained at Konnagar for some time in 1876. While he was ever ready to forgive an injury, he never forgot a favour received. His gratitude, for instance, to the cousin at whose house he used to live whilst prosecuting his studies in Calcutta, knew no bounds. Not only did he grant her a monthly allowance which she received regularly as long as she lived, but he used to present her whole family with clothes every year during the Poojahs, and on the death of her husband, he undertook to bear the entire cost of her son's education. So keen was his sense of any good office done to him, that even in his short *Autobiography* he has not omitted to mention that to his intimate friend and fellow collegian, the late Babu Hari Mohan Sen, he was much indebted for many kind offices done to him. It is worthy of mention that even out of the scholarship of Rs. 16 *per mensem*, which he held at College for two years, Shib Chunder used to grant small monthly allowances to some of his female relatives and to his family priest and spiritual guide. This system developed with the gradual expansion of his income, until the list of such pensioners upon his bounty became a pretty long one. Shib Chunder's charities also expanded with his income ; but they were administered with such secrecy that even the wife of his bosom never knew their full extent. Shib Chunder always tried to be discriminating in his charity ; but we fear that his compassionate nature not unfrequently got the better of his principles, for we have often seen him impress on a "sturdy and valiant beggar" the extreme impropriety of an able-bodied man not working for his daily bread and then stealthily slip into his hands a four-anna bit or other small coin, of which he always kept a good supply handy for the purpose. It was not merely those individual cases of distress which came under his direct personal observation that evoked Shib Chunder's warm sympathy, but he stretched his slender purse to the utmost to relieve general distress caused in remote districts or provinces by famines, floods, cyclones and the like visitations. As an instance in point, we may mention that only a few days before his death he wrote a letter to Babu Surendra Nath Banerjee, enquiring what steps were being taken for relieving the distress caused by floods in the Nuddea District and expressing his willingness to subscribe to any relief fund that might be formed.

Shib Chunder's treatment of his dependants was beyond all praise. When he was first appointed a Deputy Collector, it was the custom of the service for each Deputy Collector to receive an allowance from Government out of which he was required to maintain his own ministerial establishment. In accordance with this custom, Shib Chunder took with him to Midnapur as his *amlahs*, a number of men with whom he was personally acquainted and two of whom were his brothers-in-law. He not only provided all these men with employment under him, but also provided most of them with quarters in his own lodgings and took his daily meals in their company, no distinction being made between him and his dependants in any respect. This went on for some length of time until he suffered from dyspepsia to such a degree that at the pressing request of his sister, whose husband was one of his subordinates, he was obliged to take his meals separately, the description of rice then consumed by him being more suitable for an invalid. But in all other respects the food supplied to his dependants resembled his own. His attachment for his old *amlahs* was so great that long after his retirement from the service he received with open arms any of them who might stand in need of his help. We have seen several of them, when they were out of employ or otherwise in distress, make his house their home for months together and live upon his bounty. It is hardly necessary to add that Shib Chunder's kind and considerate treatment of his domestics made them look upon him more as a father than as a master. The innate sweetness of his temper never gave place to the peevishness and irritability which are the usual incidents of age or lingering illness, and his self-reliant habits made him less dependent on his servants than most men of his years and position in life. A strict teetotaller all his life, he lived on a proverbially spare diet. But his love of hospitality was no less remarkable than his abstemiousness and he took every opportunity of indulging in it. His capacity for work was also not at all commensurate with his frugal fare. By his economical use of time and methodical habits he was enabled to get through a good deal of work with the greatest ease. Besides keeping his own private accounts and those of some of his absentee relatives, he kept the accounts of all the public institutions founded by him and wrote all the reports and conducted all important correspondence connected therewith. He

hated perfunctory or slovenly work. Whatever he did was characterized by neatness and thoroughness. Even his college note-books,
which were carefully preserved by him to the end of his life, possessed these characteristics. His love of knowledge continued undiminished to the last, though he was prevented by ill health and
general debility, during the last few years of his life, from gratifying
his love of reading to the desired extent.

His average monthly income from all sources after his retirement
from the public service was very moderate, and his large public and
private charities were out of all proportion to his income, considering
the decent and respectable style in which he always lived. It was
only by enforcing the most rigid economy in all matters where a
retrenchment of expenditure was practicable,—and in this he was
ably seconded by his wife, who was an admirable and ever-watchful
housewife,—that he was able to make the two ends meet. His guiding
principle was—waste not, want not. It required, however, no ordinary
tact to steer clear of the Scylla of wasteful extravagance on the
one hand, and of the Charybdis of sordid parsimony on the other.

In nothing was Shib Chunder's many-sided culture so strikingly
displayed as in the attention paid by him to the laws of physical
health, for he clearly realized that the perfection of culture consists
in the harmonious development of the physical, intellectual, moral,
and spiritual sides of man's nature. The following extract from his
Autobiography shows how careful he was, to preserve his health.

"Although constitutionally I am weak, yet by a temperate and
regular mode of living I have managed under God's providence to
enjoy a pretty long life. I have studied the laws of health and have
tried my best to observe them. My food has been very simple, rice,
dál, vegetables, fish, milk and bread. I have always followed the
golden rule 'early to bed and early to rise.' I took moderate
exercise (walking) every morning, after taking a cup of tea or coffee
or cocoa, and used dumb-bells and flesh-brush after bath. At present
milk is the only beverage taken by me in the morning and I never
go out with an empty stomach. The following is the routine of my
daily life at present :—I rise at 5 A.M., in all seasons of the year, and
after washing my face I sit down to read some newspapers or religious books. At 6½ or 7, I take one *pua* (¼ seer) of milk with an arrow-

root biscuit. I then come out to take a short walk, after which I look into my private affairs and also attend to public matters if there be any. At 10 A.M. I bathe my body in tepid and head in cold water, after using the flesh-brush. The dumb-bell exercise has been discontinued in consequence of physical weakness. After bath I sit to family prayer and then take my breakfast or rather dinner at 11 A.M., which consists of a small quantity of rice, *dál*, some vegetables and fish, and a *pua* of milk, with a little sweetmeat. I never drink water till 3 or 4 hours after the meal. After this I take a little rest for half an hour or so, and then attend to business or reading. At 5 P.M. I take 5 drops of tincture opii (under medical advice) and eat some fruits, or a biscuit and *batasa* (sugar-cake). At 7 P.M. I take my evening meal, consisting of 3 or 4 small *chapatis* of bread or a few slices of loaf with a little fish-curry and a *pua* of milk and some sweetmeats. I go to bed just at 9 P.M., spending the interval in conversation with my family and friends. I am now 77 years old (July 1888) and thank God I still keep a tolerably good health, though it is sometimes out of order. My present complaint is great general debility."

Shib Chunder's stature was rather below the middle height. His slight physique consisted of little else than skin and bones ; but the muscles of his arms were well-developed and he was very active and alert in his movements. There was nothing particularly remarkable in his features, except a pair of bushy eyebrows beneath which peered a pair of beaming eyes, which "seemed to love whate'er they looked upon."

Shib Chuder's affable manners made him accessible to all. To his friends he was "sweet as summer." He survived almost all his old friends. His most intimate friends in his latter days were the late Raja Digambar Mittra and the late Babus Peary Chand Mittra and Ramtonoo Lahiri. But Shib Chunder had also many young friends ; for he loved to associate with the young and fully shared their youthful aspirations. The snows of age did not seem to have at all damped his youthful ardour and enthusiasm, and we might well apply to him the poet's lines :

> " But springtide blossoms on thy lips,
> And tears take sunshine from thine eyes."

In his family relations his conduct was no less admirable than in
the other relations of life.   He was a dutiful son and an affectionate
brother.   He long maintained his only sister and her husband, who
lived with him until he was able to build a separate house for them at a
short distance from his own.   His affection for his nephews (brothers'
and cousins' sons) knew no bounds.   Need we add that he was an
affectionate father and loving husband ?   Of his domestic life he speaks
thus in his *Autobiography* :—"My marriage with the second daughter
of the late Babu Baidya Nath Ghosh of Gopalnagar in the district of
Hugli took place in April, 1826, when I was 15 years and she 9 years
old.   This early marriage was, of course, settled and agreed to by
the parents of both parties, in which I had no voice.   But thank God
I have never had any reason to be dissatisfied with the match ; on the
contrary I have always considered myself fortunate in having a wife
who is in every respect deserving of love.   Her natural good sense,
her virtuous disposition, and her devotedness to me are beyond all
praise.   The issues of the marriage were six daughters and one son."

Shib Chunder's noble wife was really an ornament of her sex.   Born
of parents who were noted for their piety, she inherited all their virtues
and was gifted, withal, with a tenacious memory and no inconsiderable
share of mother-wit.   Shib Chunder had, therefore, very little difficulty
to encounter in educating her and moulding her character quite after
his heart.   We have already alluded to her wonderful tact in the
economical management of her household.   By dint of judicious economy, systematically practised throughout her life, she managed to
scrape up a little fortune out of the allowance given her by her husband
to meet household expenses, and she utilized the fund thus formed to
supplement her husband's charities and to gratify her *own* charitable
feelings which rivalled those of her husband.   A fine bathing *ghat*, with
a covered landing place, which she erected to her father's memory,
right opposite the Konnagar Brahmo Samaj, still attests her filial
piety, and the Charitable Homœopathic Dispensary founded and
endowed by her at her husband's house at Konnagar still testifies
to her benevolence.   She thus realised Milton's ideal of a true wife ·

> " Nothing lovelier can be found
> In woman than to study household good
> And good works in her husband to promote."

The story of her early education has all the interest of a romance. When she was quite a little girl, she had to cook, in common with Brajakisor's grown-up daughters-in-law, for Brajakisor's large family, in accordance with the custom then universally in vogue. The delicate little creature could not, without assistance, remove from the fireplace the huge earthen pot containing the rice cooked by her. In the intervals between her culinary operations, she used to scrawl on the kitchen floor the letters of the alphabet with a piece of charcoal and thus learn to write. She would afterwards carefully rub out the letters lest she should be detected in the forbidden occupation. Her only preceptor was her husband, who was then a student of the Hindu College. During his hebdomadal visits to Konnagar, she used to learn from him how to read and write, at a late hour of the night, when feeling quite weary after the day's hard work. But her indomitable zeal and perseverance in the pursuit of knowledge under such difficulties were ultimately crowned with success. In the course of a few years she was able to read all the best books then existing in the Bengalee literature, including such works as the *Yoga Vashistha Ramayana* or the *Tatwabodhini Patrika*. A retentive memory enabled her to remember in her old age a good deal of what she had read in her youth. Her keen hunger for knowledge continued to the end of her days. But that which formed the core of her character was her devotion to her husband, whose slightest wants she anticipated and supplied with the instinct of a true wife. She not only loved him as the husband of her girlhood, but adored him as her spiritual guide. Under his saintly guidance she eventually attained a spiritual elevation from which she was able to look with equal eye upon a street cooly and upon her own offspring, as she once told the late venerable Bejoy Krishna Goswami, not long before her death. During a married life of nearly sixty-five years, which in a European country would have entitled her to the honours of a diamond wedding, she never had a difference with her husband, and during the period of nearly four years by which she survived her husband, she practised all the austerities of a Hindu widow, though she was a pure theist. When she felt that her end was approaching, she became boisterously jubilant at the thought of meeting her beloved again in a better world, and her last breath was spent in singing hymns. Shib Chunder and his wife were in sooth—

"A matchless pair;
With equal virtue formed, and equal grace,
The same distinguished by their sex alone."

Here we close our imperfect sketch of the life of Shib Chunder which is about the most perfect specimen of human life with which we are acquainted. Attracted by his charming personality, we have been imperceptibly led to exceed the limits we originally assigned to this part of our subject. But, apart from the intrinsic value of his life, Shib Chunder exercised so great an influence over Grish Chunder, that we hope our readers will excuse this long digression. Not only did Shib Chunder largely inoculate Grish Chunder with his own liberal ideas, but his life presented a noble object-lesson which gave a great impetus to the moral and intellectual development of Grish Chunder. Grish himself used to say that it was his alliance, by marriage, with so distinguished a personage that first induced him to prove himself worthy of the honour by completing by private study his unfinished school education. In illustration of Grish's profound veneration for Shib Chunder, we may mention one little circumstance, *viz*, that although Grish was dearer to Shib Chunder than his only begotten son, he could never persuade himself to address his father-in-law as "My dear father," but invariably addressed him as "Honoured Sir." Shib Chunder was Grish's guardian angel and liberally helped Grish with his money and sage advice in every difficulty. After Grish's untimely death, he proved more than a father to Grish's orphan children, whom he maintained and educated for nearly ten years. So greatly were his slender resources taxed thereby that although he had retired from the public service some years previously, he was induced to accept employment as Sub-Registrar of Serampore; but after holding that office for some months he resigned it, having suffered in health from the daily journey he had to perform from Konnagar to Serampore and the remuneration not being sufficient for the trouble. Shib Chunder also defrayed the marriage expenses of Grish's youngest daughter who was unmarried at the time of her father's death. Moreover, he materially assisted Grish's children in re-establishing themselves in their paternal homestead, and even after their removal to Calcutta, he continued to pay, as long as he lived, *i.e.*, for about twelve years, an allowance of rupees ten per mensem for the education of Grish's youngest son.

CHAPTER V

OFFICIAL CAREER.

Grish Chunder does not appear to have remained long at school after his marriage. Scarcely a year elapsed since that event before the circumstances of his family necessitated his leaving school to seek his livelihood. A cousin of his, named Kali Kissen, who was the eldest son of Kasi Nath's third son Anund Chunder, and was older than Grish by some eight or nine years, was employed as a clerk in the Financial Department of the Government of India, and he procured for young Grish a small berth in that Department on Rs. 15/- *per mensem* which he was glad to accept as the office was a big one and offered good prospects of advancement. In the obituary notice which appeared in the *Bengalee* of the 25th September, 1869, and from which we have already quoted, it is stated that "after the close of his school career he obtained a small berth in the Financial Department on Rs. 15/- a month, but he soon displayed such aptitude for business that he was promoted to a place of Rs. 50. Through the interest of a friend by the name of Templeton he got a higher berth in the Military Auditor General's Office." The above statement is, in the main, correct. As, however, the pay of the appointment in the late Military Auditor General's Office to which Grish was transferred from the Financial Department on the 31st January, 1847, was only Rs. 50/- a month, it is probable that the pay he was drawing in the Financial Department at the time of such transfer was below Rs. 50. We have no means, however, of verifying the point. The transfer was brought about in the following way:—Mr. Templeton, a good-natured East Indian Assistant of the Financial Department, used every now and then to call at the Military Auditor General's Office, where he had some friends among whom was Mr. James Mackenzie, who afterwards became Collector of Abkari and Stamp Revenue, Calcutta, and who was then employed in the Military Auditor General's Office as Auditor of King's Troops Accounts. Mr. Mackenzie happened one day to mention to Mr. Templeton, in course of conversation, that he was in need of a good assistant and to enquire whether Mr. Templeton knew of a likely young man for a post of Rs. 50/- just sanctioned by Government. Mr. Templeton thereupon mentioned Grish's name and said that although he was but a boy, he was very smart and would do very well for the post. Shortly after this conversation, Grish's transfer to the Military Auditor General's Office was effected. Several years afterwards, Mr. Templeton, who had, by reason of his intemperate habits, lost his appointment and fallen into distress, applied to Grish for help. Grish, who never forgot a good turn done him and who had prospered in his new office, helped Mr. Templeton with a gift of Rs. 200. The Military Auditor General's Office was almost co-eval with the British rule in India. The appointment of Military Auditor General carried a salary of about Rs. 3500 *per men- sem.* Its original designation was "Commissary General," which was altered to "Military Auditor General" in 1788. The establishment of the office, as originally fixed in 1783, was not large, as will be seen from the subjoined summary :—

	Aggregate pay *per mensem.*
Auditors of Disbursements and Book-keepers, Indorsers	Rs.
and Examiners	1010
Portuguese writers	210
Hindoos	... 741

It is interesting to note how in those early days, the *personnel* of the office consisted of three distinct and well-marked classes. All responsible audit and account work was performed by European assistants, whilst all mechanical and copying work was done by Eurasian and Native clerks. The defective education of the latter very naturally precluded them from being entrusted with work of a responsible nature. But the traditional distinction continued to be observed long after the reason for it had ceased to exist by the spread of English education amongst the Natives of Bengal. We shall, however, see presently how the artificial barrier was first broken through in the Military Auditor General's Office. When Grish Chunder joined that office, the appointments of Military Audito General, Deputy Military Auditor General and Assistant Military Auditor General were held by Colonel A. Goldie, Major E. G. I.

Champneys, and Captain Urquhart, respectively. All these officers were exceptionally broad-minded and just in their dealings with their subordinates. Colonel Goldie had been appointed Military Auditor General only a few years back, as a reward for good services rendered during the First Sikh War. His predecessor in office, Colonel Macgregor, one of whose daughters was married to the first Lieutenant-Governor of Bengal, Sir Frederick Halliday, was an officer of the old type. He was very fond of holidays and took very little interest in his work. Colonel Goldie was, however, an officer of an altogether different stamp. He took a real interest in his work, and was well-disposed towards those native clerks of his office who did good work.

It is a most extraordinary circumstance that among the native clerks of Colonel Goldie's office should be found simultaneously employed two men of such exceptional ability and kindred genius as Hurrish Chunder Mookerjee and Grish Chunder Ghose, who joined that office within eighteen months of each other ; for Hurrish, who was older than Grish by five years, joined the Military Auditor General's office on Rs. 25 in August, 1845, and was therefore Grish's senior in the office. It is also worthy of note that the staff of Christian clerks included two such men as Messrs. George Kellner and Robert Hollingbery. Mr. (afterwards Sir. George) Kellner lived to hold successively the high offices of Accountant-General, Military Department, Government of India, and Accountant-General at Cyprus ; whilst Mr. Hollingbery held for many years the post of Assistant Secretary to the Government of India in the Department of Finance and Commerce.

It was Colonel Goldie's great aim to place his office establishment on an efficient footing. He accordingly obtained the sanction of Government to the revision of his office establishment, including the creation of two clerkships on Rs. 100 each *per mensem*. Babu Hurrish Chunder Mookerjee, who had already given evidence of the stuff he was made of, was recommended for one of these new appointments by the Assistant Military Auditor General, Captain Urquhart. Before dealing with the recommendation, however, the Deputy Military Auditor General, Major Champneys, thought it desirable to sound the views of his Chief in the matter. He accordingly spoke to Colonel Goldie on the subject and enquired whether it was his wish that an appointment on

Rs. 100 should be given to a native whose expenses of living were so much less than those of a Christian. To this Colonel Goldie replied that it was his wish to regulate the pay of the clerks of his office solely with reference to their abilities, irrespective of their creed or colour. Major Champneys thereupon asked the Registrar of the office, Mr. J. Kerr, to draft an office order promoting Babu Hurrish Chunder Mookerjee to Rs. 100. Mr. Kerr, who was wedded to the traditional idea that a native should never aspire to such a high rate of pay as Rs. 100 *per mensem*, although his own pay was five times as high, expressed his amazement at the unusual order and ventured to suggest that a native should not be promoted to a post of Rs. 100. "Why not, Mr. Kerr?" exclaimed Major Champneys, and wrote out the order himself. He never afterwards consulted Mr. Kerr in such matters. This marked a new departure in the history of the Military Auditor General's office. Grish Chunder was next promoted to a post of Rs. 100; and in due time several other native assistants were similarly promoted. Other public offices subsequently followed the good example set by the Military Auditor General's office by granting suitable salaries to deserving native assistants.

It is sad to record that so good an officer as Colonel Goldie met his death under the most tragic circumstances. He, with two of his daughters by a Hindoostanee wife, was killed in 1857 in the massacre at Cawnpore, he having proceeded on leave to that station for the benefit of his health. Colonel Champneys, who succeeded Colonel Goldie, was a nephew of Lord Stanley and possessed a fine estate in England. He was as well-disposed towards the natives as Colonel Goldie ; but he was rather short-tempered. Hurrish and Grish were his special favourites, and he lost no opportunity of promoting their interests. Colonel Champneys' manners were, as we have hinted above, not very affable. But his rough exterior concealed a tender heart, in proof of which we may mention that when Mr. (afterwards Sir George) Kellner paid him a visit at his seat in England some years after his retirement from the service, Colonel Champneys gave Mr. Kellner a most hearty reception, showed him round his orchard and insisted on his helping himself to as many of its finest fruits as he cared to have. He also made the kindest enquiries about his old office assistants, not forgetting even his old Record-clerk, Wooma Churn Mookerjee, whose broken English had been a source of constant

diversion to him. At Colonel Champneys' particular desire, as commu_
nicated through Mr. Kellner, Wooma Churn had to write to the
former a letter in his *usual* style. Colonel Champneys was verv
extravagant in his expenditure. The office sircar, Babu Rajnarain
Banerjee, once prevailed upon him to allow him to take charge of his
pay and manage his household expenses. In the course of a few
months, Babu Rajnarain was able to save Rs. 20,000 which he in_
vested in Government securities. But Colonel Champneys speedily
squandered the amount thus saved. On one occasion he went on fur-
lough to the Cape and brought from that colony no less than fifteen
horses. He was very hospitable, but his guests were, it is said, some_
times disgusted with his bad temper. The following interesting
passage *anent* Colonel Champneys, occurs in Sir William Howard
Russell's *My diary of the Indian Mutiny* :—

"Dined with Colonel Champneys, who certainly deserves his reputation as a Calcutta Lucullus, and who is more—a kindly, genial host.
He has a dreadful rôle to fill, for, as Auditor General he has to clip and
cut at pay and allowances—the latter of which, in India, are subjects of
incessant contentions. At dinner met Colonel Lugard 'who distinguished himself in Persia), Captain Malleson, a very in telligent officer
who seems to have paid great attention to Indian politics ; * * *"

Captain (afterwards Colonel) George Bruce Malleson, whom
Sir William Howard Russell met at dinner at Colonel Champneys'
in 1858, then held the appointment of Assistant Military Auditor
General. He was born in London in 1825 and died in 1898 after
a long and varied official career in India. His historical works are
too well known to be mentioned here. All that we need say is,
that his scholarly tastes made him take a special liking for Hurrish
and Grish, whom he treated more as his personal friends than as
subordinates. We are assured by Babu Neel Mony Comar, who was
then employed in the Military Auditor General's office and who is now
an old pensioner widely esteemed for his sterling and unassuming
virtues, that Colonel Malleson thought so highly of Grish's drafts
that before altering them in any way he would invariably come to
Grish and have his views in regard to the proposed alterations. It
was Colonel Malleson who, as one of the original founders of the
Dalhousie Institute, got Grish and his brother Khetter specially admit-

ted as members of that Institute in 1859, a privilege which was reserved exclusively for Europeans. In a letter dated the 6th October, 1869, which appeared in the *Bengalee* of the 23rd idem, Colonel Malleson, who was then Guardian of his Highness the Maharaja of Mysore, wrote as follows of Grish Chunder :—

"I never knew a more upright man, one possessing to a higher degree the qualities of manliness, independence, and love of virtue. He possessed, too, great abilities, and a resolution proof against all difficulties." In conclusion he stated :—"Beyond the sphere of his own relations there are none, I am sure, who regret his loss more than I do. Among his countrymen his name, I trust, will still live, and I earnestly hope to hear that some testimonial will be raised to mark the career of one, of whom they have the highest reason to be proud. I shall be glad to aid such a movement by a donation of Rs. 100."

Of Captain Urquhart, whose name we have already mentioned, we have very little to say beyond that he belonged to the Artillery branch of the Army and was so fond of mathematics that he seriously advised the aforesaid Babu Neel Mony Comar to study the Differential Calculus whenever he felt "dead-tired." On his pay being once retrenched on audit, the same officer naively asked Grish—"Grish, do the audit office cut the pay of their own officers?" Of Major Ferris, who held for some years the appointment of Deputy Military Auditor General, and who had a great liking for Grish, we have only to say that he was remarkable for his herculean strength and physique. We would mention one more name before we close our roll-call of these officers of a by-gone age.

Some time in 1859, Colonel Champneys left India for good. He was succeeded by Colonel J. Hannyngton, who was the last officer who held the office of Military Auditor General and the first who held the office of Controller of Military Finance, which was created on the abolition of the old office. The re-organization was sanctioned in 1861, but it did not take effect till the following year.

Colonel (afterwards Major General) Hannyngton was a splendid mathematician. He held the appointment of Assistant Financial Secretary and Actuary at the India Office at the time of his death, and his Tables are, we believe, still used for calculating the capitalized value of officers' pensions, &c.

Although Grish won the golden opinions of all officers under whom he had the honour to serve, Colonel Hannyngton was the only officer whose opinion of Grish Chunder was recorded in the form of a certificate, and the reason for this singular dearth of testimonials was thus explained in an application made by Grish on the 9th May, 1869, for an Under-Secretaryship to the Government of Bengal :—

" I am sorry that as I never solicited certificates from those under whom I had the honour to serve, believing that my own right hand would stand me in better stead for the promotion of my interests in life than any laudatory lines that I could muster through the courtesy or indulgence of those placed above me, I cannot support this application by any such testimonials. But a certificate was sent to me, unasked, by Colonel Hannyngton, late Controller of Military Finance, on the eve of his departure for Europe, which I therefore value, and a copy of which I beg to annex"

The certificate referred to, is given below :—

" I have much pleasure in stating that Babu Grish Chunder Ghose is a most efficient public servant—diligent and upright in the discharge of his important duties as Auditor in the Pay Department.

April 8th, 1862.
J. Hannyngton, Col.
Late Controller Mily. Finance."

Hurrish and Grish hunted in couples. Whenever Hurrish was promoted, Grish stepped into his place. The following extract from a letter dated the 8th November, 1855, which Grish wrote to his brother Sree Nath, is given by way of illustration :—

" Mr. Sturmer, that lean and hungry-looking fellow, the sworn enemy to native progress, has fallen ill and the doctors have advised him to take a change of air. He has obtained 4 months' leave to visit the Upper Provinces, and Hurris, in supersession of all the other auditors, has been appointed to take charge of his duties. I have been pitch-forked to Hurris' place with the additional responsibility, which Hurris never had, of supervising the audit of my former Disbursement—the Benares—which has been made over to a raw young fellow, Mr. Gordon, who understands nothing of the work. We were asked to make our own arrangements with Mr. Sturmer regarding the remuneration for the additional labour imposed upon us by these transfers. But we generously declined touching a pice of his money. I am however the most unfortunate, having now a vast amount of work before me in the Presidency Circle, swollen up like a July torrent by the accession of a host of Regiments on account of the Sonthal insurrection—over and above the labor imposed on me by Major Champneys' plan of getting me to overlook Mr. Gordon's work also."

In order to ascertain the different dates on which the pay of Rs. 50 on which Grish was first transferred to the Military Auditor General's office on the 31st January, 1847, was successively increased, we referred, many years ago, to the old records of that office. But the oldest pay abstract of the establishment of that office on which we could lay our hands was the one for August 1854, all previous ones having been destroyed. In the pay abstract for August 1854, Grish was shown as Auditor, Sirhind Division, on Rs. 200. There is, therefore, no means, of ascertaining the exact dates on which Grish's initial pay of Rs. 50 was increased successively to Rs. 100, Rs. 150, and Rs. 200—for we know that the rate of increment throughout his service was uniformly Rs. 50. As, however, we know that when Grish bought his first garden at Ooltadanga on the 5th January, 1852, he was in receipt of pay at Rs. 150 a month, it follows that he received two increments of Rs. 50 each, within five years of his joining the Military Auditor General's office.

We learn from the *Autobiography* of Khetter Chunder Ghose that when he joined the Military Auditor General's office in June 1853, his brother Grish Chunder was an "Auditor" in that office, presumably on Rs. 200 a month, the lowest rate of pay then attached to the post. We may, therefore, safely conclude that Grish Chunder was advanced to this rate of pay before he had put in seven years' service. No uncertainty exists in regard to the dates of his subsequent promotions. He was promoted to Rs. 250 from the 3rd November, 1857, to Rs. 300 from the 22nd April, 1861, and to Rs. 350 from the 1st January, 1862. But although he continued in the service for nearly eight years after his advancement to Rs. 350 in 1862, and although he was, on the transfer during that year of Mr. Robert Hollingbery to the Financial Department of the Government of India, appointed to the highly responsible post of Registrar of the office of Examiner, Pay Department, which was formed on the abolition of the old Military Auditor General's Office, Grish Chunder never drew more than Rs. 350, that being the highest pay included in the scale tentatively sanctioned for the establishment of the new office, while the scale eventually sanctioned for that office—which provided for the Registrar a maximum pay of Rs. 600—did not, thanks to the potent influence of red tape, come into effect until five years after Grish's death. Thus it happened that although Grish lived to attain a much higher official position than Hurrish ever did, he was not destined to draw even Rs. 400, the pay drawn by the latter as a senior auditor in the old Military Auditor General's Office. The promise held out by his rapid promotion in the early part of his official career, when he had comparatively less need of money, was belied by the dead block which faced him towards the latter end of his service, when the increasing wants of a growing family would have made him welcome even a modest addition to his pay. So the fountain became dry when his need was the sorest, and the hope of advancement deferred too long was enough to sicken the heart of even so contented and restful a man as Grish. Very naturally, therefore, Grish used to recall with delight the happy years he had spent in his old office, although the head of his new office, Major (afterwards Major General) T. B. Harrison, always treated him with the greatest kindness and consideration. The son of a Scotch clergyman, Major Harrison was a truly God-fearing man. He was as intelligent as he was hard-working. He was a *pucca kerani*. He was conversant with every detail of the multifarious work turned out by his large office establishment, and he used to keep notes of all important Government orders and rulings bearing on such work. His intimate knowledge of the capabilities of each individual assistant of his office enabled him to promote the most deserving man in every case, irrespective of creed or colour. So kind and considerate was he in his treatment of his subordinates, that he *compelled* them to take privilege leave by rotation, lest their health and working capacity should suffer for want of such occasional relaxation from work. So fearless and independent was he in the discharge of his official duties that he once issued a retrenchment against the head of his department, Colonel Broome, Controller General of Military Expenditure, who took the mean revenge of moving Government to reduce the staff salary of the First Examiner, Pay Department, from Rs. 1000 to Rs. 800 a month.   On another occasion, a native auditor of his office having made an unfortunate slip in audit which resulted in a loss to Government of two lacs of rupees, Government called upon Major Harrison to furnish the name of the auditor at fault, but he declined to do so, taking all responsibility for the mistake upon himself as the sole responsible head of the office.   Need we say that Grish Chunder considered it an, honor to serve under such an officer? The most perfect harmony also existed between Grish Chunder and the Second Pay Examiner, Captain W. W. Aubert, an officer of the Invalid Establishment.   Captain Aubert had a wooden leg, his natural leg having been mauled by Master Stripes at a tiger-hunt.   The accident happened in this way.   The elephant on which Captain Aubert rode took fright at the sight of the formidable beast and rushed through the jungle with such headlong fury that the gallant Captain was in imminent danger of being crushed to death by the over-hanging boughs of trees.   He was accordingly obliged to leave his howdah and save himself by holding on to a projecting branch, following the example set by his Mahout.   His vindictive enemy, seeing how matters stood, patiently lay in wait for his victims at the foot of the tree.   After a while, Captain Aubert found it impossible to hold on any longer and he let go his hold of the branch, just as succour was coming into view.   The wary beast sprang upon Captain Aubert as soon as he dropped from the tree and succeeded in fearfully mauling one of his thighs before the animal could be despatched by the shots fired by some of the *shikaris* who had now approached close to the tree.   On the eve of his departure for Europe, Captain Aubert presented Grish Chunder with some valuable books and wrote on the fly-leaf of each volume—"Presented to Babu Grish Chunder Ghose by his friend W. W. Aubert."   Major (afterwards Colonel) A. E. Osborn, who succeeded Captain Aubert as Second Pay Examiner, was a brother of Rear-Admiral Sherard Osborn, the well-known author of the *Arctic Journal* and other works, who commanded vessels in two expeditions sent in search of Sir John Franklin, also commanded the British Squadron in the Sea of Azov during the Crimean War and took a leading part in the Chinese War of 1857-59.   Colonel Osborn also had a high regard for Grish Chunder and subscribed the handsome sum of Rs. 200 to the Grish Memorial

Fund. Among the other Military officers who subscribed to the Fund may be named Colonel Malleson, Guardian to H. H. the Maharaja of Mysore, Major Harrison, First Examiner, Pay Department, Colonel Mundy, Presidency Pay master, Colonel Hill, Military Accountant, and Captain Cowper, Examiner of Ordnance, Barrack, Clothing and Dockyard Accounts.

So great was the interest that Colonel Osborn took in the Grish testimonial that, noticing a delay in the realization of subscriptions thereto, he wrote an indignant letter which was published in the *Bengalee* of the 22nd January 1870 and which ended as follows :—

" Those who swear at Asiatics for being more ready with their tongues than their purses will be pleased to learn that—after the lapse of weeks—barely one half the necessary amount has been collected. For my part I am filled with shame that the wealthy and intelligent among the Bengali gentry of Calcutta have allowed so humiliating a fact to be charged against them. Is it possible that the truth has not reached them ?"

It is worthy of remark that in former days, that is to say, before the promulgation of the present stringent rules prohibiting Government servants from having anything to do with the press, there were heads of offices who used to take a pride in having clever journalists for their subordinates. The first question that Colonel Osborn put to Grish's eldest son when the latter joined the Pay Examiner's office, was " Do you write for the papers ?" and on receiving a reply in the negative, he remarked : "You should follow in your father's footsteps." Colonel Champneys used, it is said, to supply Hurrish Chunder Mookerjee with London telegrams for publication in the *Hindoo Patriot* and there is reason to suspect that Colonel Malleson occasionally contributed to the columns of that paper. The following remarks made by Grish Chunder regarding the right of Government servants to freely criticise the measures of Governmet are quoted from an article which appeared in the *Hindoo Patriot* of the 11th May 1854. They have a peculiar significance and interest at the present day.

"All civilized Government ought to bear in mind that their power is merely derivative and that because a member of the general polity consents for the benefit as well of himself as that of the public to accept service under the State, he does not thereby forfeit the title of a free-born citizen to give expression to his opinions regarding measures to which he may take objection. On the contrary, his official experience should peculiarly qualify him for leading the public mind into the correct channel of thought; and to a Government that builds not its power on the complement of bayonets at its service, but on the reverence and affection of its grateful subjects, such discussion is fraught with manifold advantages. But Evil seeks darkness and the East India Company is certainly not in a position to bear the light."

Grish Chunder's genial nature made him extremely popular alike with the officers and subordinates of his department. Many Military officers who had occasion to see him in course of business, became his personal friends. Among these may be named Major Delane, Military Secretary, and Lieutenant Colonel Hedayet Ali, Native A. D. C. to H. E. the Commander-in-Chief. The former officer once presented Grish with a fine shawl *Chogah* specially made up for him at Simla, for no ordinary *Chogah* would fit Grish's Afghan proportions. Grish's thorough knowledge of the Military Pay and Audit Regulations and his wonderful facility in drafting official correspondence enabled him not only to finish his own work quickly, so that he never had occasion to take work home, but also to accord his ready help to all who sought for it. Assistants from neighbouring or allied offices not unfrequently came to him to have their drafts corrected or put into shape. One of these young assistants was eventually appointed Examiner of Ordnance Factory Accounts in India. He has since retired from the the service and is now residing in England. The note-books in which Grish used to jot down the pith of all important Government rulings and orders in a remarkably clear and concise style, formed two bulky volumes which were constantly referred to by the office long after his death.

It was, after all, a fortunate circumstance that Grish Chunder's lot was cast in a public office; for, had he followed a lucrative profession, he would undoubtedly have earned a fortune, but it is very doubtful whether in that case he would have had much time left for literary pursuits. "For my own part," says John Stuart Mill, "I have, through life, found office duties an actual rest from the other mental occupations I have carried on simultaneously with them." The late Sir John Kaye, who succeeded Mill at the India Office, also found time for considerable literary work. The literary work of another India Office clerk, Charles Lamb, is too well-known to be referred to here.

GRISH CHUNDER GHOSE.

KUNTALINE PRESS, CALCUTTA.

CHAPTER VI.

————•·•·•————

Early Journalism—The Bengal Recorder—The Hindoo Patriot— The Calcutta Monthly Review.

WE trace Grish's 'prentice hand in journalism as far back as his school days, when he used to contribute to the manuscript journal edited by his school fellow, the late Babu Koylas Chunder Bose. After leaving school, he contributed stray letters to the " Hindu Intelligencer, '' a weekly newspaper edited from about the year 1846 by Babu Kashi Prasad Ghose, the well-known author of the " *Shair* " and other poems, whose reputation as a votary of the Muses was once so great that Fisher's *Drawing Room Scrap Book* for 1835, which adorned every drawing room in London and which was edited by the then celebrated " L. E. L." or Letitia Landon, included a fine steel engraving of the handsome bust of the Hindu bard. When Babu Koylas Chunder Bose started " The Literary Chronicle," a year or so before the establishment of the " Bengal Recorder " in or about 1850, Grish Chunder regularly contributed to it. The " Literary Chronicle" was a small monthly publication, which existed for some years and was mainly confined to notices of new literary works published in England or India. We remember having read in an early issue of the " Literary Chronicle," a slashing review by Grish Chunder of the " Encyclopædia Bengalensis" or " বিদ্যা কল্পদ্রুম," which was then being edited by the late Dr. Krishna Mohan Banerjee under the auspices of Lord Hardinge. Unfortunately, however, our file of the " Literary Chronicle" has since been lost. But Grish made his real *debut* as a journalist in the *Bengal Recorder*, which was founded under circum- stances which we have already described. Sree Nath, who started the paper, carefully preserved a complete file of the *Bengal Recorder* until in an evil hour he was induced by a near relative to lend the file to the late Babu Sambhu Chunder Mookerjee, who never returned it to the owner. We have therefore no means of judging of the extent and excellence of Grish Chunder's contributions to the *Bengal Recorder*, beyond the statement made by Babu Koylas Chunder Bose in his obituary notice of Grish Chunder to which we have already referred, that they " were innumerable and much applauded. The then Editor of the *Friend of India*, Mr. Marshman, never lost an opportunity of commending the style and spirit of those writings." That Grish Chunder had no inconsiderable share in conducting the paper, is also apparent from the fact that in the obituary notice which appeared in the *National Paper* of the 22nd September 1869, he is described as " Joint Editor with his brother Babu Sree Nath Ghose, of the *Bengal Recorder*." This description is borne out by what we have often heard from Sree Nath himself, *viz*, that both he and his brother Grish had to work at the press at Cossitola where the *Recorder* was printed, till a very late hour of the night preceding the morning on which the paper was due. As the locality swarmed with drunken sailors, the two brothers, in order to avoid being molested by them, used to palm themselves off as a pair of jolly British tars by trolling divers sea-catches in sailor fashion. But they were obliged, ere long, to discontinue this dangerous trick ; for, one night they were accosted by a veritable blue-jacket with the unexpected query " What ship do you belong to, boys ?" Finding it rather difficult to answer the question, our young journalists thought it safer to have recourse to their heels than to their wits. They accordingly made off for their distant home as fast as their legs could carry them. Sree Nath used to relate many a funny anecdote in connection with his first journalistic venture. An old pedagogue who had known the two brothers from their boyhood, could scarcely believe that the clever articles which appeared in the *Recorder* were written by two such raw youths ; so he had the impertinence to ask them one day " Do you pay for your editorials ?" The incident, to the horror of the questioner, was duly published in the next impression of the *Recorder*. When the paper was first started, it had a very limited circulation. One of the distributors of the paper, on being asked to take copies for sale to the various public offices in Calcutta, refused to do so point blank, saying that he was not prepared to make a laughing stock of himself ("আরে মহাশয় ! আমি কি হাস্যাস্পদনীয় হ'ব ?"). Gradually, however, the new weekly found favor with men of culture. We have already referred to the favourable notice taken of it by Mr. John Clark Marshman, the then editor of the *Friend of India*. Mr. Arthur Grote, Collector of Calcutta, who was a brother of the eminent historian of Greece and who afterwards became the Senior Member of the Board of Revenue and President of the Asiatic Society of Bengal, was also favorably impressed with the merits of the new journal. One day Mr. Grote happened, in course of conversation with Babu Shib Chunder Deb, who was then employed as Deputy Collector of the 24 Pergunnahs, to enquire of the latter whether he knew by whom the *Recorder* was conducted and how he was employed. Babu Shib Chunder Deb thereupon informed Mr. Grote that the paper was conducted by his son-in-law Grish Chunder, who held a respectable post in a Government Office, and by his elder brother Sree Nath, who was without any employment. Mr. Grote thereupon asked Babu Shib Chunder to be so good as to send word to Sree Nath that Mr. Grote would like to see him. This led to Sree Nath's admission temporarily to Government service in 1852 as a clerk in the Calcutta Collectorate on Rs. 150 *per mensem* and his subsequent appointment as a Deputy Collector on Rs. 200 *per mensem* in 1854

In a long article which appeared in the *Reis and Rayyet* of the 14th March 1903, it is stated that Hurrish Chunder Mookerjee " wrote legal and judicial articles in the 'Recorder.' " We doubt, however, the correctness of this statement, as we never heard Sree Nath say anything of the kind. We are inclined to accept the statement made by the late Rai Kristo Das Pal in his obituary notice of Grish Chunder, that in the *Bengal Recorder* " the late Hurrish Chunder, whose literary talents were then just budding forth, was assigned the humble place of 'correspondent.' "

Not many months after Sree Nath's admission to Government service in 1852, the *Bengal Recorder* had to be discontinued owing to circumstances over which the two brothers had no control and which have no interest for the general reader.

We take from the article in the *Reis and Rayyet* referred to above, the following account of the origin of the *Hindoo Patriot* :—

" In 1853, one Madu Sudan Ray, of Burrabazar, having, by accident, come into possession of a printing press and some types, and knowing no other mode of working them, proposed to the Ghoses to start a newspaper in English. It was then agreed to drop the name of the 'Bengal Recorder,' and with its subscribers for a nucleus to begin a new paper. It was of an evening in January 1853, in Khetter's *baitakkhana*, the three brothers being present, that the 'Hindoo Patriot' may be said to have been conceived. What should be the name of the new paper ? was debated. There were as many suggestions as the number of brothers.

It might seem that the name 'Hindoo Patriot' must have been taken as indicative of a particular and bold policy of opposition to Government and Europeans and of vindication of native usages and ideas. Nothing of the kind. As usual, the name arose by accident. Grish suggested ' The Hindoo Standard,' Sreenath proposed ' The Hindoo Gentleman.' A bright idea struck Khetter. He said, why not call it 'The Hindoo Patriot?' and, as that name appeared appropriate, it was adopted by acclamation.

A statement appeared that Hurrish had christened the paper. It cannot be true ; for, Hurrish joined the staff afterwards. In a letter dated the 7th March in the ' Indian Mirror' of the 10th March last, Gobin Chunder Dhur writes :—' The young members of the Auddy family of Pathuriaghata who were pupils of the Oriental Seminary started the 'Hindoo Patriot.' Babu Hurrish Chunder Mookerjee who was also a pupil of the Seminary joined them.' Babu Dhur is as right in the one statement as in the other. It does not appear, except in his statement, that Hurrish was ever in the Oriental Seminary."

The following account of the origin of the *Hindoo Patriot* is given in Rai Kristo Das Pal's obituary notice of Grish Chnnder :— " About the time the well-known Charter campaign was meditated by the leaders of native society, an enterprising native gentleman of the banker caste, Babu Madhu Sudan Ray, conceived the idea of starting the *Hindoo Patriot*. He was acquainted with the Ghose brothers and invited them to undertake its editorial management. They readily consented, but they or rather Grish Chunder recommended him to Babu Hurrish Chunder Mookerjee. We have the authority of this gentleman for stating that it was Hurrish Chunder who gave to the paper the name '*Hindoo Patriot*' so dear to us, and was elected its first responsible editor. It is superfluous for us to say that the hard intellectuality, rare power of reasoning, and a thorough knowledge of local politics, which Hurrish Chunder possessed, pre-eminently qualified him for the chiefship of the only native political organ of the day, and Grish Chunder, who watched with interest and admiration the rapid development of his friend's intellect, cheerfully served under him."

The *Bengalee* of the 9th October 1869 republished the following correction which appeared at the time in the *National Paper* :— " The 'Patriot' in a memorial of the lamented deceased has unconsciously done him a wrong which requires prompt correction. We know the connection that Babu Madhu Sudan Ray had in the first starting of the 'Hindoo Patriot,' but he seems to have forgotten the fact, that in the early days of that journal Babu Hurrish Chunder held a very subordinate position in the management of the paper. The name of the journal was wholly of Grish's coinage and it was some time before Hurrish joined. Those who know anything of the circumstances connected with the early growth of the ' Patriot,' must remember that Hurrish was for a long time a mere subaltern."

We may add that we had the honour of knowing personally Babu Madhu Sudan Ray, who died in green old age only a few years ago, and on our questioning him, some years before his death, how he could have made the statement ascribed to him when he knew very well that Hurrish joined the staff of the *Hindoo Patriot* sometime after it had been brought into the field, he at once repudiated the statement.

The *Hindoo Patriot* was started on Thursday the 6th January 1853, and Grish Chunder was undoubtedly its first editor. To remove all doubt on the point, we extract the following from the obituary notices of Grish Chunder which appeared in the leading native journals of the day :—

The Bengalee—" Babu Grish Chunder on his own account started a new paper and christened it the *Hindoo Patriot.*"

The Indian Mirror—"He [Grish Chunder] it was who first started the *Hindoo Patriot.*"

The National Paper—" The *Hindoo Patriot* was first brought into the field by him. He was a regular contributor to that paper in the time of Babu Hurrish Chunder Mookerjee. After the death of

Hurrish the paper was held up by him jointly with another gentleman who is now on the staff of the *Patriot*. For some reason or other he broke off his connection with this paper, and sought to make the *Bengalee* its successful rival."

The Reflector (published at Allahabad)—" He projected and brought into light the *Hindoo Patriot*. * * * Having reared and nurtured his dear little bantling, with the tenderest paternal care and solicitude, during the first few years of its existence, he made it over to his excellent friend and *co-laborateur*, the illustrious Babu Hurrish Chunder Mookerjee * * * *"

It was not long before Hurrish joined Grish and shared with him in the editorial management of the paper; but it was after the *Hindoo Patriot* had been in existence for some few years and had already become a power in the realm, that Hurrish Chunder became its sole responsible editor. "The genius and energy of Hurrish," as Babu Koylas Chunder Bose justly remarks in his obituary notice of Grish Chunder, "soon proved him to be a worthy compeer, when Babu Grish Chunder conferred on him the Captainship of his own accord, contenting himself with occasional displays of wit and strength of mind which could not be mistaken." As instances of such "occasional displays of wit and strength of mind" we may refer to "those scathing and crushing articles against the Volunteers" which, Rai Kristo Das Pal says, Grish Chunder chiefly wrote for the *Hindoo Patriot* during the Mutinies.

In Mr. Skrine's Life of the late Babu Sambhu Chunder Mookerjee, the early history of the *Hindoo Patriot* is thus related ·—" The paper arose from the ashes of the *Bengal Recorder*, one of the ephemerides which heralded the awakening of a nation's literary spirit. The proprietor found it a losing speculation ; and in 1854 offered the Press and good will for a mere song. Harish Chandra, who had been one of the leading contributors, saw an opportunity of gratifying a darling ambition and became the purchaser. The transaction was veiled in secrecy, for his master, the Military Auditor General, would hardly have approved of a proprietor-editor of a journal as one of his subordinates. The 'man of straw' put forward was an elder brother Babu Haran Chandra Mukherji ; but the entire labour of editing and management fell on Harish."

We are not aware of the authority on which Mr. Skrine's statement is based, that the Press and good will of the *Hindoo Patriot* were bought by Hurrish, in his brother's name, in 1854. The incorrectness of this statement will, however, at once appear from the extract given below from an obituary notice of Hurrish Chunder which appeared in the *Hindoo Patriot* of the 19th June, 1861 :—

"As a pecuniary speculation the *Patriot* was a failure. The first proprietor, therefore, after sustaining a loss of a few thousand Rupees, at the end of three years offered it for sale. No purchaser appearing, the paper was determined to be abolished and the press and the materials sold. Hurris who by economy had made a little money, rather than see the paper perish, at once resolved to invest it in a speculation which had proved a failure and was not at all likely to prove anything better in his hands, supported by a hope that his exertions might at least make the *Patriot* pay its bare expenses. For himself he never meant to make a pice by his literary labors. In June 1855 he bought the *Patriot* in the name of his brother the present proprietor and removed the press and office to Bhowanipore near his house."

From the foregoing extract it is clear that the transfer of property did not, at all events, take place before June, 1855, if not sometime in 1856—for, as the paper was started in January, 1853, and as its original proprietor is stated to have offered it for sale after it had been in existence for three years, it is probable that the sale was effected sometime in 1856, although this cannot be verified in the absence of the files of the *Hindoo Patriot* for 1855 and 1856, which are not available. The file for 1857 shews that the paper was then printed at Bhowanipore. The sole editorship of the *Hindoo Patriot* devolved upon Hurrish, in all probability, when he became the proprietor of that paper, and we suspect this to have happened sometime in 1856; for, in a letter which Grish wrote on the 16th October, 1855, to his brother Sree Nath, who was then Deputy Collector, Balasore, we come across the following passage :—"Write me a history of Balasore and I will engage to puff it in the columns of the 'Patriot.' Do you receive your copy regularly and do you *read* it ? Now be sincere for once and tell me the truth as to my latter query."

Grish's anxiety to know the truth as to his "latter query" makes us suspect that if he was not, at the time, the chief editor of the "Patriot," he had, at any rate, a big finger in the pie.

We notice that in the account given of Babu Haris Chandra Mukerji in Mr. Buckland's *Bengal under the Lieutenant Governors*, Vol. II, it is stated that "it was in 1855 that the *Hindu Patriot* was issued under his sole editorial charge."

Babu Ram Gopal Sanyal, in his *General Biography of Bengal Celebrities,* writes as follows anent the origin of the *Hindoo Patriot* :— "We transcribe below what we have written on this subject in our work on the life of Kristo Das Pal. Dr. Sumbhoo Chunder Mukherji the Editor of *Reis and Rayyet* is our authority and informant on the subject.

'Babu Modhoo Shoodun Roy of Bara Bazar who had a press at Kalakur Street first conceived the idea of starting a newspaper, and it was from his press that the *Hindoo Patriot* was first issued in the beginning of the year 1853. The first Editors were the three well-known brothers of the Ghose family at Simla, viz, Babus Srinath Ghose, Girish Chunder Ghose, and Khetra Chundra Ghose. Babu Srinath Ghose was then head clerk of the Calcutta Collectorate, under Mr. Arthur Grote, who has now retired. They were assisted now and then by Babu Hurish Chunder Mukherjee, a clerk in the Military Auditor General's office (now called the Military Comptroller General's office) on a monthly salary of Rs. 100. After 3 or 4 months, the brothers Ghose gradually severed their connection with the paper, and the entire task of editing then fell on Hurish Chunder Mukherjee. *   *   *   *'

It was about the year 1854 that Babu Modhoo Shoodun became seriously ill and had to go upcountry for a change. The press was therefore sold to a third party, and the *Hindu Patriot* was published from Satyagyan Shuncharini Sova's press at Bowanipur. Hurish Chunder then established a press of his own, now known as the *Hindu Patriot* press. *   *   *   *."

With regard to the first editorship of the paper, we have already shown that the consensus of contemporary press opinion ascribed it to Grish Chunder. Had he been materially assisted by his brother

Khetter Chunder, the fact would have doubtless been mentioned in the latter's *Autobiography*. Nor could Grish Chunder have received much help from his brother Sree Nath, who in 1853 was employed in the Calcutta Collectorate as a temporary clerk on Rs. 150 a month in connection with the settlement of Calcutta—a special work which engrossed all his time and energies. In the following year, Sree Nath was appointed a Deputy Collector and posted to Balasore, where he remained for some years. In this connection, we may quote the following from a letter written by Grish to his brother Sree Nath on the 12th December, 1855 :—

" Why, my dear Nodada, you seem to be pursued by the harpies from the moment you entered upon busy life. There was firstly that accursed Boothby (may the Furies play at bat and ball with his sinful soul!) who would give you no holidays and make you work from 8 A.M. to 7 P.M. Then there came the deluge at the Collectorate, and after a merciful Providence had sent you an Ark in the shape of the Board's office whereon to rest after your grievous ducking, lo! an unkind angel tears you away from friends and home and deposits your already too well-battered brains and person in a Biscay of work and labour at Balasore."

The statement that " after 3 or 4 months the brothers Ghose gradually severed their connection with the paper, and the entire task of editing then fell on Hurish Chunder Mookherjee " is manifestly incorrect, as from an incomplete file of the *Hindoo Patriot* for 1854, to which we have had access through the courtesy of Babu Jogesh Chunder Dutt of Wellington Square, we find that many of the cleverest articles in that file were penned by Grish Chunder, whose sign manual is unmistakable. The file in question also shews that in 1854 the paper was printed at Cossitolah and not at Bhowanipore. But we have, after all, Grish Chunder's *own* recorded testimony to the fact that it was he who started the *Hindoo Patriot* and that he practically severed his connection with that paper only three years before Hurrish's death which occurred on the 14th June, 1861. Immediately after that event, Grish Chunder was induced, in the interest of Hurrish's bereaved mother and his helpless widow, to take up the editorial charge of the *Hindoo Patriot*, and he continued to edit the paper for some months, with the help of Babu Sambhu Chunder Mookerjee

who had acted as an Assistant Editor during the latter days of Hurrish Chunder. The following extract from an article headed "Our
Drainage," which was written by Grish Chunder and which appeared
in the *Hindoo Patriot* of Wednesday the 26th June 1861, will speak
for itself :—

"Our Drainage—We publish at Bhowanipore, and 'Our drainage'
might startle many a reader who knows not the secrets of the
Hindoo Patriot's present *sanctum*. The fact is, the *Patriot* will
henceforth be conducted wholly in Calcutta. *The paper has reverted
to those hands that first started it.* But the hand of hands is, alas,
wanting! The reader will in vain seek for those brilliant political
crushers which awed and astonished the local Press and sent dismay
into the factories. Providence in his own inscrutable wisdom has
taken back to himself that spirit which flashed like a meteor over the
country and disappeared as suddenly as it had burst upon the eye.
The tear of friendship is not yet dry, and we are called upon to re-
sume the pen which had been all but laid aside for the last three
years in admiration of the talent which raised the *Hindoo Patriot*
to the position of a power in the realm. The public will perhaps
excuse our shortcomings when we tell them that their forbearance is
craved in the interest of the bereaved mother and the unfortunate
widow of the remarkable man who devoted his fortune and his life to
the service of his country. With his fast-ebbing breath he loudly and
repeatedly called for the last proof! 'Don't print yet! Give me the
last proof!' and Hurris Chunder Mookerjea died three minutes after
with the *Hindoo Patriot* still uppermost in his delirious thoughts!
The gushing tear compels us to close the heart-rending scene, for we
mean to proceed with our article manfully."

Grish Chunder continued thus to edit the *Hindoo Patriot* up to
the middle of November 1861, i.e., for about five months. During
this period Babu Sambhu Chunder Mookerjee, who was allowed by
Babu Kali Prasanna Singh to reside at his Barrodwaree Palace,
acted as "Managing Editor," as will be seen from the following
Notice which appeared for the last time in the *Hindoo Patriot*
of the 14th November, 1861 :—

"All communications of whatever nature, regarding the *Hindoo
Patriot*, are to be addressed to the Managing Editor who is authorized

to sign all bills, grant all receipts, and transact all business connected with the paper.

Barrodwaree Palace.
Jorasanko, Calcutta
The 24th July 1861.

From the middle of November, 1861, new arrangements were made for the editing of the paper, as will be seen from the following extract from an editorial paragraph which appeared in the *Hindoo Patriot* dated Monday the 2nd December, 1861 :—

"Ourselves—We have to announce today a change in the ministry of the *Hindoo Patriot* which dates from the last issue [Thursday, November 21]. * * *"

In the account given of Rai Kristo Das Pal in the second volume of Mr. Buckland's *Bengal under the Lieutenant Governors*, the history' of the *Hindoo Patriot* subsequent to the death of Hurrish, is thus briefly outlined :—

"When Haris Chandra Mukerji, the founder of the *Hindu Patriot*, died on the 14th June 1861, its new proprietor Babu Kali Prasanna Sinha, after managing it at a loss for some time, made it over to Pundit Iswar Chandra Vidyasagar, who invited Kristo Das Pal to take over the editorial charge in November 1861, and subsequently transferred the proprietorship in July 1862 to a body of trustees."

In January 1858 a new periodical was started, entitled the *Calcutta Monthly Review*, to which Grish Chunder was invited to contribute, as will be seen from the following extract from Babu Koylas Chunder Bose's obituary notice of Grish Chunder :—

" During the time of the mutiny when men of the blood and scalp school were denouncing wholesale vengeance upon 'pandies' and ' niggers,' Baboo Grish Chunder was invited to contribute to a periodical started under the auspices of a few patriotic Hindu gentlemen under the name of the *Calcutta Monthly Review*. His articles on race antipathy and race antagonism were most telling, and such was the indignation of the English press upon him that a member of it seriously proposed to give him a sound thrashing, perhaps in ignorance of the fact that the man was full six feet high with a proportionate breadth of stature and firmness of limbs."

Rai Kristo Das Pal also alludes to Grish Chunder's contributions to the *Calcutta Monthly Review* :—"His power of word-
painting, of clothing the commonest ideas in gorgeous and glittering
costume, radiant with flashes of wit and humour, and occasionally of
originality, was equally conspicuous in the pages of the *Calcutta
Monthly Review* and the *Bengalee* of which he was the founder and
editor."

We very much regret that we have been able to lay hold of only
the fifth issue of the *Calcutta Monthly Review*, viz, that for May
1858.   It shews, however, that Grish Chunder largely contributed to
this small monthly, which consisted of only sixteen octavo pages.
We subjoin an extract from an interesting notice of the first number
which appeared in the *Hindoo Patriot* of the 14th January 1858
evidently from the pen of Hurrish Chunder Mookerjee :—

"*The Calcutta Monthly Review*—We have perused the first
number of this periodical with considerable interest.   The articles
are four in number.   1st. Contemporary Indian Literature. 2. Life of
Malcolm. 3. Hindu Music. 4. Indian Tenant Right

    *   *   *   *   *   *   *

The matter must interest Indian readers; the style is racy,
vigorous and wonderfully idiomatic for writers in a foreign tongue.
In politics, the journal has decided upon taking a side.   Its attack
upon the Indian press is in some parts rather violent, shows that it is
no admirer of the 'policy of coercion and repression' which that press
patronises, or the doctrines of the 'blood and scalp school,' which find
so much favor with the majority of our contemporaries.   The article
upon Indian Tenant Right places the Review at once in the position
of an advocate of democracy.

    *   *   *   *   *   *

The style of the brochure is such that few will pronounce it the
work of native Bengalees.   "

    *   *   *   *   *   *   *

Grish Chunder appears to have finally severed his connection
with the *Hindoo Patriot* about the time that he formed the project of
starting a new weekly to be named the *Bengalee.*

In closing our brief and necessarily incomplete account of Grish Chunder's early journalism we would say a word or two about his relations with Hurrish Chunder Mookerjee. Although Hurrish was older than Grish by some five years, a similarity of official and literary occupations produced the closest intimacy between the two friends in early youth. Both were remarkable for their manly independence, for their devoted and enthusiastic patriotism, and for their keen hatred of oppression or injustice in any shape. Both possessed a ready pen, though Hurrish did not possess Grish's gift of a ready tongue. Hurrish was a great admirer of Jeremy Bentham and formed his style on the model of that of the great jurist. His style did not, therefore, possess those airy graces and that idiomatic racines for which Grish's style was so remarkable. Hurrish was not also gifted with Grish's wit and humour and his wonderful power of word-painting. On the other hand, nobody was a greater admirer than Grish of Hurrish's solid sense, his dignified, weighty and sententious utterances, his wide grasp of each subject with which he dealt, his calm judicial fairness and candour and his power of close reasoning—qualities which enabled Hurrish to render material help to our last Governor General and first Viceroy in steering the ship of the State during a most stormy period of the history of British India. Hurrish was a constant guest at the Ghoses,' whom he epigrammatically described as being addicted to eating *loochies* and listening to *Jattras* or operas. Grish Chunder, in like manner, spent many a holiday at Bhowanipore, where Hurrish lived and latterly had his press. Grish was admitted to the society of Hurrish's most intimate friends among whom may be named the late Babu Annada Prasad Banerjee, Senior Government Pleader at the High Court of Calcutta, to whom Hurrish gave the nickname of "Durbal Singh" on account of his weak physique, and the late Justice Sumbhoo Nath Pundit, of whose princely hospitality Grish Chunder frequently partook. Hurrish's untimely death at the age of thirty-seven was, it is well known, brought on by drink. Grish also died prematurely at the age of forty, although he never tasted a drop of liquor in his life.

12

CHAPTER VII.

LETTERS.

As a journalist and publicist, Grish Chunder necessarily had to receive and dispose of a large number of letters every day. He had also to conduct an extensive private correspondence with his numerous friends and relations. As, however, he never took care to preserve either the letters received by him or copies of his replies thereto, we have no means of gratifying the curiosity of our readers on this head, beyond a batch of letters which Grish Chunder wrote to his brother Sree Nath whilst the latter was stationed as a Deputy Collector at Balasore and Bhadrak. These were all carefully preserved in Sree Nath's file of letters which, however, accidentally caught fire, some years ago, with the result that some of the letters were either wholly or partially destroyed. We have debated for some time the propriety of publishing any of the letters which still remain unscathed, seeing that they were all written in the confidence of brotherly intimacy and were never intended for the public eye, seeing also that they dealt largely with topics of a strictly private nature or of purely family interest. After giving the matter our most earnest and careful consideration, we have, however, decided to place before our readers, *extracts* from some of these letters,* excluding such portions as relate to matters of a strictly private nature. By being thus mutilated, the letters will, no doubt, have their integrity greatly impaired, but they will not, we trust, be found wanting in that perfect abandon or freedom from restraint which constitutes by far the most attractive charm of all familiar epistolary composition. They will also be found to give us glimpses of the youthful writer's inmost nature and predilections and to abound with flashes of his exquisite humour. The distinguishing characteristic of Grish Chunder's style of letter-writing is the easy flow of the words used to give expression to his thoughts. The secret of this is to be found in what Grish himself says in one of his letters to his brother :—" Don't think before you write. But let the words

---

* See Appendix A.

spontaneously flow from your pen. I myself am aware in my own person of the procrastinating tendency of thought. The blue devils are a clog to our activity and mar despatch."

The extracts we are about to give, will give our readers no idea of the enormous length of many of the original letters. Grish is perfectly right in what he says on this point in one of his letters ·—

" You do not give me longer stuff than I do you. I admit you occupy a larger space. But that is owing to the clever habit you have of putting three words to the line—whilst I, with greater condensation of calligraphy, carry out to the letter the principle of *multum in parvo.*"

Yet such was his marvellous facility in letter-writing that we have hardly come across a blot or an erasure in any of his long—or as he calls them, "one sheet"—letters.

Grish Chunder's playful humour is frequently in evidence in these letters. In informing his brother, for instance, of his mother's recovery from illness, he has a humorous fling at one of his cousins :—

" Shezdada, sick of having nothing to communicate to you in the melancholy way, must have added some varnish to his version of mother's illness. Perhaps too a latent wish to enjoy a magnificent *shrad* influenced his pen and the vision of such a festivity whetted his wit."

In noticing a delay on the part of the Post office in delivering one of his brother's letters, he humorously writes :—" What does Mr. Riddle deserve for his serious delay? Oughtn't he to be impeached for high crimes and misdemeanours in having put Grish Chunder Ghose of Simlah out of his brother's letter for three days beyond time? Indeed the Post office, like Doctorjee, is callous in respect to the feelings of the parties whose patronage supports it."

While expressing regret at his brother's want of success in growing green peas and cabbages in his kitchen garden, he asks—" What expense have you incurred on their account? I would advise your hypothecating the dear vegetables to our good friend Bissonauth Baboo to whom my compliments of the season, pray."

The effervescent humour of the following passage is characteristic of Grish :—

" We have nice accounts indeed of the manner in which you contrive to keep body and soul together in that dirty corner of yours. You have hitherto been amusing us with *couleur de rose* representations of your comforts. Father says that you keep lent all the week round, the fish of your place being worse than dog's meat. Fah ! throw up your magistracy, brother, and come down to Calcutta for rare pillaos and kallias, hilsa fish and mango fish—*khursela*, *rooee*, and *parsia*. Oh you unfortunate man, oh ! you monk of Balasore, there you have no good fare, but only a bubble to subsist upon—the bubble reputation. Yet I dare say God will reward you in the end and compensate you for these harassing privations by making a great man of you. This hope should sustain you through *Kristo moog* dall and vegetable curry, and reconcile you to your destiny. I, for my part, would have revolted against the bill of fare and gone to any expense to keep myself from the gastronomic condition of a Hindoo widow !"

The delineations by Grish Chunder of certain traits of his father's character are remarkable alike for their vividness of colouring and delicacy of humour. In one of his letters to his brother he says :—

" Father has not wronged you in the matter of the *kochoorie* and *nimkee* which you get up at home for lunch. On the contrary he has been shaming the girls here on the score of their incapacity and raising to the skies your wife's excellence in *cuisine* affairs. But he damned the fish of your tanks, the sweet-meats of your confectionery shops, and the *chaool* and *daool* of your bazars—and he damned them all with a vengeance. But he is returning nevertheless to the scene of your ' *mead*,' as Russic Pundit would put it. He can't abide in Calcutta. He won't be able to abide in Balasore. God has given him a quick-silver spirit, and now that his blood is up with a taste for travelling, he will, I conceive, tramp about the country like a " wandering Willie,' here and there, to the no small detriment of your purse."

In another letter he says :—" Father is wroth at your negligence in making arrangements for the return to us of the palkee which Bissonauth Baboo had borrowed of you for the purpose of bringing his family down to Calcutta. The Baboo has been unnecessarily put to an expense of five or six rupees in sending back the palkee to Balasore and father has been deprived of the means of proceeding to your station again which he must now do by purchasing or hiring (which comes almost to the same thing) a palkee. He is afraid lest the paucity of wisdom exhibited in this small affair may lead you to difficulties and hence his further anxiety to be by your side as soon as possible.   *   *   *   *

Father is quite uneasy here. The want of a *garrie* has vexed him sorely. He cannot go to the auctions, he cannot go to the *sahib-barries*. Can human misfortune proceed further? He wants an excitement and the *Jattra fureur* has made us lose many a goodly rupee. We had Kartick Ghose in the compound last Saturday night to humour the old gentleman. We had another *Jattra* about a month ago to satisfy the same appetite. The garden no longer pleases him because you have taken prisoner his playmates. And in his bewilderment he will one of these days give us the slip and post to Balasore. He already fancies you are playing the prodigal and he cannot bear to see your money wasted in gratuities to this man and that. He will probably be with you in another month."

In a third letter he writes :—

" Father is bent upon the ' grand pilgrimage ' as you call it and has sermoned mother into a similar state of mind. They will leave this as soon as your reply is received. Father thinks that his honor is concerned in the matter as the people of Balasore must be thinking very poorly of his religion after his sudden disappearance from the station without stepping over to Poorie to have a peep at the Great God. I in vain hinted to him the possibility of the people of Balasore being too much engaged with their own affairs to devote that earnest consideration to his which his morbid imagination seems to give them credit for doing. Further, that even if the good men and women of the place had such a marvellous taste for talking about the conduct and religion of a stray sojourner amongst them, now absent however, he had very little to suffer from their opinions, inasmuch as your transfer to a station nearer to Calcutta will remove the possibility of his coming *vis à vis* with his busy critics a thousand chances off. But you know the old man—when he has set his heart upon anything not all the Gods and little fishes can reason him out of it. So look up, look up. You may expect guests at the very moment probably, at which you are packing up for Calcutta."

We would only refer to two more passages in his letters to show how Grish Chunder could give a humorous turn to the commonest ideas and incidents. In one of these passages, he warns his brother of the danger of having no good doctor at Balasore by telling him that he has "scarcely a grown-up son of Esculapius within hail of his quarters." In the other he thus humorously explains why he had to send for a doctor for the treatment of a sick child :—"The urchin was fasted into a very devil and at night he became so unmanageable that I was thro' sheer fright compelled to send for the doctor in order to exorcise him."

But the chief interest which these letters possess, from a biographical point of view, lies in the glimpses which they give us, as we have already observed, of the inmost nature and predilections of their youthful writer.

The most noticeable feature of Grish Chunder's character, as disclosed by these letters, is his devoted affection for his brother which made him absolutely identify himself with the best interests of his brother.

The letters also bear witness to (i) his rigid uprightness in money matters, or as he calls it himself, his morbid sensibility in matters of money ; (ii) his love of gardens and gardening ; (iii) his keen relish for picnics, garden parties and all similar social enjoyments; and (iv) his utter want of self-glorification.

With regard to (i), it will be sufficient for our purpose to refer to letter XV from which it will be seen how firmly yet gratefully Grish Chunder declined to avail himself of his brother Sree Nath's generous offer to help him with an accommodation when he was in danger of having to fork out a large sum of money to make good certain defalcations of government revenue made by a villain for whom he had stood security at the pressing request of his father. All his brother's arguments failed to induce him to accept the proffered help. His conscience stood in the way—" King conscience who keeps a much too nicer pair of scales than Justice in the Courts cares to furnish herself with." The same trait of character is also in evidence in letter XII in which he insists on paying his quota of his father's pilgrimage expenses to Juggurnauth. "Why indeed, my dearest brother," says he, "you have not the shadow of a right to pay father's pilgrimage expenses from your individual pocket. I have just as good a claim to the thing as I have to my father's property and I shall stick out as litigiously for the one as I would for the other —wherefore no use quarrelling, give up the point at once like a good boy. We will go shares. That's the only concession I can make to you." He would not even allow his brother to send unnecessarily large remittances to him. "Pray don't send any more remittances," he says in letter XVIII, "unless you choose to give me a charter for a Bank."

With regard to (ii), we need only refer to letters IV and IX. In what minute detail does Grish Chunder describe in the former letter, the process of plastering anew his garden *atchalla*! "Every portion," he says, "of the old plastering had fallen off, exposing hideous gaps in the wall. This time I believe it is all right, as the Mistry who did the job was completely up to such things, not a charlatan in his profession like the last rascal. There are small cracks visible now as the wall is getting dry, but they are not serious ones and may be remedied by an application of cow-dung, a process which the *Mallee* under my direction is now going through. In another ten days I hope to have the room in possessable order and duly whitewashed." Further on he says:—"The jungle in front of the *atchalla* I shall keep inviolable, for that will keep me from the public gaze—but the seven or eight old mango and jack trees that greet your sight just as you enter the garden I intend demolishing to make room for younger blood."

Letter XXVI furnishes a typical illustration of trait (iii). With what gusto does Grish Chunder describe each detail of the subscription garden picnic at Wooltadanga on the 1st January 1858 and of his pleasure trip to Baraset and the adjoining villages on the two following days!

Grish Chunder's utter want of self-glorification is curiously illustrated by his letters containing no allusion whatever to his literary achievements during the period covered by them, although his pen must have then been as busy as ever and although the letters contain several interesting allusions to contemporaneous events, such as the wild rumours in connection with the Sonthal insurrection of 1855, the Sir Lawrence Peel memorial meeting and the sudden breakdown of the Baliaghatta bridge in the same year, the got-up address to Lord Dalhousie on his departure for England early in 1856, the floods in the Nadia district in the same year, the English scare during the mutiny of 1857, the wig received by Mr. Henry Mead from Govern‐ment for a violent article which had appeared in his paper, the *Friend of India*, the censure passed on Babu Shib Chunder Deb, Deputy Collector of Alipore, for some unguarded expressions used by him in a railway carriage, &c. &c.

CHAPTER VIII.

———•◦•———

CONNECTION WITH LITERARY AND POLITICAL ASSOCIATIONS.— THE BRITISH INDIAN ASSOCIATION—THE DALHOUSIE INSTITUTE—THE BETHUNE SOCIETY

Before we proceed to give an account of Grish Chunder's later journalism, it would be as well to advert very briefly to his connection with with some of the leading literary and political associations in Calcutta. His connection with the British Indian Association, which was founded towards the end of 1851, commenced in December 1853, and in May 1854 we find him seconding a resolution moved by the late Babu (afterwards Raja) Rajendra Lala Mitra at a meeting of the Association which was presided over by the late Raja Pertaub Chunder Singh. In 1861, he was elected a member of the Committee of the Association. He retained a keen interest in the Association to the end of his life and often took a prominent part in its proceedings. On various occasions he formed a member of the deputations sent by the Association to wait upon Governors-General and Lieutenant-Governors to present petitions and addresses. Some of his most brilliant speeches were also delivered in the rooms of the Association—notably those made by him at the memorial meetings held there in honour of Babu Hurrish Chunder Mookerjee on the 12th July 1861, of Raja Sir Radha Kant Deb Bahadur. K. C. S. I., on the 14th May 1867, and of Babu Ram Gopal Ghose on the 22nd February 1868.

We have already related how he became a member of the Dalhousie Institute in 1859. It was in the hall of that Institute, " when it resounded with the eloquence of Dr. Duff and Sir Mordaunt Wells, that Grish Chunder's oratorical powers first attracted notice," as remarked by the late Rai Kristo Das Pal. Grish Chunder often took with him to the Institute his lovely little daughter, who also attracted no little attention from the assembled ladies and gentlemen. Although Grish Chunder often took an

13

animated part in the debates of the Institute* and sometimes delivered discourses of his own, we regret we have not been able to gather any detailed information on the subject. He once competed for a prize offered by the Institute for the best Christmas story that might be written by one of the members. The story written by Grish Chunder, entitled "The Borrowed Shawl," was published, a few years after his death, in an early issue of the second series of *Mookerjee's Magazine*, *viz*, in that for December 1872, with a prefatory note in which the Editor remarked that although the prize was won by Colonel Malleson, he believed that Grish lost the race only by a neck.

But the Society with which the name of Grish Chunder is most closely associated is the Bethune Society, which was founded by Dr. F. J. Mouat, the then Secretary of the Medical College, Calcutta, and of the Government Council of Education, on Thursday the 11th December 1851.

A meeting of native gentlemen, convened by Dr. Mouat, was held on that date in the Theatre of the Medical College. Dr. Mouat having been called to the chair, opened the proceedings by briefly reviewing the nature and object of the Societies already existing in Calcutta, *e.g.*, the Asiatic and the Agricultural Societies, and explaining the necessity of devising some means of bringing the educated natives more into personal contact with each other, for purposes less ambitious, but perhaps not less useful, than those of the Societies named. He concluded by proposing to the meeting the establishment of a Society for mental improvement and intellectual recreation, generously undertaking at the same time to bear the entire expense of organizing and maintaining the Institution for one year.

After a lengthened conversation, in which Babu Debendra Nath Tagore, Dr. Chuckerbutty, Dr. Sprenger, the Revd. Mr. Long and

---

* The newspapers of the day show that Grish Chunder not unfrequently *opened* the debates of the Institute. We can find space, however, for only the following brief extracts from the file of the *Bengal Hurkaru* for 1862 :—

" *Public Engagements.*

Friday 3-1-62. Discussion at the Dalhousie Institute. Subject—" That the Zamindaree system of Land Tenure is most conducive to National Prosperity." Mover—Baboo Grish Chunder Ghose, 7 p.m.

Friday 21-3-62. Adjourned Debate at the Dalhousie Institute. Subject—" That up to the year 1860, the English had not improved on the Financial system of the Mogul Empire." ' Mover—Baboo Grish Chunder Ghose."

others took part, it was unanimously resolved that " A Society be established for the consideration and discussion of questions connected with Literature and Science." In order to perpetuate the memory of the Honourable Mr. Bethune, then lately deceased, it was further resolved to name the Society after him. Dr. Mouat was then chosen President, and Babu Peary Chand Mittra, Secretary. Although Grish Chunder was not one of the foundation members of the Bethune Society, he joined it shortly after its establishment.

On the 12th January 1854, Dr. Mouat resigned his office, and Mr. Hodgson Pratt, C. S., Colonel Goodwyn, Chief Engineer to the Government of Bengal, Dr. Bedford, and Mr. James Hume, Police Magistrate of Calcutta, were successively chosen President of the Society, until at a meeting held on the 9th June 1859 it was resolved to offer the Chair to Dr. Alexander Duff. Dr. Duff infused a new life into the Society, which had well nigh been on the brink of lapsing into total extinction owing to the great majority of the members never attending at all and declining to pay up their small arrears of subscriptions. At a monthly meeting held in November 1859, Dr. Duff unfolded a programme of monthly lectures to be delivered by some of the ablest and ripest of Calcutta scholars whose services, as lecturers, he had happily succeeded in securing. He further proposed that, after the model of some of the greatest and oldest Associations of the kind in Europe, the members should divide themselves into different sections, for the prosecution of special enquiries and the cultivation of particular branches of liberal, useful and professional study. After explaining in detail the advan. tages to be derived from such an arrangement, he formulated the following scheme for acceptance :—

1st.—A section on " General Education", which, if sanctioned, Mr. Henry Woodrow was willing to head.

2nd.—A section on "Literature and Philosophy," which Professor Cowell was willing to head.

3rd.—A section on "Science and Art," which Mr. Scott Smith, Professor of Natural Science in the Engineering College and Registrar of the University of Calcutta, was willing to head.

4th.—A section on "Medical and Sanitary improvement," which Dr. Norman Chevers, the distinguished Secretary of the Director General, Government Medical Department, was willing to head.

5th.—A section on "Sociology,"—recently elevated to the rank of a Science and replete with practical benefits to man,—which the Rev. James Long was willing to head.

6th.—A section on "Native Female improvement," inclusive of all that tends to improve and elevate the Female mind and character, which, from the very peculiar and delicate enquiries involved, a native gentleman of the highest qualification, Babu Rama Persad Roy, was willing to head.

The scheme having met with instantaneous and cordial approval, Dr. Duff next went on to say that all the members ought forthwith to intimate to the Secretary their choice of a section or sections; so that, at the next meeting, it might be possible to announce the complete organization of the sections. In furtherance of the scheme detailed above, Grish Chunder was appointed Secretary of the Philosophy and Literature Section, of which the late Professor Edward Byles Cowell was the President. Grish Chunder thus enjoyed frequent opportunities of cultivating the acquaintance of a man who was not only one of the most accomplished Sanskrit scholars that ever visited these shores, but who was also a true Christian, remarkable no less for his unaffected piety, modesty, gentleness and courtesy, than for his profound erudition. Professor Cowell was only thirty years old when he came out to India in 1856 as Professor of History in the Presidency College, Calcutta. He was shortly afterwards appointed Principal of the Government Sanskrit College. He left India for good in 1866, and in the following year was appointed Boden Professor of Sanskrit at the University of Oxford—an appointment which he held when he died in 1903. He is now chiefly remembered as the elegant translator of Kálidása's *Vikramorvas'i'* and the editor and translator of Mádhaváchárya's *Sarvadars'ana-Sangraha* and Vararuchi's *Prákritaprakás'a*. To the student of Indian history he is well-known for his valuable edition of Elphinstone's monumental work. But it is, perhaps, not so generally known that he was a sound Arabic and Persian scholar and that it was he who first introduced Edward Fitzgerald to Omar Khayyam. Bengali literature is also much indebted to him; for, it was at his instance that the first Bengali treatise on rhetoric was published; and it was his appreciative review, in *Macmillan's Magazine*, of the *Durgesh Nandini*—which he hailed as "the first fruits" of University education in India—that first brought the genius of our great romancer to the notice of the British scholar. He was also perhaps the first Englishman who appreciated the genius of our great national bard, Kabi-kankan, and rightly called him the " Chaucer of Bengal."

It is hardly necessary to say that the most cordial relations existed between Grish Chunder and Professor Cowell. In a long article headed " Professor Cowell," which appeared in the *Bengalee* of 24th March 1866, Grish Chunder paid a handsome tribute to that eminent scholar's many virtues.

In his first Report (dated the 10th January 1861) of the Section of Literature and Philosophy, Professor Cowell, after remarking that Dr. Duff's plan of establishing sections for encouraging private industry and research was essential to the healthy development of the educated natives of Bengal, made the following pregnant observations on the subject :—

" Now *originality* is the great lack in the present state of the Bengali mind. I have a very high opinion of the native intellect, and I am confident that the future will see it achieve great results ; but at present it seems to me to be in a far from healthy state. It has hitherto lain as it were passive in our hands, imbibing and perhaps assimilating the nutriment given it, but giving few signs of living energy and original vigour. We have had in consequence many admirable translations,—first-rate adaptations of already existing materials but beyond this there is a *blank*. If I look for some books which shall be the bonâ fide utterance of the Bengali educated mind, I can hardly name a volume which has any claim to such a title. But, if our English education is to be really useful, it must lead to some such result as that—if it does not bring out Bengali originality, our education is only a failure after all. The friends of native educa-tion have no desire to see the Hindu anglicised,—by all means let the educated Hindu keep himself true to his country ; but let him seek to raise that country from the torpor in which centuries, aye millennia, have sunk it. This is not to be done by blindly imitating the past,—India has tried her own field and has exhausted it, and the simple imitation of the past is not what India wants to renovate her. The old Hindu thinkers were giants for their day,— but like the giants of Greece and Rome, their day is over,—and modern India, like modern Europe, has need of a firmer hand, to guide her in her present path. Nor must she simply follow the West, as it seems to me too many Hindus are contented to do, as if a denationalised Hindu were the true result to which our education were to tend. But this is not the result which will really benefit India. What India wants is that the oriental should remain the oriental—with an occidental training beneath him."

After dwelling at some length upon the gains to science and the still more important intellectual and moral gain that would accrue from the adoption of such a course, he gave the following account of the proceedings of the Philosophy and Literature Section :—" Early in the year, a meeting was held at which different members undertook to prepare papers on a variety of subjects, but I am sorry to say that only two have been sufficiently completed to be presented to the Society this evening, but I may add that both these essays are highly creditable to their authors, and are just the sort of productions which we wish our Section to produce. These are, the one by Baboo Grish Chunder Ghose on the present state of dramatic representations among the natives of Bengal, the other by Baboo Tara Prosad Chatterjea, B.A., on the rise, progress and doctrine of Chaitanya, * * * * * "

At the conclusion of his Report, Professor Cowell read extracts from the two essays. The essay on Chaitanya was published in the volume of Transactions of the Bethune Society for the Sessions of 1859-60 and 1860-61, but the paper contributed by Grish Chunder was not so published, the reason for the omission being explained in the following foot-note :—

" As the author has promised to add a second part, giving some further information on this interesting subject, the publication of the present part has been deferred, in order that it may be all presented together."

We find from a subsequent volume of the Proceedings and Transactions of the Society that Grish Chunder did submit a Second part of his dissertation on the Native Drama in January 1862, which was specially noticed by Dr. Duff at a monthly meeting held on the 13th February 1862, but which unfortunately shared the fate of its predecessor in not finding a place among the papers appended to the volume. We also find from the same volume that Grish Chunder gave in another paper on " The Bengalee at Home" on the 14th January 1864. This paper also does not appear to have been published, and has thus been lost to us.

Similarly, we have no record of any of the lectures delivered at the Society by Grish Chunder, from time to time, or of the speeches made by him in course of debate, although we have heard from several reliable ear-witnesses that they were, when delivered, listened to with great interest and applause. Even in the volumes of Transactions we have before us, the record of the discussions which followed the delivery of a Lecture is, in general, so meagre that it does no justice whatever to this vital part of the proceedings. We are, therefore, obliged to content ourselves with giving a single extract— the only one, in fact, which we have found at all suitable for our purpose—from the proceedings of a monthly meeting held on the 15th March 1860, just to show, by way of illustration, the part which Grish Chunder took in the discussions which followed the delivery of a lecture by Mr. Macleod Wylie on " Hannah More and Female Education." After recording the substance of certain remarks made by Raja Kali Krishna Bahadur, the Revd. C. H. A. Dall and Babu Rama Persad Roy, the proceedings go on to say—

" Babu Grish Chandra Ghose next addressed the meeting at some length in an animated speech, in which he depicted in a lively way, the difficulties still to be encountered in the education of the young females from the ignorant prejudices and antagonism of mothers, grand-mothers, aunts and other aged relatives. He also asked, whether any of the native Managers of the Bethune Female School sent their own daughters to it? If not, as he had reason to suppose was the case, he asked again, how would they expect the Institution really to prosper and effect all the good it was fitted and designed to produce, if the very Managers, through want of moral courage or any other cause, declined to avail themselves of the benefits which it offered? In order to encourage the natives generally and inspire confidence in the Institution, surely the first duty of the native Managers was to set the example, which they expected to be copied, by sending their own daughters and young female relatives to be instructed and trained there. No valid excuse could be made for holding back from setting an example so much needed. They had it all in their own hands. Over the admission of pupils, the books and sub-jects to be studied, the system of instruction and discipline, they had absolute control. He concluded, therefore, by expressing a hope that the Rajahs and other native Managers of the Bethune Female School would be able to stimulate their neighbours to avail themselves of the advantages which the School so clearly offered, by pointing to their own example."

Among the innumerable speeches that Grish Chunder made at the Bethune Society, there is only one of which we have succeeded in procuring a tolerably full newspaper report, *viz*, his speech at the meeting held to vote a memorial to Dr. Duff on the eve of his final departure from India in 1863, and it is some satisfaction to us that we are able to present it to our readers as a fair specimen of the oratorical powers of Grish Chunder.

When the present Government School of Art was originally pro-jected as a private institution, early in 1854, Grish Chunder took a lively interest in the scheme and did his best to forward it. The first step taken by Colonel Goodwyn, the originator of the movement, was to deliver a lecture at the Bethune Society on the " Union of Science, Industry and Art, with a view to the formation of a School of Indus-trial Art and Design." He next caused the assembly of a meeting in the house of Mr. Hodgson Pratt,—which was very respectably attended and presided over by Mr. C. Allen, the then Financial Secretary to the Government of India,—for the purpose of giving working impetus to the proposals. Grish Chunder reviewed the Lecture and warmly supported the scheme in a long article which appeared in the *Hindoo Patriot* of the 6th April 1854 and in the course of which he said—

" We are fully alive to the great fact that the Hindoos, in order to regain their rightful position amongst the peoples of the world, must be less a nation of dreamers and more a nation of practical men ; we are painfully cognizant of the meaningless aversion to independent labour with which the middling classes of our community are griev-ously possessed. We shame to own it—but own it we must—that a native gentleman will serve rather as the factotum of a European guilder, cabinet-maker or house-builder than become a guilder, cabinet-maker or house-builder on his own account."

When the Society formed for the purpose, submitted to the public a proposal for the establishment of a School of Design to instruct the youth of Bengal in drawing, etching, engraving and modelling, Grish Chunder expatiated on the manifold advantages of such an institution in a second article which appeared in the *Hindoo Patriot* of the 4th May 1854 In this article he remarked—" * * * but while we have no sympathy with those who are the uncompromising advocates of a levelling system, we must admit that the almost religious abhorrence with which a high caste Hindoo looks down upon the calling of the artizan is calculated to produce effects injurious to the real interest of the country. It prevents a man from entering an honest and independent profession to which he was not born, though he may be the best fitted for it by nature. Such a state of things is peculiarly hurtful to the middle classes of the community—those who have to live upon their own labour. The numerous educational institutions in and around Calcutta and in the Provinces send forth annually a large number of educated youths who consider a clerkship in the Treasury or any other public office as the ultimatum of their aims and expectations. They would submit to the most insulting treatment which the caprice or the mean-ness of the heads of offices can inflict, but can never be prevailed upon to undertake the honourable and independent profession of the arts, even of the liberal kind." We may add that so thoroughly convinced was Grish Chunder of the usefulness of the " Industrial School," as the institution was originally called, that he actually joined it in the early part of the year 1857 for the purpose of learning the art of Drawing ; but he left it after a few months, not finding much profit from the lessons of Monsieur Rigaud—a French plaster-coat maker who was its first teacher.

CHAPTER IX.

LATER JOURNALISM—THE MOOKERJEE'S MAGAZINE AND THE BENGALEE. TRIP TO BENARES.

In 1861, a new literary monthly under the name and style of "Mookerjee's Magzine" was started by the late Babu Sambhu Chunder Mookerjee, with the liberal pecuniary help of the late Babu Kali Prasanna Singh who provided, free of charge, the Press at which the Magazine was printed. The first number of the Magazine, *viz* that for February 1861, appeared on the 20th of that month. The new journal died a premature death, after the issue of the fifth number, *viz.* that for June 1861. Not only did Grish Chunder largely contribute to it while it was in existence, but almost all the most attractive articles that appeared in it were from his pen. We quote below, from the "Prospectus of Mookerjee's Magazine, New Series," dated Barahnagar April 1872, the account given by Babu Sambhu Chunder himself of the old series of his magazine :—

"So far from drawing out any new writers in the field, the contributors of the *Hindoo Patriot* were all the writers in *Mookerjee's Magazine,* which became as it were the Literary Journal of the weekly, to which it bore the same relation that the *Calcutta Literary Gazette* so long as it lived bore to the *Bengal Hurkaru*, and the *Englishman's Saturday Evening Journal* now bears to the daily *Englishman*—the receptacle of the more purely literary articles of the same staff—my late lamented friend Babu Grish Chunder Ghose, since Editor of the *Bengalee*, and myself writing nearly the whole of the numbers published, Babu Khetra Chandra Ghosh giving a translation of one of Madame George Sand's Novels, Babu Kashiprâsad Ghosh, the veteran poet, some poems, and Babu Omesh Chunder Dutt of the Rambagan family, some stanzas from the French. Under these circumstances when, at the death of Babu Hurris Chunder Mookerjea, the Editorship of the *Hindoo Patriot* devolved upon me, we (Grish Babu and myself) found it too much to keep up both. So, though most desirous of continuing the Magazine,—Grish Babu, as a suitable vehicle for the attractive,

rollicking, often brilliant, always brimful of humour, writing in which
he delighted, and I, in addition to the literary convenience, as my own
property,—it had to be given up. "

The following articles were contributed by Grish Chunder to the
several numbers of *Mookerjee's Magazine* (old series):—

No. I. *My first Railway to Rajmehal.*

(A humorous account of the actual incidents of a trip taken by
Grish Chunder in October 1860, which was characterized by Babu
Sambhu Chunder in his *Magazine* for July 1872 as "one of the most
felicitous things from the prolific pen" of Grish Chunder. A reviewer
in the *Hindoo Patriot* of the 12th June 1861 also highly extolled it as
"a piece of sustained vivacious and brilliantly graphic description.")

Reconciliation.

No. II. *The Currency.*

The Smash in the Indigo Districts.

No. III. *The Civil Finance Commission.*

The Omedwar (a humorous character-sketch which
was pronouced by a reviewer in the *Hindoo Patriot* of the 12th June
1861 to be one that would "do honour to any Magazine in the world.")

No. IV. *Gardens and Gardening.*

The White Act miscalled Black.

The Civil Finance Commission.

No. V. *Hurris Chunder Mookerjea.*

We have already mentioned the fact that a Christmas story by
Grish Chunder—entitled "The Borrowed Shawl"—was published
posthumously in an early issue of the second series of *Mookerjee's
Magazine.* His name accordingly appeared in the List of Contributors
to Vol. I of that series, and it was connected by an asterisk with the
following foot-note ·—

"*Of this gentleman who is dead some years, we have published
one of the posthumous works, of which we have some others in store.—
For a study of his life and character see p. 8. Editor."

From this it appears that the late Babu Sambhu Chunder
Mookerjee was in possession of some of Grish Chunder's manuscripts
which he never published : they are now lost for ever.

About the end of March 1862, Grish Chunder delivered at a Literary Society at Bhowanipore an admirable lecture on the career of Lord Canning, who had just departed for England. The impression made by it on the audience will appear from the following letter :—

BHOWANIPORE,
9th April, 1862.

My dear Sir,

Family mishaps and other pressing circumstances have so long prevented me from giving expression to my private opinion of your lecture on the Career of Lord Canning.

Know you, Sir, that I take a little credit from our members on your success on the last occasion, as it was through my instrumentality that so good a lecture was procured for the Society. Though my private opinion will be of no value to you, yet as a member of the Society, I perform my duty when I congratulate you on your late admirable lecture. The vigor, perspicuity, and pointed truth which adorned your lecture I have seldom heard of the like before from the mouth of my countrymen. Perhaps you will think that I am lavish in your praise and therefore give little heed to it, but let me quote what is written in the proceedings of that meeting with reference to your lecture. The passage runs thus :—

" It (the lecture) was excellent and commanded the intense attention of the audience. In point of style and argument the speech was admirable and elicited the warmest applause of the hearers. On the whole Baboo Grish Chunder did full justice to the great man who a fortnight ago was the ruler of this vast empire. " And to this opinion of your lecture by the Society I do fully endorse my humble name. It has not a whit exceeded in praise of you but has done only justice and nothing more.

In conclusion I beg that the name of our Society be ever in your remembrance and that in future it may proudly say that such a one is its zealous patron.

I herewith beg to forward for your information a letter nominating you an honorary member of our Society.

Yours sincerely

KRISHNA CHUNDER CHATTERJEE.

P. S. The Report of the Fourth Annual General Meeting also accompanies.

BABOO GRISH CHUNDER GHOSE.

It was in the early part of the year 1862 that Grish Chunder conceived and put into execution the project of starting a new weekly on behalf of the Ryot, who then had no special organ or advocate to voice his grievances. In order to leave himself entirely free to attend to the more important and arduous intellectual work connected with the *editorial* management of his new venture, Grish Chunder was glad to associate with himself, for the management of all *business transactions,* the late Babu Becha Ram Chatterjee, who, although he was then but an obscure young man, had been well-recommended to Grish. On the needful preliminaries being settled, a prospectus of the new weekly was duly issued in April 1862. In the absence of a copy of this document, we take the following notice of it from the weekly summary of the *Hindoo Patriot* of the 21st idem :—

" We have received a copy of the prospectus of a new weekly to be called the 'Bengalee.' The projectors state, 'all that we can say is, that the 'Bengalee'—that shall be our cognomen, and we hope to confound Macaulay and his mimics—will stand in nobody's way, but with unflinching honesty, without party bias or foul-mouthed petulance, defend Truth and Justice wherever those may be, and faithfully and fearlessly represent the *Ryut* to the Ruler and the Ruler to the *Ryut*.' "

About a fortnight later, the " Bengalee " made its first appearance before the public on Tuesday, the 6th May 1862.

The late Mr. W. C. Bonnerjee, who had the unique honour of being elected President of the first Indian National Congress held in Bombay in December, 1885, and who was remarkable no less for his single-hearted devotion to his country than for his forensic success, was employed on the staff of the *Bengalee*, during the first two or three years of its existence, in the humble capacity of compiler of the summary of weekly news, receiving for this duty a small monthly stipend— not exceeding rupees twenty, if we remember aright. This happened when Mr. Bonnerjee was yet in his teens. It is well-known to all who, like ourselves, had the honour of his personal acquaintance, how sadly his school education had been neglected, like that of many a great man before him and since, and how amply did he make amends for his early neglect by hard study in later life. It was after Mr. Bonnerjee had abruptly closed his school career, that he was taken by Grish Chunder on the staff of his newly-started paper in the capacity mentioned above ; for, Mr. Bonnerjee's father was an old and valued friend and neighbour of Grish Chunder's and he therefore took a fatherly interest in the youth. We distinctly remember how young Bonnerjee (who was then familiarly known as " Mutty Babu ") used to come to Grish's house every morning and make the necessary extracts from the various periodicals of the day under his personal direction and advice. This went on for two or three years. Grish used to encourage young Bonnerjee to write short paragraphs and submit them to him for revision. Under such excellent training, young Bonnerjee's natural intelligence was gradually directed into the proper channel, till at last Grish Chunder became so highly satisfied with the progress made by his young friend that when in 1864 Mr. Bonnerjee became a candidate for one of several scholarships founded by a Parsee gentleman of Bombay to enable Indian youths to study law in England, Grish Chunder strongly recommended him to the right quarter and got him nominated to the scholarship which put him at once on the high road to his future eminence. Mr. Bonnerjee, who was one of the very few men who are " royal born by right divine, " never forgot the kindness shown him in his early youth by Grish Chunder and gratefully cherished his memory to the end of his days.

Grish Chunder was pre-eminently a " home-keeping youth," though he had by no means a " homely wit. " He never travelled beyond a day's journey from home, except only thrice in all his life. On the first occasion, he took a pleasure trip by rail to Rajmehal during the Doorga Poojah holidays of October 1860, of which he has left us a charming record in print. On the second occasion he took. in February 1863, a trip to the Upper Provinces, which lasted for nearly three weeks and extended as far as Benares ; it will be described presently. On the third or last occasion he took, in November 1868, a boat trip to Krishnagar, for the benefit of his health ; an account of this trip will be given later on. Grish Chunder started on his second trip on the night of the 4th February 1863, travelling by what has since been called the " Loop line " of the East Indian Railway. He arrived at Monghyr on the following day and put up at the late Babu Prosonno Coomar Tagore's fine house at Peerpahar. In a letter dated at Peerpahar on the 8th February, he wrote to his brother Sree Nath—" We start from Peerpahar for Benares tomorrow. I have got an excellent companion in Baboo Raj Coomar Shurbadhicary. We intend proceeding as far as Agra to see the world-renowned Taj Mehal."

Owing, however, to an outbreak of epidemic at Allahabad, Grish had to content himself with a three nights' stay at Benares, under the hospitable roof of the well-known Babu Kashi Nath Biswas, and then retrace his course homewards, travelling by boat with his young friend Babu (now Rai) Raj Coomar Sarvadhikari, whose intelligent and lively talk greatly heightened the pleasures of the voyage. It was at Benares that Grish Chunder made the acquaintance of the late Babu Ramkali Chowdry, retired Sub-Judge, who fondly cherished Grish's memory ill he died in October 1900. The following letter gives Grish's impressions of the Holy City ·—

ON THE RIVER OFF RAJGHAT,

13th February 1863.

My dearest Brother,

We have been prevented going to Agra, as we had intend-ed, by the breaking out of an epidemic at Allahabad. We are therefore on our way homewards by boat. The trip is delightful and has already given us such a sharp appetite that we can eat an elephant. We stayed three nights at Benares and were sumptuously entertained with the best of sweet-meats and meats. It is emphatically a holiday city. Everybody wears on his face that which makes you believe he cannot be otherwise than happy. The streets are beauti_ fully paved with Chunar stone and the drainage is so excellent that Mr. Municipal Clarke may well take a page out of the holy city and save us a heavy and unnecessary tax. The river front is one conti_ nued range of Ghats built at an enormous expense by the first princes of India. The stone buildings which crown these Ghats are architectural models. I never saw such things before in my life. We expect to reach Rajmehal in about twelve days from this, touching at Dinapore, Buxar, Monghyr, Bhaugulpore and other places. We prefer this mode of travelling to the eternal *ghur ghur* of the Railway. From Rajmehal, however, we will take the rail so as to reach Calcutta by the end of this month. Tell everybody at home that I have wonderfully improved and expect to astonish them by my health.

What about that business of Dennis Hely ? Bacharam appears to be in an awful fright about it. I received his letter the night before starting from Peerpahar and wrote off a reply immediately. Tell him there is nothing to fear. I hear that the man has not one pice to rub against another—and he bring an action in which the old story is sure to be brought up in a manner not very pleasant to either this reputation or his pockets ! I would consider it good fortune for the *Bengalee* to be the means of confirming the guilt of a man who has providentially escaped scot-free. Providence will not save him a second time.

We shall be at Dinapore in three or four days and remain there one night with my Bayes who have removed to that station. Kindly direct your letter to me to await arrival at Monghyr. I shall call for it at the Post Office when I reach the place. Hoping yourself and the dear family are quite well.

Your most affectionately

GRISH CHUNDER GHOSE.

To

BABOO SREENAUTH GHOSE.

The programme chalked out in the foregoing letter was, for some reason or other, not carried out in its entirety. The original plan of proceeding by boat from Benares to Rajmehal after touching at

Dinapore, Buxar, Monghyr, Bhaugulpore and other places, and then taking the rail to Calcutta, was apparently abandoned at Dinapore, where Grish Chunder spent a few days as the guest of his friend the late Babu Baladeb Palit, who was the head clerk of the Military Pension Paymaster and who also enjoyed in his day some reputation as a Bengali poet. He appears to have performed the rest of his journey by rail, arriving in Calcutta by the 23rd February, under which date the following entry occurs in his private account book :—

"Trip to Benares   Rs. 90."

CHAPTER X.

——: o :——

TROUBLES AT HOME.

The year 1863—in the early part of which we find Grish Chunder
in the enjoyment, since his return from the trip described in the preceding chapter, of perfect health and happiness and at peace with all
the world, including his co-sharers in the joint family dwelling house—
gave birth to certain events which had a most disastrous influence over
his future life. We cannot narrate them fully without laying open old
sores over which time has already shed its healing influence. But the
exigencies of our subject make it indispensably necessary that we
should advert to them, however briefly. We accordingly proceed to
do so as briefly and as colourlessly as possible. We have already
stated how Kasi Nath, commiserating the childless condition of his
eldest son Hurrish, made his second son Ramdhone allow Hurrish
to adopt his youngest son Grish while he was an infant. We do not
know whether all the formalities usually observed on such occasions
were gone through; but this much we know that no father ever
loved his only son more dearly than Hurrish did his nephew. Grish
also was filially attached to Hurrish and all along supported him
and his wife like a dutiful son. Kasi Nath's youngest son Gobin,
who was a congenital idiot, died without issue a year or two after
his father's death. Each of his five surviving brothers thus became
entitled to a fifth share of the family dwelling house, the only property left by Kasi Nath when he died. Apprehending lest Hurrish,
whose habits were rather wild, should some day or other transfer
his share to a stranger for a song, Ramdhone advised Grish to have
his uncle's share transferred to him. This was easily effected.
Hurrish cheerfully made over his share to Grish by means of a deed
of gift. This fatal document eventually proved to Grish " the direful
spring of woes unnumbered," for it roused the jealousy and enmity
of Kali Kissen, Nobin Kissen and Jeebun Kissen, the three sons of
Kasi Nath's third son Anund Chunder, who had hitherto hoped, however unreasonably, to participate in their childless uncle's share

after his death. To deprive Grish Chunder, as long as practicable, of any practical use that he might seek to make of the rights acquired by him under the deed of gift, his cousins aforesaid hit upon a rare device. They were well aware of Ramdhone's inordi- nate desire to keep the old house and its honours intact at any cost ; and by appealing to this weakness of his, they succeeded in per suading Ramdhone to enter, along with his three sons, into an agreement with Anund Chunder and his three sons, that the house was not to be divided without the unanimous consent of all the parties to the agreement. The only party whose interests were injuriously affected by this agreement was Grish Chunder, who was then in possession of only one bed-room, although he owned one- fifth of the whole house. As, however, he was in the habit of rendering implicit obedience to his father—a species of romantic folly which has now become a thing of the past—Grish Chunder decided not to disoblige his old father by refusing to sign the agree- ment, but to rely upon the chapter of accidents ; for, there was a second agreement which was simultaneously signed by the same contracting parties and which provided that if, owing to any cause, a portion of the house should become detached and appropriated to any party or parties who had not signed the first agreement, that agreement would then become null and void. Not only was Grish Chunder made to sign the two agreements, but to draft them as well, his cousins complimenting him, to that end, on his superior skill in drafting. The agreements were executed in 1862.

In 1863, Kasi Nath's fourth son Prawn Kissen's one-fifth share in the family dwelling house was jointly purchased, from his widow and only daughter, by the three sons of Ramdhone and the three sons of Anund Chunder. After the purchase of Prawn Kissen's share, Ramdhone caused the two rooms vacated by Prawn Kissen's family in the inner department of the house, to be repaired, one for the use of his second son Sree Nath, who was badly in need of a second bed- room, and the other for Jeebun Kissen, the youngest son of Anund Chunder. Grish, who knew nothing about the latter arrangement and who had for some time past been feeling very sorely the want of a second bed-room inasmuch as it had prevented him from inviting his son-in-law to spend occasionally a night at his house, could not let slip this last opportunity of supplying the desideratum. He accordingly went to his father and asked him to let him have the smaller of the two rooms in question—explaining how hard pressed he was for some little extra accommodation. Ramdhone saw at once the reason-ableness of the request and told Grish to occupy the room without tel-ling him, however, that he had already promised it to Jeebun. He did not think it necessary to do so, as, after the heavy sacrifice which he had so lately induced Grish to make at the request of his nephews, he did not anticipate that there would be any difficulty in making them agree to let Grish have the use of a small room scarcely ten feet long and eight feet broad, more especially as Jeebun had no immediate need for additional accommodation, his family then consisting of a sickly wife and only one little boy. But Ramdhone soon afterwards found to his cost that he had been reckoning without his host. Grish Chunder put the room in question under lock and key, as soon as he had ob-tained his father's permission to occupy it, and went to office as usual, little dreaming that on his return from office he would find the lock broken open and the room in the forcible possession of his cousin Jeebun Kissen. We will not describe the disgraceful scene which followed the discovery. Ramdhone now saw clearly how he had been duped by his nephews and realised the great wrong he had done Grish by making him sign the agreement for the non-partition of the house. He who had hitherto been so morbidly anxious to preserve the integrity of the family dwelling house, was now most anxious that Grish Chunder should file, without delay, a plaint in the High Court for a partition of the house. He not only joined Grish Chunder in the suit (offering to bear his full share of the costs) but also asked Khetter and Sree Nath to do so. Sree Nath most readily joined his father and brother in the suit. As, however, Sree Nath's actual interest in the house was comparatively small, Grish Chunder would, on no account, allow him to be made liable for any portion of the costs that might be incurred in the prosecution of the suit. Khetter Chunder did not think it right to accede to his father's request. "My father," he says in his *Autobiography*, "endeavoured to prevail upon me to join him and my brothers in the suit in question, but I had the moral courage to resist his importunities, on the score of our agreement, which prevented us from claiming a partition of our family dwelling house without the *unanimous* consent of all the share-holders who subscribed to the same. I was consequently, with my cousins and

my uncle, made a defendant in the suit, and although my position
with reference to those who were much nearer and dearer to me in
relationship than the rest of the litigants was thus rendered very
delicate and distressing, I could not help myself from siding with my
uncle and cousins." It may be added that as Khetter Chunder was
then in the exclusive possession of the whole of the top flat of the
house, with the exception of the *Thakoorghur* or the room in which
the family idols were located, and as moreover he occupied one of the
two largest parlours on the first floor, he had no inducement to join
his father and brothers in the partition suit. Grish Chunder now be-
took himself to the glorious uncertainties of the law, and in spite of
the able arguments of Mr. Cowie, the then Advocate General, who
fought hard to get the agreements set aside mainly on the ground
that they were opposed to the public policy, the case of *Ramdhone
Ghose and others* vs. *Anund Chunder Ghose and others*, which made
a great sensation at the time and became a *cause celebre*, was decreed
against the plaintiffs, with costs, by the presiding Judge of the High
Court. An appeal preferred against this decision ended with the same
result. The learned Judges of the Appellate Court remarked, however,
in the course of their judgment, which was published in the *Hurkaru*
of the 18th May 1864, that although the agreements under dispute
would hold good with reference to the then plaintiffs and defendants,
they were not sure how far they would stand when any of the parties
concerned in the present suit had their shares transferred on account
of debt or otherwise to other parties who were not subscribers to the
agreements in question. Taking his cue from this, Ramdhone asked
Grish, about two years after the dismissal of the appeal with costs, to
cause his (Ramdhone's) share in the family dwelling house to be
seized and sold at a public sale by the Sheriff of Calcutta in satisfaction of the amount due to Grish on account of Ramdhone's share of
the costs of the two suits. Grish had all this time forborne demand-
ing a pice from his father on this account, although he was himself
over-burdened with debt. He agreed, however, to Ramdhone's present
proposal simply because it offered the only means of getting a partition effected, on the attainment of which end he intended providing
suitable accommodation for his father and brother. The chief
difficulty lay in finding a friendly purchaser who would be willing to
undertake all the risk and trouble involved in the purchase of an
undivided share in a family dwelling house. Such a man was found

in the person of the late Babu Prawn Kissen Dutt, who was not only a resolute man of substance but also lay under a great personal obligation to Grish and who was therefore ready to do any thing for his benefactor. This gentleman succeeded in purchasing Ramdhone's share by outbidding Jeebun Kissen, who had attempted to purchase it at the Sheriff's sale in question with the object of preventing a partition of the house. To obtain possession of Ramdhone's share Babu Prawn Kissen Dutt had to file a regular partition suit against Khetter Chunder and his cousins, but before the institution of such a suit Ramdhone died from a sudden failure of heart. The partition suit instituted by Babu Prawn Kissen Dutt was strongly opposed by Khetter Chunder and his cousins, but the suit was decreed in favour of the plaintiff, with costs. An appeal preferred against the decree was also dismissed with costs.

Thus when everything seemed to be in train for the attainment of Grish Chunder's darling wish, he unexpectedly succumbed to an attack of typhoid fever while he was almost within sight of the Promised Land. By a curious dispensation of Providence the mission of Joshua devolved upon Khetter Chunder—for, he it was who took the initiative, five years after Grish's death, to have the work which Grish had left unfinished, completed with the help of his brother Sree Nath. "I hope," says he in his *Autobiography*, "that having been the humble instrument in the hands of God, of Grish's heirs being put in possession of their share in the property, my brother, who, I am sure, is now in heaven, has forgiven any troubles that I might have given him by opposing his wishes, whilst he was in existence in this world, and that my father also, has likewise excused me for having formerly, in obedience to certain conscientious scruples, also resisted his proceedings during his life-time." Never did a contrite heart more richly deserve forgiveness than the heart of Khetter Chunder, who has since been gathered to his fathers.

In closing this melancholy chapter of the life of Grish Chunder, we cannot help remarking that he was ill-fitted by nature to stand the strain and the worry imposed upon him by the long-continued litigation which was in a manner forced upon him by a strange combination of circumstances, and the unfortunate family-feuds of which he was the victim not only drained his purse and destroyed his peace of mind, but also told upon his splendid health and thus contributed in no small degree to shorten his glorious career.

CHAPTER XI.

BELLORE. THE CANNING INSTITUTE, HOWRAH.

After the dismissal of the appeal preferred by Grish Chunder against the decision of the High Court in the partition suit instituted by him, the ill-feeling which had, for some months past, been growing up between him and his cousins, became so greatly aggravated that in order to relieve the abnormal tension and recover his peace of mind he found it necessary to remove with his family to his garden-house at Bellore across the river, early in July 1864. It was a one-storied building, built in the English style over an elevated and vaulted plinth, and flanked on two sides by an extensive and well-laid-out flower-garden. The place was altogether a thing of beauty and a joy for ever, and the rural sights and sounds with which it abounded were well-calculated to restore the tone of Grish Chunder's overwrought nerves. The following letter written by him to his brother Sree Nath, three weeks after his removal to Bellore, shews how kindly he had taken to his new home :—

23rd July, 64.

My dear Brother,

Of course I am not going to Calcutta tomorrow, for I have been expecting you at the *Assrom* for the last three weeks. Come over as early as you can. I shall keep the garrie at Sulkea or Howrah Ghat as the case may be. If the steamer does not ply at Sulkea, Meerun will drive over to Howrah. I hope you will bring over all the dears— *viz.*, Chundy, Ada and Kheroo. I should very much like to keep some of them to see if the air of the wilderness does not make them healthier. My boys and girls are in prime health, as you will see.

Hoping you will on no account fail and that you will spend to-morrow night with me and to that end bring your office clothes.

Yours most affectionately
GRISH CHUNDER GHOSE.

P.S. Ask father to bring the usual supply of meat.

Little did Grish Chunder dream when he wrote so cheerily to his brother, that before another ten days elapsed he would be prostrated by a dangerous attack of typhoid fever. So completely was he floored by the fell disease on the 2nd August 1864, that we find an entry in his private account book under that date to the effect that he was then too ill to write up his accounts. The dubious struggle between life and death continued for days and weeks together. It was the height of the rainy season and the downpour was incessant. Not only was there no good medical aid at hand, but there was not even a good dispensary available within some miles of the obscure village where Grish Chunder now lay on the sick bed, separated from all his friends and relations in Calcutta. The solitude of the situation was well described by Grish Chunder himself in the *Bengalee* of the 6th October 1866:—

"Honestly and faithfully as before will the *Bengalee* continue to do his duty though there are not twenty persons within hail of his resting-place. The God of Heaven protects him however, and that is a species of security of which mere religionists and worldlings cannot and do not know the practical and permanent value."

The God of Heaven did indeed protect Grish Chunder on this occasion, through the instrumentality of the late Babu Sooresh Chun der Dutt of Wellington Square and the late Dr. Chunder Coomar Dey, the accomplished scholar and eminent physician who translated from the German, Vogel on *Diseases of the Blood*, and who was, we believe, the first graduate of the Medical College, Bengal, on whom the degree of Doctor of Medicine was conferred. Baboo Sooresh Chunder Dutt was a member of the well-known Dutt family of Wellington Square, whose library was at one time justly considered the finest private library in all Calcutta. Like a good many members of his family, Babu Sooresh Chunder was remarkable for his public spirit and taste for letters. He was one of Nature's aristocrats and he looked a nobleman every inch of him. It has seldom been our lot to come across so handsome a specimen of the genus *homo*; his faultless beauty of form, feature and complexion might well furnish a model for the sculptor and the painter. The eldest daughter of Grish Chunder was married on the 4th July 1861 to the late Babu Sreesh Chunder Dutt, who was a nephew of Babu Sooresh Chunder.

Grish Chunder thus became connected, by marriage, with Baboo Soo-resh Chunder Dutt—a connection which soon ripened into the most steadfast friendship. As soon as Babu Sooresh Chunder heard of Grish Chunder's serious illness he went to Bellore, taking Dr. Dey with him. He continued to do so, day after day, in spite of the un-favourable weather, until Grish Chunder was pronounced by Dr. Dey to be quite out of danger. We may add that Dr. Dey had a high re-gard for his patient and he therefore took a more than professional interest in the case. But the consummate skill and judicious care displayed by Dr. Dey in his treatment of the case would have been of little avail had not Baboo Sooresh Chunder arranged for the prompt supply of the medicines prescribed by him from Messrs. Scott, Thomson and Co's Dispensary in Calcutta, by posting relays for the purpose, on the route leading from that excellent dispensary to Grish Chunder's garden at Bellore. It would, therefore, not be too much to say that under God Grish Chunder owed his life mainly to the un-remitting exertions of his devoted friend. During his convalescence, Grish Chunder used to relate the following particulars of a curious dream which he had at the most critical stage of his illness. He dreamt that a nymph of heaven, resembling in loveliness his own el-dest daughter, came down to him from the top of a mountain with a golden jar of water and asked him to drink his fill of the cool and crystal liquid as she poured it gently into his parched mouth. That very day his medical attendant declared that he had passed the crisis of the disease.

Before Grish Chunder had completely regained his former strength after his recovery from the dangerous illness described above, Calcutta and its neighbourhood were visited, on the 5th October 1864, by one of the most terrible Cyclones on record. No less than thirty-one ships and steamers were wrecked in the river ; all the vessels lying in port were driven off their moorings and one of the P. and O. Co's large mail steamers was, by the force of the wind, driven from the Calcutta side of the river and landed high and dry on Shalimar Point. Upwards of 48,000 people were drowned in the terrible flood caused by the storm-wave which rolled in over the low-lying parts of Midnapur and the 24 Pergunnahs ; some 25,000 more were carried away by the fever and scarcity which followed in the wake of the

flood.   The cyclone played havoc with many of the oldest and finest
fruit-trees in Grish Chunder's garden, which for many months afterwards wore a most dreary and desolate look.   But nothing made him
feel so desolate as the irreparable loss he sustained by the death of
his dear friend Babu Sooresh Chunder Dutt, on the 15th December
1864, at the early age of thirty-two.

It was in the year 1865 that Grish Chunder was induced to take
up the management of the Bellore Anglo-Vernacular School by
becoming its Secretary. The School had been in existence for some
time before his advent in the village, but owing to the very little
interest taken in it by its then Secretary, it was in a most deplorable
condition, although it enjoyed the rare advantage of being located,
free of rent, in a fine building—belonging to Ranee Katyanee of
Paikparah, the widow of Kristo Chunder Singh better known as
" Lalla Baboo "—which possessed an extensive compound abutting on
the Grand Trunk Road.   Grish Chunder infused new blood into the
institution.   Not only did he succeed, with the help of the late Babu
Khetter Mohun Mullick, the energetic Head Pundit and *de facto*
Superintendent of the school, in inducing the respectable inhabitants
of the village to take an active interest in the School, but he also suc
ceeded in obtaining from Government a suitable grant-in-aid, thereby
placing the finances of the institution on a satisfactory basis. His stre-
nuous endeavours to place the teaching staff on an efficient footing
were likewise crowned with success.   Men like the late Babu Hara
Sankar Dutt, a distinguished old senior scholar and veteran educationist, or the late Babu Shoshi Bhushan Chatterjee, who afterwards became
an eminent criminal lawyer and was appointed Government Pleader,
Hooghly, successively held the post of Head Master of the Bellore
School.   So great was the interest that Grish Chunder took in the
school of which he was practically the founder or reviver, that in spite
of the numerous pressing calls on his time, he always welcomed with
pleasure the daily visits of the Head Pundit with whom he spent
nearly an hour every morning in talking over or transacting the affairs
of the school.   To test the progress made by the boys, he not un
frequently took part in the annual examinations of the upper forms
and also induced some of his scholarly friends to come over from
Calcutta for a like purpose.   The prize-books were all personally

selected and purchased by him, his great aim being to present the boys with the choicest treasures of English literature at as small a cost as possible. He introduced the salutary practice of making the boys recite passages from the works of eminent British poets and dramatists at the annual distribution of prizes, coaching them himself in the art of elocution at no small sacrifice of his time and patience. With a view to enlisting public sympathy on behalf of the school, he spared no pains to make the prize-day as imposing and attractive as practicable. Had he been spared a few years longer, he would undoubtedly have made the Bellore Anglo-Vernacular School one of the most flourishing rural schools in Bengal. Grish Chunder once thought of establishing a female school at Bellore, but owing to the insuperable difficulties which met him at the outset, he had to give up the idea. He organized a Debating Club which used to meet every other Sunday afternoon at the Bellore School-house. Grish Chunder and his brother Sree Nath used to open the debates. Among the educated young men of Bellore who used to take part in the debates were the late Babu Joy Kissen Gangooly, the well-known solicitor of the High Court, and the late Babu Shib Chunder Chatterjee, who was for many years an ornament of the Hooghly bar and commanded an extensive criminal practice. These two young gentlemen often displayed considerable acuteness—notably on one occasion when the subject for debate was the expediency or otherwise of abolishing capital punishment. The Club ceased, however, to meet regularly as the enthusiasm of the younger members gradually cooled down, until it ceased to meet altogether.

Grish Chunder was appointed a Municipal Commissioner of Howrah sometime in 1865 and he held that office up to the date of his death. He devoted his wonted energy to the consideration of Municipal affairs and regularly attended the Commissioners' meetings, although they were held at mid-day and he had therefore to come over to the Municipal office, Howrah, from his office in Calcutta, and then go back to the latter at the end of the meeting, thus incurring considerable personal inconvenience and loss of time, not to speak of the risk involved in crossing the river four times in the course of a day. But Grish Chunder's strong sense of duty made him overlook all considerations of personal inconvenience.

What pained him most was to see the arbitrary way in which the all-powerful non-official European majority at these meetings opposed successfully every measure which they thought was not conducive to their own interests, to the manifest detriment of the interests of the rate-payers at large. As an instance in point, we may mention that Grish Chunder tried in vain to get the Municipality to metal the *kutcha* road which led from the Bellore Bazar to Goosery, and on which his own garden was situated, although the thoroughfare was more than a mile long and proportionately broad. In vain did Grish Chunder urge that during the rainy season the road became quite impassable, to the extreme inconvenience of the hundreds of passers-by who daily used it. A Mr. William Stalkart, who used the road for riding purposes during the cold season, found the soft sand of which it was composed good for his horses' hoofs, and he therefore induced his European brother Commissioners to negative the proposal each time it was mooted. The road in question was, after Grish's death, named after him to commemorate his services to the Municipality, and it has since been duly macadamised.

Grish Chunder was latterly appointed a member of the Local Committee of Public Instruction which controlled the Government Zillah School at Howrah. But the institution with which his name was most closely associated was the Canning Institute, Howrah, a literary society founded in April 1865 by the then Chaplain of Howrah, the Revd. Mr. W. Spencer M.A., who afterwards became the Senior Chaplain of St. Paul's Cathedral. Grish Chunder joined the Institute a year later and was elected one of its Vice-Presidents on the 1st July 1868. In May 1866, he read at the Institute a paper on " The Social and Domestic Life of the Hindoos " which was so admirably written that the Revd. Mr. Coe of the Bishop's College, Seebpore, who formed one of the audience, begged of Grish Chunder to let him have the paper for perusal. The paper does not appear to have been received back by Grish and we are therefore unable to present it to our readers. We present them, however, with a summary of an extempore lecture on " The Rural Economy of Bengal " which he delivered at the Institute on the 30th April 1867. The Proceedings record that " the Lecturer, who was repeatedly cheered, sat down amidst loud and prolonged applause. "

Besides delivering the two lectures mentioned above, Grish Chunder frequently took an active part in the debates which followed the lectures delivered by eminent scholars at the monthly meetings of the Institute. The record of such debates in the Proceedings of the Institute is necessarily imperfect. The following extracts from the published Proceedings for the sessions 1866-67 and 1867-68 will, however, give our readers some faint idea of the part played by Grish Chunder in such debates :—

30th May 1866—Lecture by G. M. Tagore Esq., Barrister-at-Law, on the " Future Prospects of India."—" At the conclusion of the lecture, Baboo Grish Chunder Ghose moved that a hearty vote of thanks was due to Mr. Tagore for the very able lecture with which he had favoured the meeting, and expressed a hope that the day was not very distant that would witness an entire reconstruction of Hindoo society ; when Hindoos would become Englishmen in mind, and Englishmen not feel ashamed to learn from Hindoos."

26th September 1866.— Lecture by H. L. Harrison Esq. C.S. on 'Indifferentism."—" Baboo Grish Chunder Ghose, in rising to propose a vote of thanks to Mr. Harrison for his able lecture, endeavoured, as a representative of the Hindoo Community, to exculpate the Bengalee from the charge of being indifferent to religion. He was compelled, he said, to repudiate through the influence of a Western education all the religious dogmas which he had been taught to regard with reverence in his infancy, and the conflict of opinion on religious matters now prevailing in England rendered him helpless in the selection of his form of worship."

26th December 1866—Readings from Tennyson by Mr. Tudor Trevor M.A., and Lecture by Miss Mary Carpenter on " Education." " At the termination of the address, Baboo Grish Chunder Ghose expressed his admiration of the manner in which Mr. Trevor had delivered his readings which were about as good as those given by Captain Richardson and Mr. Hume at the Town Hall many years ago. He cordially welcomed Miss Carpenter, and observed that the natives were never influenced by apathy, as was represented to be the case, but that the most serious drawback to the education of native females was, their withdrawal from school, that is, at an early age as soon as they got married, and the elder females with whom they had to associate being generally illiterate, did not at all sympathise with them, but on the contrary discouraged them in the acquisition of knowledge. What was learned at school or elsewhere was thus thrown away or lost ; in fact the progress of female education had been arrested and retarded by the want of proper female teachers."

*9th January 1867.—Lecture by Mr. J.F.B. Tinling on " Life is Real, Life is Earnest."—*In the absence of the Revd. Mr. Spencer, Baboo Grish Chunder Ghose was chosen to preside. " The Chairman then rose and made a defence of Hindooism. He confessed that Hindooism allowed idolatry, but he urged the audience to remember that in worshipping the idols Hindoos only worshipped the Almighty God and not the idol. With regard to Christianity he observed, that miracles could not be the best gauge of that religion since Colenso, Renan and many learned scholars of Europe had repudiated them."

12th February 1868.—Lecture by the Right Revd. the Lord Bishop of Calcutta on " Individuality."—" At the conclusion of the lecture, Baboo Grish Chunder Ghose rose, and in a few pointed words proposed that the warmest thanks of the society should be accorded to the Right Revd. the Lord Bishop of Calcutta for the very admirable lecture to which he had treated them that evening. Already the natives were indebted to the European missionaries for their laudable efforts to regenerate India, and again the Right Revd. the Bishop had added to the obligation by an interesting lecture. The Right Revd. the Bishop was not only the diocesan of all the Christian churches in India, but also that of the Hindoos. He rejoiced that through the influence of Western education the most baneful idolatry of which India had been the stronghold, had been dispelled. He rejoiced that through Christian enlightenment, the most pernicious superstition which ruled the minds of his countrymen had given place to a belief in an over-ruling God— the Governor of the universe. But while with gratitude he acknowledged the benefits done to his country by Western education, he begged to be pardoned if he said it had not also equally removed all the doubts regarding Christianity. The excellencies with which the Bible was replete, were also to be found in the Hindoo Shasters, and particularly in the *Bhagabat Geeta*. He concluded by moving that the best thanks of the meeting were due to the Right Revd. the Lord Bishop for his able and impressive lecture."

25th March 1868.—Lecture by the Hon'ble Mr. Justice Phear on "Female Culture."—"Babu Grish Chunder Ghose, in a spirited speech, combated the position taken up by the learned lecturer that Hindoo females were wholly without culture. The lecture they had heard, proceeded on the assumption that Hindoo females were just as the Europeans fancied them to be—entirely ignorant—without a scintilla of education, without a scintilla of thought. This was not so. Hindoo females, at the present moment, possessed, as he (the speaker) could vouch from experience, a high degree of culture. It was a mistake to suppose that knowledge was withheld from Hindoo females ; Europeans were not aware of the media through which education is imparted to them. There were express institutions among Hindoos for educating females in classes, and those classes were periodically held. He believed the fact was unknown. Passages from the *Ramayana*, the *Mahabharata*, and other works were read by a thoughtful and impressive Brahmin—generally in the compound of the house—for the edification of Hindoo women. The god was, at the same time, brought out and crowds of women were always present at this rendezvous of learning. The importance of chastity was inculcated and the proceedings of these assemblies were always of an impressive character—more impressive, perhaps, than those that were carried on in the English churches. Hindoo ladies who possessed learned and intelligent husbands, could not but be equally intelligent and learned. The speaker had himself had opportunities of reading Shakespeare's works to Hindoo ladies, and had drawn tears from their eyes in reciting the fate of *Desdemona*. One lady, after he had read the *Taming of the Shrew*, had asked him for a translation of the speech of *Katharina* in which she sets forth the duties of a wife to her husband. The *zenana* was not an institution natural to Hindoo society, but had been forced upon them by the conduct of their Mahomedan conquerors. He doubted, however, looking to the conduct of some of the English in this country, whether Hindoo ladies could even now, with safety, be brought out of their seclusion and admitted into society."

[After this speech by Grish Chunder, the Chairman, Sir Richard Temple K.C.S.I., observed that " he believed that all gentlemen present would admit that native ladies were not so destitute of education as was commonly supposed, and it was quite true, as mentioned by Baboo Grish Chunder Ghose, that native ladies had as much capacity for learning and for understanding and for appreciating everything that is great and noble as the ladies of any other country." We may note here that the *Hindoo Patriot* of the 13th April 1868, in an article headed " The Reign of Commonplace," condemned the offensive tone of the Hon'ble Mr. Justice Phear's lecture, and referred to Grish Chunder's speech in the following words :—" In the name of the nation we offer our gratitude to Baboo Grish Chunder Ghose for vindicating the character of our countrymen and countrywomen before the abject natives and merry Europeans who delighted to libel them. * * * "]

29th April 1868—Readings from the " Mohabharat " by the Hon'ble Sir Richard Temple K.C.S.I.—" Babu Grish Chunder Ghose, in proposing a vote of thanks to the Hon'ble lecturer, said that if the Hon'ble lecturer had been a Brahmin, a chain of gold would have been placed round his neck and clothes would have been heaped upon him, the usual way in which his country-men expressed their gratitude to the readers of that celebrated epic, the ' Mohabharat.' That great book, he said, was not held by the Hindoos merely in the light of an epic poem. Hardly any single book was of greater importance to a nation than the ' Mohabharat ' to the Hindoos. In it are contained the arts of war, of government, of administration, the political, the mental and the moral philosophy of the Hindoos. It is a book known and revered everywhere, its name familiar as a household word even to the females of the *zenana.* Viewing it in whatever light, no great poem was superior to the ' Mohabharat.' He concurred with the Hon'ble lecturer as to the country having the richest materials for poetry ; for he said, there is no mere history among us ; in fact, all that was written was written in poetry, even the very dictionaries. The author of the poem was Vyasa, who dictated, and Ganesa, the God represented with an elephant's head, was the writer. Ganesa, previous to his undertaking to write, made this express condition, that he would not wait for a minute, his pen would continually flow without the least respite. Vyasa agreed to this, but bound Ganesa in turn to the agreement that he would not proceed to compose fresh lines till Ganesa had understood the previous ones. Thus Vyasa went on dictating ; the time that Ganesa took to understand his lines was ample enough to enable him to compose new ones. He then said that the marriage of Droupodee with the five Pandavas formed only one instance in ancient India of a woman having more husbands than one, and that the custom was not, as the Hon'ble lecturer had said, in those days an ordinary custom. The father of Droupodee made this vow, that whoever would be able to pierce the eyeball of a fish in the heavens by looking at the image reflected on a still sheet of water below, would have the hand of his daughter. Several princes were assembled to try this extraordinary feat, but Urjuna only was successful. In those days, be it remembered, the law of primogeniture was not known, and the rational and equitable law of equal division amongst equal claimants prevailed. The brothers used to bring the trophies of their victory to their mother, and had them, in conformity with this law, equally divided amongst them. Accordingly, when Urjuna returned home with the princess, as the prize of his feat, the mother, little knowing that the prize won that day was a beautiful princess, ordered the spoil to be shared equally between them. Respect and obedience to a mother are inculcated in strong terms in the *shasters*. The brothers, with due deference to the injunction of their mother, married the princess. Thus he (the speaker) shewed that this extraordinary marriage took place under extraordinary circumstances. In conclusion, he tendered his humble tribute of praise to Mr. Wheeler, for the very admirable way in which he has concentrated all the facts of that celebrated work in the compass of a single volume. He thanked him, on behalf of his educated countrymen, for the trouble he had taken in throwing new light upon such a subject, and in opening a new source of intelligence to his European brethren in a form that is at once readable and acceptable to all. He resumed his seat, proposing a hearty vote of thanks to the Hon'ble lecturer. "

1st July 1868. Lecture by the Revd. K. S. Macdonald on " Auguste Comte the Positivist."—" Baboo Grish Chunder Ghose, in rising to move a vote of thanks to the Revd. lecturer for his able paper on the life of Comte, warned the meeting against the fallacy of gauging the philosophy of a great thinker by the incidents of his private life. The insanity or the infirmities of Comte must be kept out of view altogether, when examining his luminous system; what great man was without blemishes of character? The giants of thought were not to be tested by the ordinary criteria of human conduct. They compassed such a large amount of good to society at large, that society could afford to overlook that which, in ordinary men, would excite ridicule or disgust. Comte may, at a certain period of his life, have been insane, but the positive philosophy, of which he was the missionary, bore no traces of insanity. It was given to few men indeed to elaborate a system such as that involved in the religion of humanity. Comte found that all other systems were at strife with each other, that they offered battle-fields to dogmatists who, reasoning from no assured or well-recognized principles, were led into errors which disturbed the peace of humanity. The system of Comte was founded on the doctrine of universal equality, not that kind of equality which subverted the order of nature, and like the democrats of the French Revolution made every man a despot, but the equality of order as bodied forth by the great English constitution, the equality of all men before the law, yet the due subordination of the poor to the rich, the governed man to the governing man. All Comte's speculation took the form of order. There was no entanglement in his system. Taking his stand on the symmetry of nature, he carried that symmetry into the manifestations of the human mind, and the needs of human sociology.

An attempt had been made to ridicule Comte's veneration of woman as developed in the mother and the daughter. The speaker was surprised that the chivalric Englishman could not take kindly to such a worship. The religion of the Hindoo raised woman to the highest pedestal of veneration and worship. The chief deity of the Hindoo Pantheon was a goddess, the great *Sakti*, who was greater than *Mahadeo*, the god of gods. The chivalry as well as the philosophy of the Hindoo mind created this deity, for who can else in creation be greater than woman, the progenitor of creation's lord— man? In worshipping the mother we carry legitimate adoration to the antecedent of man, and in worshipping the daughter the same veneration is carried down to the being who is destined to propagate the future man, and make the genus man immortal. The tether and the fling of Comte's mind appalled the moral cowards who dared travel with him to a certain distance only, and turned back in horror from the fame with which he dazzled them. The lecturer said that Mill had declared Comte to be ignorant of political economy. The fact, on the other hand, was that Comte despised political economy— the science of buying and selling, not yet raised to the dignity of a positive science. The laws of political economy are still unsettled. That which thinking men now call a law had not long ago devastated Orissa and turned one of the finest countries under the sun into a charnel-house, filling it with the groans of the dying and the deade. The philosophy of Comte has no mists about it. It is destined to envelop the civilized world, to upset the empire of the sword, to drive out the needle-guns and the iron-clads, and weld humanity into one harmonious, law-obeying, affectionate brotherhood of nations ".

We have already shown at what sacrifice of personal comfort and time Grish Chunder used to attend the Howrah Municipal Commissioners' meetings. His attendance at the meetings of the Canning Institute involved scarcely less personal discomfort and loss of time. As the village of Bellore is situated at a distance of more than three miles from Howrah, the carriage and pair of ponies maintained by Grish Chunder for conveying him daily to tne steamer ghat at Howrah, had to be kept at Howrah all day long until they were used for conveying him back to Bellore on his return from office at about six o'clock in the evening, in order to save the poor animals the strain of a double journey each way. The proceedings of the Canning Institute generally commenced at eight o'clock in the evening. Apart, therefore, from the danger of imposing extra work on his jaded roadsters, Grish Chunder had scarcely the time to allow of his returning home after the day's work, snatching a hasty meal, and then driving over to the Institute so as to reach it by the appointed hour. He was accordingly obliged to take his evening meal at the house of his hospitable friend the late Babu Raj Mohan Bose of Howrah, better known as "Bangal Babu," and wait there until the meeting hour approached, when he proceeded to the Institute and after taking a prominent part in the evening's proceedings which generally occupied more than a couple of hours, drove homewards, seldom reaching his home before midnight.   This not only meant that he was away from home for fourteen or fifteen hours at a stretch, but also that he was in harness, *i.e.*, had his office dress on, nearly all that time, even in the most grilling weather.

CHAPTER XII.

WHEN the late Bengal Social Science Association came into existence in 1867, Grish Chunder was invited to join it and he was elected a member of its Council. The following account of the origin of the Association is taken from Vol. I Part I of its *Transactions* (1st Session July /67) —

"The Bengal Social Science Association owes its origin to the late visit of Miss Mary Carpenter. When in Calcutta last December, she expressed a desire to meet the leading members of both Native and European Society, with a view to the discussion of the advantages to be derived from the establishment of such an institution in this country. A meeting was accordingly held in the rooms of the Asiatic Society on the 17th December 1866, at which His Excellency the Viceroy, the Lieutenant Governor of Bengal, and a large number of Native and European gentlemen were present."

The late Babu Peary Chand Mittra was the permanent Secretary of the Association, and the office of President was succesively held by the Hon'ble Messrs. Justices Norman, Beverley and Phear. The object of the Association, as described in the Prospectus, was " to promote the devolopment of social progress in the Presidency of Bengal by uniting Europeans and Natives of all classes in the collection, arrangement and classification of facts bearing on the social, intellectual and moral condition of the people." With this object the Association was divided into the following four sections, viz, I. *Jurisprudence and Law*, II. *Education*, III. *Health*, and IV. *Economy and Trade* (including Social Economy). Grish Chunder elected to be attached to the last named section and read on the 30th January 1868 a paper on " Female Occupations in Bengal" which was published in accordance with the rules of the Association, not only in its *Transactions* but also

as a separate pamphlet.   It forms the only paper read by Grish
Chunder before a learned Society which we are able to lay before our
readers, the rest having been irretrievably lost.   We transcribe below
the remarks which the paper elicited when it was read, as recorded in
Vol. II, Part I of the *Transactions* (2nd Session, January 1868) :—

" Babu Shama Churn Sircar expressed his general concurrence
in the remarks which were contained in the paper.

Babu Kissory Chand Mittra had much pleasure in testifying to
the correctness of the photograph of domestic life—not perhaps a very
flattering one—which had been presented to the Association.   There
was a proverb about a bird fouling its own nest, but he would rather
liken the writer to the skilful surgeon who only probed the wound to
heal it.   The Hindus had one great virtue which the paper had
brought out.   Charity was a conspicuous trait in the national character
and provision was made for the poor in all parts of the country.

The Revd. J. Long thought that a Poor Law would nevertheless be soon required in Bengal—not perhaps for the sake of
professional beggars, but for a class above them who had greater
claims to consideration."

Grish Chunder was, for several years, connected with the
Ooterparah Hitakari Sabha and was a Vice-President of the Sabha at
the time of his death.   He took a warm interest in its proceedings
and not unfrequently took part therein.   We remember having attended a meeting of the Sabha held about the middle of the year 1866.
The late Babu Koylas Chunder Bose read on that occasion a paper
on " The Claims of the Poor."   He was followed by the late Babu
Keshub Chunder Sen, who dwelt briefly on the subject in a neat little
speech in the course of which he remarked that his countrymen had
a large proportion of camphor in their constitution ; for, their zeal in a
good cause evaporated in a wonderfully short time.   But the best
speaker of the evening was Grish Chunder, who made an eloquent
and stirring appeal to the rich on behalf of the poor.   We may
remark in passing that that God-gifted orator, Babu Keshub Chunder
Sen, came out in all his glory only when he spoke on a religious or
kindred subject.   " Within that magic circle none durst walk but he."
It appears from the Reports of the Sabha that Grish Chunder

delivered a lecture on "Education" in November 1867 and another in the following year.

We also recollect having been present at a meeting of the Ooterparah Literary Club held in the Hall of the Ooterparah Government School in the summer of 1869. The late Colonel Malleson read on that occasion an admirable discourse on Dr. Johnson and some of his contemporaries, *e.g.*, Richard Savage. Grish Chunder, who had been called to the chair, thanked the learned lecturer, at the conclusion of his lecture, for the rare intellectual treat with which he had favoured the meeting. Colonel Malleson thereupon made a suitable acknowledgment in the course of which he complimented Grish Chunder in a way which took the audience, of whom Babu Shib Chunder Deb happened to be one, by the most pleasant surprise, for they had seldom heard an eminent European speak so highly of a Native. The incident is referred to in the following extract from the *Bengalee* of the 6th November, 1869 :—

"A correspondent of the 'Reflector' thus speaks of the late Baboo Grish Chunder Ghose :—

'He was held in so great esteem among Europeans, that at a public meeting of the Ooterparah Literary Club, Colonel Malleson said with emphasis, that he had travelled over different parts of the world—Italy, Germany, &c.—but he had never seen a man more independent or more honourable than Baboo Grish Chunder. As Registrar of the office of the Examiner, Pay Department, his impartiality and urbanity of behaviour towards the assistants of the office were so remarkable, that notwithstanding the party feeling which still prevails to a certain extent among Christians and Natives in office, he was held in high esteem and awe by both the Christian and Native sections of the office.' "

Grish Chunder's removal to Bellore while the *Bengalee* Press still continued to be located in Calcutta, naturally made him to a certain extent lose touch with his paper. It is true that he still continued to be in editorial charge of the *Bengalee* and to write leading articles for it during his leisure hours; yet there is no gainsaying the fact that when an editor finds a goodly distance interposed between himself and his inexorable dun, the printer's devil, he is tempted to draw more largely upon his staff of contributors and to depend less upon the produce of his own pen. The gradual decrease in the number of leaders written by the editor himself sensibly affected the popularity of the *Bengalee* and Baboo Becha Ram Chatterjee noticed with dismay the falling-off in the number of subscribers. He accordingly implored Grish Chunder to allow the *Bengalee* Press to be removed to his garden, promising not to trouble him in any way about its *management*. Grish Chunder agreed to the proposal. About the end of September 1866, the needful arrangements were completed and the Press was located in a thatched hut built for its accommodation—as a temporary measure. It was subsequently accommodated in a *pucca* building which Grish Chunder caused to be erected for the purpose at his own expense. The first number of the *Bengalee* that was published at Bellore bore date the 6th October 1866. In the opening article of this number, after humorously accounting for the change in the *locale* of the paper, Grish Chunder thus dilates upon the advantages attending the change :—

"We have the advantage besides of being in close proximity to the important and growing township of Howrah with its varied population and gigantic Railway interest and operations. Calcutta also lies at our feet and the hum of the great city reaches our ears with a murmuring music on the still evening air. We can survey the politics of the city from our solitary stand-point uninfluenced by party, by prejudice, by self-interest or the heat which distracts the senses and devours the energies of its residents. In our cool retreat we can sift the most intricate questions and disentangle the web of the most involved politics of the day, local or imperial. Nothing will mar the equanimity of our temper or take away from the purity of our motives. Observing rigidly and carefully all the doings and sayings of the famous mofussil, ourselves placed in the midst of the formidable Bengal Police, under the clutches of a magistracy supposed to be incompetent and despotic, in daily intercourse with Amlah whose moral condition is known and described to be one of bribery and corruption, our opportunities for exposing misgovernment will be vast and our motives for doing so invulnerable. Here we plant our Head Quarters in a village the population whereof scarcely exceeds one thousand souls but on whose right is Howrah and on whose left is Ooterparah, which stands on the Ganges in shaggy magnificence, within a quarter of an hour's rowing or riding of Calcutta itself—the enemy of oppression and the friend of the poor. The ryut crouches round about us. His wrongs and his sufferings will be hourly poured into our willing ears. If we cannot practically help him ourselves we shall not mind screaming out hoarse to those who can. The Government may depend upon our giving correct information whatever the color or texture of our politics. Honestly and faithfully as before will the *Bengalee* continue to do his duty though there are not twenty persons within hail of his resting-place. The God of Heaven protects him, however, and that is a species of security of which mere religionists and worldlings cannot and do not know the practical and permanent value."

Nor was the song of welcome or priestly benediction wanting to greet the *Bengalee* on its change of location. The following verses appeared in the *Bengalee* of the 3rd Novr. 1866.

To

The Editor of the Bengalee.

Welcome! "Bengalee" to our side
Of holy Gunga's sacred tide!
After a course of patriot fire,
Of ardent hope, and high desire,
And aspiration for the best,
To God in his supreme behest,
Amid the devastating jars
Of nations, and destructive wars,
Of Austrian armies, 'gainst the Prusse,
While both are half afraid of Russe,
When Captain Jervis, aide so fickle,
Has eaten the Commander's pickle,
Missioners cloke themselves in shrouds,
And preachers lecture from the clouds, *
While Competition-wallahs fill
Fine old appointments at their will,
And 'stead of English gentlemen,
We get green-grocers for our gain,

Apothecaries for Assistant Surgeons,
Like self-ordained vulgar Spurgeons,
Who of examination prate,
Themselves the while half-educate,
Police officials who can get,
In their own districts, deep in debt,
For Plowden, Grant, and Lushingtons,
We get Smith, Jones, and Robinsons,—
Oh! that such difference should be,
Since days of old John Company!
Welcome Bengalee! hold your own,
No change of site can change your tone,
Tho' now your influence may be less
Than th' English or Columbian Press,
Write words of truth and soberness,
Nor fear lest sanctimonious oil
Your lawful pages should sweat to spoil,
And common liberty of speech
Make theirs alone who pray and preach.
Forward, and Onward, be the word,
The laws obeyed, the Gods adored!

　　　　　　　　　　R. I. B.

The above lines were composed by the late Revd. Robert Bland of whom the following obituary notice appeared in the *Bengalee* of the 29th December 1866 :—

"With deep regret we have to announce the death at Chundernagore of the Revd. Robert Bland, a nephew of Bishop Bland, whose name is familiar to every native student in connection with his text-book on Algebra. The Revd. gentleman was long the Government Chaplain of Gowhati where he distinguished himself by his Christian zeal in the cause of native education. From that station he was removed to Dum Dum and finally to Muttra, where he met with a fall from his horse, which shattered a not very robust constitution. He had retired from the service two years ago after labouring effectually to free the Church from Judaism. Full of noble ideas, he often ventilated these through the Press, fearlessly and without favour. In him the natives of the country have lost a real and hearty friend."

The year 1866 is memorable in the history of Bengal as the year of the Orissa Famine, the saddest feature of which awful calamity was the enormous mortality for which the culpable incredulity displayed at the outset by Sir Cecil Beadon's Government in regard to the true character and extent of the dire visitation must, in a great measure, be held answerable.   Grish Chunder's keen sympathy for human suffering made him unsparing in his criticism of the conduct of Government in the matter.   The same feeling made him unsparing in his exertions to relieve the poor villagers whom the Cyclone of the 1st November 1867 had made homeless.   Not only did he subscribe his mite to the Cyclone Relief Fund, but, as an active member of the Relief Committee, he also trudged on foot for days together through Bellore and its adjacent villages, distributing the much-needed relief from door to door with his own hands.   About the middle of that year he was shocked to hear of the sudden death, from heart failure, of his dear old father.   The old gentleman had, scarcely a fortnight before his death, visited his son at Bellore, walking all the way from Sulkea Ghat to Bellore,—a distance of more than a mile.   He then seemed to be quite hale and hearty—barring a pain in his chest, which, he said, had lately been troubling him off and on.   Even on the day of his death he had no suspicion that his end was so near.   After taking in the afternoon of that day a hearty meal—consisting of *loochis*, mangoes and milk—he had a smoke with his *hookah* and then reclined himself against a bolster, in which position he expired, before an old Brahmin, who was his constant companion and to whom he had handed over his *chillum* just a second or two previously, could realize the dreadful fact.   As soon as Grish Chunder received intelligence of the sad occurrence, he hastened to Calcutta to condole with his poor, bereaved mother.   It was agreed that the three brothers should jointly celebrate their father's *shrad* in style, on the expiry of the usual period of mourning, and preparations were made accordingly for a grand funeral feast.   Owing, however, to the death of Sree Nath's wife on the very day on which the feast was to have been held, the feast had to be stopped after considerable expense had been incurred for the purpose.

It was about the time he lost his father that Grish Chunder acquired an inestimable friend.   He first became acquainted with the late Principal Lobb at the Canning Institute, Howrah, in 1867.

Professor Lobb—for he was at the time a Professor at the Presidency College, Calcutta,—then used to reside at Howrah, where he had the reputation of being a profound and versatile scholar of retired habits and unobtrusive manners. So favourably impressed was he with Grish Chunder's frank and genial manners, his breadth of views and his high intellectual attainments, that he soon ceased to treat him as a mere casual acquaintance, but honoured him with his unreserved friend ship and esteem. Grish Chunder, on his part, so highly valued his intimacy with Principal Lobb that the letters addressed to him by the latter are almost the only ones which he took care to preserve. We are thus enabled to present our readers with some of these letters. It was at the instance and under the guidance of Principal Lobb that Grish Chunder first studied the Positive Philosophy and mastered its leading principles, though of course he was not sufficiently well grounded in science to be able to follow all the abstruse details of the system. With a view to bringing the main principles of Positivism within easy reach of the educated Indian, Principal Lobb contributed to the *Bengalee*, during the years 1867 and 1868, a series of admirable articles which were afterwards revised and republished by him in the form of a book entitled " A Brief View of Positivism." These articles, together with several others contributed by Babu Krishna Kamal Bhattacharya, who was then the Senior Professor of Sanskrit at the Presidency College, did much to popularize the philosophy of Auguste Comte in Bengal. It was while Grish Chunder was thus interesting himself in the cause of Positivism that he was induced by a mutual friend to pay a visit to the late Justice Dwarka Nath Mitter who was then living in a garden-house at Cossipore opposite Bellore. The visit was eminently auspicious, for it led to the establishment of the most cordial relations between the two gifted men. Justice Dwarka Nath, who survived Grish by a little over three years, took an active interest in the Grish testimonial.

On the 14th March 1868 Grish Chunder delivered a lecture on the " Life of Ram Doolal Dey the Bengalee Millionaire " in the Hall of the Hooghly College, at the request of Principal Lobb. It was the result of several months' patient research and untiring industry. The public welcomed with delight the appearance of the veteran journalist in the new character of a successful biographer.

The Revd. Mr. James Long, in a foot-note to his celebrated paper entitled "Peeps into Social Life in Calcutta a Century ago," which he read on the 24th July 1868 before the Bengal Social Science Association and which was published in Vol. II, Part II, of the Trans-actions of the Association, hailed the appearance of the *Life of Ram Doolal Dey* as supplying a real desideratum. The Hon'ble Mr. Justice Phear, in acknowledging receipt of a presentation copy of the lecture, wrote from Ballygunge on the 19th July 1868 —" I look for-ward to reading it with pleasure and I am sure from the reputation it has earned I shall gather from it much instruction." Mr. J. Talbovs Wheeler, the eminent historian, likewise wrote to Grish Chunder as follows, from the Foreign office, on the 18th July 1868 :—

" I should very much like to see more biographies published of a similar character as they would do more to show to Europeans the true character of the social life amongst native families than has hitherto been done by any works with which I am acquainted.

If you would kindly favour me with a call some morning at the Foreign office I should have much pleasure in making your acquaintance."

In Volume II of his monumental *History of India from the Earliest Ages* (see pp. 514, 528, 572-3 and 579) Mr. Wheeler noticed the *Life of Ram Doolal Dey* and quoted several passages from it in illustration of Hindu social life. The late Babu Anup Chand Mitter, who was a member of the now defunct firm of *Ashutosh Deb & Nephews*, told us that the late Lord Northbrook, who, before his appointment to the Vice-royalty of India had, as a member of the celebrated firm of *Baring Brothers*, dealt largely with the aforesaid firm, was once pleased, during his Vice-royalty, to honor the firm with a visit. Happening to be shown, in the course of his visit, a copy of the *Life of Ram Doolal Dey*, His Excellency evinced so great an interest in the pamphlet, that Babu Anup Chand had a copy of it splendidly bound and presented to His Excellency. We may add that the late Maharaja Sir Jotendro Mohun Tagore had, scarcely a month before his lamented demise, asked Grish Chunder's eldest son, through Rai Baikuntha Nath Basu, to let him have for a few days a copy of the *Life of Ram Doolal Dey*, the American Consul General having expressed a particular desire to refer to the account given therein of a portrait of George Washington which was presented to Ram Doolal by his American constituents, and which is now in the possession of Babu Subodh Chunder Mullick of Wellington Square.

Babu Kalimoy Ghatak, the compiler of several short biographies of eminent Bengalees, applied to Grish Chunder, shortly after the publication of his lecture, for permission to base on it a Bengali biography of Ram Doolal. The permission asked for was readily granted and the main facts of the life of Ram Doolal, as related by Grish Chunder, thus became accessible to such of his countrymen as might be ignorant of the English language.

The first National Gathering that was held in the suburbs of Calcutta in April 1868 under the name of the " Hindu Mela," marked the dawning of that National spirit in Bengal which has since attained the splendour of " another morn risen upon midnoon." Few could, however, then realize the full significance of the movement, the originator of which—the late Babu Nobo Gopal Mitter who also founded the *National Paper*—was ridiculed by many as a visionary enthusiast. The following extract from the *National Paper* of the 22nd September 1869 will show that Grish Chunder was one of the earliest supporters of the movement. :

" In him we have lost a veteran Indo-English journalist and an ardent sympathiser with all national movements. It may be said here, that he was one of the few supporters of the National Gathering when the project was first conceived. He observed with great delight its subsequent progress, and always used to observe to us, that in time the movement will be a source of great power to the people."

Now that he had reached the summit of his fame, the splendid health of Grish Chunder who had hitherto been a stranger to ailment of any kind, sudenly broke down. The causes which contributed to bring about this disastrous result have been well summarised in the article headed " A Great Indian but a Geographical Mistake" which appeared in *Mookerjee's Magazine* for February 1872 and to which we have already referred :—

" What with his everyday desk labour at his office,—the greater the more a man's sense of duty is acute,—what with the writing of leading articles for his weekly paper, what with constant speeches at public meetings, and not infrequent lectures at

Societies, sometimes the result of long and patient enquiries, what with the duties of an Honorary Magistrate and active member of a municipality as a representative and champion of the dumb thousands, what with long-continued family feuds, and law-suits, and costs, and consultations, and letters on nothing which have a price notwithstanding, and partitions and partition-commissioners, remarkable only for snail's pace, what with the writing of applications and memorials for everybody and pamphlets for Kumars, what with excitation of the imagination by a constant contemplation of the suffering which it was his delight to alleviate, the strain upon his nerves was too much even for him"

The result was that he who had never known before what was meant by giddiness of the head, now suffered constantly from vertigo and extreme nervous debility. He was distracted by a hundred ugly apprehensions. In his alarm he consulted Dr. Chunder Coomar Dey, who had once before rescued him from the jaws of death. Dr. Dey prescribed for him some preparation of iron, but told him that what he really required was absolute rest. He advised Grish Chunder to abjure all intellectual work, to take gentle exercise every morning and, as soon as he felt himself a little stronger, to take a long trip by boat up the river. It was now decided to send the *Bengalee* Press back to Calcutta, although the removal was not actually effected till May 1869. It had, indeed, been a most potent factor in undermining the health of Grish Chunder. Ever since its removal to Bellore he had to work harder for his paper than was good for his health. In order that the paper might make its appearance punctually on Saturday morning, he had to sit up on Friday night till the small hours, attending office all the same on the following day. No wonder then that he was now overtaken by the Nemesis that inevitably dogs such persistent violation of the laws of physical health. In vain did he forswear all literary work, for he was still hampered with his office work. In vain did he now take a two miles' walk regularly every morning ; in vain did he dig up a few feet of ground every morning with an English spade which he bought for the purpose. His nervous debility still continued to trouble him. At last on the 17th November 1868 he started on a trip to Cutwa up the river. He hired for the purpose a large budgerow containing two cabins and licensed to carry thirty passengers

and ten crew.   Besides taking his entire household with him, consisting of his wife and children, his uncle and aunt and his domestic
servants, he engaged the services of two stalwart up-country
Durwans and carried with him a pair of pistols as a protection
against dacoits.   He also took in an ample stock of provisions, not
forgetting even to provide himself with several tins of condensed
Swiss milk which was then considered a novelty.   The voyage was
altogether a most delightful one.   The river was quite calm and the
budgerow dragged its slow length along the smooth surface of the
water.   For the first time after several years of unremitting toil,
Grish Chunder found himself absolutely without occupation.   He
had all his loved ones nestling round him in his little wooden home.
The bracing November breeze soothed his over-strained nerves.   For
the first two or three days of the voyage he enjoyed the sights
presented by the lovely villas which dotted both banks of the river.
They were then replaced by a monotonous succession of steep banks
occasionally relieved by thick jungles.   But the glorious sunrise and
the still more glorious sunset presented sights which never failed to
interest Grish Chunder.   When the budgerow approached some
village far removed from civic influences, numbers of village women
would flock to the river-side to witness the strange phenomenon and
these often formed very picturesque and interesting groups.   The
daily meals of the voyagers were cooked on shoals or sand banks
alongside of which the boat was moored for the purpose, and the
novelty of the situation invested these meals with all the interest
and romance of a picnic and gave them a zest which amply made up
for all their shortcomings.

Above Tribeni the river ceased to be a tidal one and the
budgerow had to be towed up by the crew.   Grish Chunder would
now and then leave the boat and explore the interior of a river-side
village.   One such village he found to be absolutely destitute of any
path-ways.   On reaching Krishnagar, Grish Chunder gave up, for some
reason or other, his original idea of proceeding as far as Cutwa and
decided to retrace his course homewards.

We have said that for some reason or other Grish Chunder
decided to make Krishnagar the farthest limit of his trip up the
river.   It is probable that in arriving at this decision he was influenced

by the circumstance of some of his children, as well as his aged uncle, having contracted fever in the interim, which naturally made him anxious to hurry home in order that they might be placed under proper medical treatment as soon as practicable. Hearing that good medical aid was available at Culna, which lay on his home_ward route, he ordered the boatmen to touch at that port. A dispen_sary was maintained there at the expense of the Burdwan Raj. Dr. Mohendra Nath Gupta, L. M. S., who was then attached to this dis_pensary, was a highly intelligent and capable physician. As soon as he was called in, he assured Grish Chunder that the strong fever from which some of his children were suffering was not at all dange_rous, but he feared that the low fever from which the old gentleman was suffering and which even the patient himself did not consider at all serious, would prove fatal. The prediction proved only too true. While the children were all brought round in a short time by the skilful treatment of Dr. Gupta, Grish Chunder's uncle Hurrish succumbed on the third day of his illness and died at the green old age of seventy-six on the 28th November 1868, in the lap of the holy Ganges. His remains were cremated at Santipore, a place which is considered no less holy by the Vaishnavas of Bengal. To the eternal honor of Dr. Gupta we must here record that on accidentally learning the name of Grish Chunder, he not only declined to charge him any fees, but loaded him with presents of loaves of bread and various other articles of diet. He resisted Grish Chunder's repeated importunities that he should accept some remuneration for his trouble and observed with emphasis that he would forfeit his title to be called a Bengalee if he accepted any payment from the patriotic editor of the *Bengalee.*

The homeward voyage of Grish Chunder was thus darkened by a heavy affliction. He reached Bellore after an absence of twenty days, and during the prescribed period of mourning practised all the austerities enjoined by the Hindu *Shasters,* notwithstanding the bad state of his health. At the end of the period of mourning, he gave a sumptuous feast in honor of his uncle's funeral. The upshot of the matter was, that he derived no lasting benefit from his expensive boat voyage. The position is well described in the article in *Mookerjee's Magazine* from which we have already quoted. "Returned home, he also returned to his old work, if not to quite its old extent. His paper and his village and his country and his clients once more claimed his attention, no less than the state work on which he was engaged. But he brought back not his old powers of body and mind. He wrote as gaily, even as lustily as ever, but he wrote much less and at long intervals, and what little he did write, over-tasked his mind, taxed his very life, as the event proved." But little did he or any of his friends and relations apprehend at the time that he had not many more months to live. Scarcely five months before his death, he was induced by his brother Sree Nath, in May 1869, to apply for an Under-Secretaryship to the Government of Bengal which he understood was about to be created and bestowed upon a Native. The late Mr. H. L. Dampier, who was then the Chief Secretary to the Government of Bengal, promptly acknowledged the application and wrote back in reply that the Government of India had declined to sanction the post. Scarcely three months before his death, Grish Chunder celebrated, in July 1869, the marriage of his eldest son, a youth of fifteen. Only a month before his death Grish Chunder was appointed, in August 1869, by the late Babu Hurray Kristo Auddy (the brother of Gour Mohun and the last Proprietor of the Oriental Seminary) a member of a small committee of Native gentlemen to whom the entire management of the Seminary was entrusted in order to save it from the verge of ruin. Up to Saturday the 11th September, he attended office as usual. The following Sunday he passed at his brother's, dining in company. On Monday the 13th September, he felt, however, too indisposed to attend office and at night complained of feverishness, accompanied by an acute pain all over his body. The pain gradually increased. Suspecting that it was due to an attack of rheumatism and believing that in cases of rheumatism homœopathic medicines proved more efficacious than allopathic ones, Grish Chunder wrote to his friend, the late Dr. Mohendro Lal Sircar, on Tuesday the 14th September, asking him to come over and see what ailed him. Dr. Sircar attended the next day, and believing the case to be one of rheumatism he prescribed fresh lime-juice to be taken in large doses. He also prescribed a mild aperient, viz., Seidlitz powder. On the morning of Friday the 17th September, the patient felt himself so well that the doctor advised him to take some light food. Grish Chunder's mother-in-law paid him a visit that day, and found him in a very hopeful mood. Grish Chunder took the opportunity of describing to her how well he had been nursed by his devoted wife. At night, however, he had fever again. The doctor was duly informed of this fact when he came to see the patient on Saturday morning, but he attached no importance to it. On Saturday night the patient became delirious, and this so alarmed his near relatives that they sent for Dr. Chunder Coomar Dey without further loss of time. Dr. Dey came early on Sunday morning, ominously shook his head, pronounced the case to be one of typhoid fever in its most virulent form, and said that he feared he had been called in too late. Dr. Sircar came a little while later and flew into a towering - passion when he heard that another doctor had been called in without his concurrence. He vented his wrath upon the poor old father-in-law of the patient in the presence of the latter and then went away in high dudgeon. This stormy scene made such a deep impression upon the susceptible mind of Grish Chunder that his last delirious ravings had exclusive reference to the partition suit instituted by Babu Prawn Kissen Dutt and to the extreme impropriety of Dr. Dey having been called in without the knowledge and consent of Dr. Sircar who had been attending *gratis*. It may be observed, in passing, that in his delirious moments Grish Chunder never uttered a single Bengali expression, but invariably used the language of his adoption which had a firmer grip upon him than his mother tongue. On Sunday evening he called his eldest boy to his bed-side and said to him in English, "Obeen, I shall die tomorrow." These were the last words that passed his lips. Dr. Dey called again that evening and said: "The case is very serious, the patient should be watched very carefully." True to his word even in death, as he had ever been in life, poor Grish Chunder renounced his earthly pilgrimage at the age of forty, at half past two on the morning of Monday the 20th September 1869. But he cannot altogether be said to have died prematurely who had for nearly twenty years worked incessantly for the good of his country. Truly does the poet sing—

"We live in deeds, not years, in thoughts, not breath."

When the people of Bellore heard of the death of Grish Chunder, who had, during his five years' sojourn in their midst, done so much for them, many of them burst into tears.   Young and old, high and low, flocked to the river-side to do honor to the last remains of their benefactor, and when the cremation was over, they wended to their homes in the deepest dejection.

CHAPTER XIII.

----o----

TRAITS OF CHARACTER—CONDUCT IN PRIVATE LIFE—VIEWS ON RELIGION AND SOCIAL REFORM.

Having narrated the main facts of his life, we now proceed to notice the salient features of Grish Chunder's character and conduct in private life. The key-note of his character is furnished by a single line of Tennyson's—" And manhood fused with female grace "—which occurs in a beautiful passage quoted from the *In Memoriam* by Principal Lobb in his speech at the Town Hall meeting held in honour of Grish Chunder's memory. While his manly independence challenged the unbounded admiration of such distinguished Europeans as Colonel Malleson and Sir John Phear, his uniformly courteous demeanour towards all, his suavity of manners, his frank geniality and bland affability, alike endeared him to all classes of people from the highest to the lowest. Although there was not a tittle of pride or vanity in his composition, he possessed in no ordinary degree that manly self-respect which not only made it impossible for him to cringe to or flatter the great, but which also made him scrupulously careful not to wound the self-respect of even the lowest menial of his office. He possessed in an eminent degree that free and brave spirit of which F. D. Maurice speaks :—" The free and brave spirit is the spirit of Charity and Truth, the spirit who fights in us with our selfishness ; a spirit which makes men feminine, if feminine means courteous, deferential, free from brutal insolent pretensions ; but which also gives women manliness, if manliness means the vigour to live for the cause of Humanity and die for it." Grish Chunder always endeavoured to act in accordance with the dictates of his conscience. Endowed by nature with a singularly unselfish heart which overflowed with the milk of human kindness, it was his mission in life to champion the cause of the weak and the oppressed without fear or favour, to battle for the true and the just, unconnected with any party and uncontaminated by sectarian influences. If he never hesitated to adopt a slashing style in pitilessly shewing up what he considered to be unjust or unrighteous, his pen was never steeped in venom distilled by private malice from an acid heart. As one who knew him most intimately has justly observed, " he wrote strongly because he felt strongly, but there was no venom in what he wrote." He never used, however, the sledge-hammer style in his daily intercourse with his fellowmen, which was characterized by the utmost urbanity and never-failing courtesy. Nor did he ever delight in blunt or slanderous speech. As remarked by the late Babu Koylas Chunder Bose, "he disarmed malice of its sting by his open and straightforward nature, and while he could scarcely make an enemy he was sure to make a friend even on the most slight acquaintance." The same authority tells us that although " he never allowed the insidious cup to touch his lips, yet he was a most jolly companion ever ready with an inexhaustible fund of jokes, anecdotes and stories to brighten the faces of the circle in which he happened to be placed." No wonder then that Grish Chunder was the idol of society. But although he was fond of all innocent social pleasures, he was remarkable for his domestic virtues. He never forgot old Cotton's advice—

> " From ourselves our joys must flow,
>
> And that dear hut—our home "

May we not describe Grish Chunder as one—

> " Who reverenced his conscience as his king ;
>
> Whose glory was, redressing human wrong,
>
> Who spake no slander, no, nor listen'd to it ;
>
> Who loved one only, and who clave to her."

We have already shewn how affectionate a brother and how dutiful a son was Grish Chunder. In nothing, however, was the spotless purity of his character more signally displayed than in his conjugal relations. The marriage vow that he took at the early age of fifteen he faithfully fulfilled to the end of his life, and never did a happier couple exist even in this land in which, of all lands under the sun, connubial bliss is not a rarity, than Grish Chunder and his wife during their uniformly happy married life of twenty-five years.

Grish Chunder's wife was, indeed, in every respect, a worthy helpmate of her gifted husband. In loftiness of soul she was the exact counterpart of her husband. In point of literary culture, she was, no doubt, far inferior to her husband, yet her natural intelligence was so great that she could fully sympathise with her husband's loftiest views and aspirations.

> " Her soul, though feminine and weak,
>
> Can image his, even as the lake,
>
> Itself disturbed by slightest stroke,
>
> Reflects the invulnerable rock."

Nor was she by any means destitute of culture. It is true that her husband's efforts to teach her English, when she was quite a young girl, had proved abortive owing to the thousand and one obstacles thrown in their way by the Hindu joint family system. But she ac-quired a sufficient knowledge of her own vernacular to be able to read and appreciate many of the best Bengali books that were pub-lished in her day. When the *Masik Patrika*—the first Bengali magazine which aimed at the instruction of Hindu females—was started in 1854, Grish Chunder subscribed to it for his wife. Similar-ly, when the *Bamabodhini Patrika* made its first appearance in 1863, Grish Chunder became one of its earliest subscribers. But it was at Bellore that Grish Chunder enjoyed the amplest opportunities of imparting to his better half no inconsiderable portion of his own Western culture. It was there that, unrestrained by the trammels imposed by the joint family system, he spent an hour or two every evening, after supper, in reading and translating to his wife passages from some of the master-pieces of English literature, among which we may mention Shakespeare's *Othello, Romeo and Juliet, Macbeth,* and *The Taming of the Shrew,* Scott's *Rob Roy,* Dickens's *Oliver Twist,* Beaconsfield's *Contarini Fleming,* Lytton's *Caxtons,* Miss Mitford's *Country Stories,* Warren's *Diary of a Late Physician* and Marryat's *Japhet in Search of a Father* and *Jacob Faithful.* These family readings were the only recreation that Grish Chunder allowed himself to indulge in before commencing his serious literary work at night. Sometimes he would spread his mat on the terrace of his garden-house or in a cosy corner of a flower-bed and there keep his little family spell-bound for hours together, by pouring forth the rich treasures of his mind with all the ease and exuberance of a born prose poet. It is thus that—

" The tidal wave of deeper souls

    Into our inmost being rolls,

    And lifts us, unawares,

    Out of all meaner cares."

But if Grish Chunder did all he could to enrich and improve the mind of his wife, she amply repaid him for his trouble by ardently sympathising with his noble mission in life, which she also furthered in no small measure by entirely relieving her husband of the management of all domestic concerns, by nourishing him in his hours of ease, and by nursing him in his hours of illness One of Darwin's sons has told us lately, in an excellent biography of his father, how that illustrious naturalist was enabled to achieve his great scientific work, in spite of his delicate health, mainly by the incessant care bestowed upon him by his devoted wife. But how little does the world know of the way in which the secluded and self-denying Hindu wife helps her husband to fulfil his life's mission. " The mill-streams that turn the clappers of the world arise in solitary places."

Grish Chunder's wife was an adept in the art of making the most toothsome confectionery, mango-jellies of the most exquisitely delicate flavour and divers other dainty dishes. The following passage in Grish Chunder's paper on " Female Occupations in Bengal," presents to us a picture drawn from his own home-life :—

" Though the middle classes of Bengalis usually keep an establishment of hired cooks, yet their wives are not altogether relieved from the duty of cooking. The ordinary rations of their families are of course produced without their help, but the dainty dishes are altogether their handiwork. The cookrooms are invariably at the base of the house ; but the lady has a small apartment on a higher floor, close to her sleeping room, where sweetmeats and bread and meat preparations and other interesting articles of food are got ready by her own individual labour. Even in joint families, this separation of delicate· eating is effected with the tacit consent of a majority of the members. The wife cooks for her own children and husband that which is agreeable to them, in excess of the joint allowance of rice and fish. It is a delight to her to make her children sit in a ring round her husband, as she distributes the warm bread and sweetmeats, listening to the eulogies pronounced upon them. The joint ration is always miserably cooked and coarsely issued. It is the wife's labour that gives the Hindu a taste for delicacies." The description given by Grish Chunder, in the same paper, of the way in which the Hindu female discharges the duties of a sick nurse applies, in every particular, to his own wife :—" On the sick bed her attendance is priceless, she seems to be formed by nature for the office of a nurse. Cool, patient, and self-denying for days and nights together, she hangs over the object of her solicitude ; nothing escapes her eagle eye ; every need of the patient is anticipated. Indeed the devotion and strength of character manifested on such occasions by the affectionate creature prove more efficient means of the patient's recovery than the prescriptions of the doctor. The rich who are thrown upon the attentions of their servants during severe illness, seldom survive ; the poor whose wives are their sole attendants on the sick bed generally escape death."

Grish Chunder's wife was indeed adorned with every virtue and every grace which forms the peculiar heritage of her sex. She was a pattern daughter, a pattern wife and a pattern mother. The pen refuses, however, to record that this " stately flower of female fortitude and perfect wifehood," after enjoying the most perfect and unalloyed happiness for the first thirty-four years of her existence, survived her gifted husband by nearly twenty-six years, during which latter period she successively lost an infant daughter and three most promising sons whose ages ranged from twelve to fifteen. These repeated bereavements so completely shattered her health and spirits that she became a perfect wreck and nervously apprehensive of what more bereavements might yet be in store for her. When, therefore, she was overtaken by death in the sixtieth year of her life, on the 17th May 1895, she welcomed it as a long-wished-for relief. It may, however, be added that at the time of her death she had the satisfaction of leaving three sons and two daughters, all well-established in life, with the exception of her youngest son who was then studying for the degree of Bachelor of Law which he afterwards attained.

Although Grish Chunder was an affectionate father, he never doted upon his children. He condemned as highly injudicious

the plan followed by many well-to-do parents in this country of
bringing up their children with a good deal of coddling, instead of
allowing them to grow up in a healthy and natural way. He made
no distinction between his sons and daughters, or if he did make any
distinction at all, it was rather in favour of the latter. He was as
solicitous about the education of his daughters as about that of his
sons. His eldest daughter was scarcely five years old when he sent
her, in May 1857, to the Bethune Female School, which was then
patronised by few respectable Hindus. In the absence of a female
school at Bellore, he allowed his second daughter to live with her
mother's family at Konnagar in order that she might enjoy the
advantage of studying at the good female school established there in
1860. He strongly advocated the employment of respectable Hindu
females as zenana teachers, as in the absence of such teachers what
little a girl learnt at school was generally forgotten by her after
marriage at an early age. Grish Chunder took an active interest in
all educational matters, and his private accounts shew that he
supported not a few of the schools in Calcutta and its neighbourhood
by monthly subscriptions and donations. He attached greater
importance to the moral education of his sons than to their intellectual
training. He never inflicted corporal punishment upon a boy for
neglecting his studies, but the slightest indication of untruthfulness or
disingenuousness was visited by him with condign punishment. A
fault committed, if frankly and prompty acknowledged, was sure to be
condoned by him. Grish Chunder never engaged a private tutor for
his sons and he always impressed upon them the value of self-help.
He would on no account allow them to use "keys" or "cribs,"
but always made them refer to the dictionary for the meaning of a
word, helping them only after every honest attempt made by them
had failed. He treated his eldest boy, when he was barely thirteen
years of age, more as a friend and companion than otherwise, and
freely discussed all manner of literary topics with him, with the
object of inspiring him with a taste for literary pursuits even at that
early age. To create in him a laudable ambition, he used to tell him
that as he intended giving him an education superior to what he
had himself received, he expected that the son would excel the father
in the same way that Lord Canning had excelled George Canning.
Grish Chunder's busy life allowed him but very little time which

he could call his own. He could therefore ill afford to waste a single minute. During his long drive to Howrah in the morning, he generally read the daily papers. In the evening, when light failed, he utilized the time occupied by the homeward journey in conversing with his eldest boy on literary subjects, his wonderful memory enabling him to edify the youth with no end of literary anecdotes and quotations from the English classics. There was no defect in his early education of which Grish Chunder was more keenly sensible than his ignorance of Sanskrit and consequent imperfect acquaintance with the literature of his own vernacular language. It was therefore his great aim that his eldest boy should be well-grounded in Sanskrit, and with this object in view he had him admitted, when he was only nine years old, to the Government Sanskrit College, Calcutta, in 1863. Owing, however, to the exodus to Bellore, which took place in the following year, the boy had to be withdrawn from the College and put to school at Howrah.

With all his literary tastes and predilections, Grish Chunder was no mere bookworm, but he was of an eminently practical turn of mind. It was this turn of mind which induced him in 1857 to attend for a few months the "Industrial School." The laying-out of his gardens and the construction of his garden-house also bore witness to it. He had a complete set of carpenter's tools with which it was his delight to execute petty jobs without the aid of a joiner. In his published writings, also, Grish Chunder seldom put forward a theory without making some practical suggestion to give effect to it. We are convinced that the practical side of Grish Chunder's genius would have risen more prominently to view, had it been given ample room and verge enough. He felt a genuine admiration for men of great practical ability, such as Ram Doolal Dey or Boulton and Watt. Grish Chunder's second son, who was scarcely twelve years old at the time of his father's death, displayed practical ability of no mean order even at that early age. He was therefore his father's especial favourite, confidential adviser and factotum. So great was the confidence reposed in him by Grish Chunder that he went the length of entrusting him with the keys of his safe. It pains us to record that this bright and amiable boy who, his father always thought, had a glorious future before him, survived Grish Chunder by scarcely three years.

Grish Chunder's conduct twowards his servants was quite of a piece with his general character. He was the gentlest of masters ; yet he possessed a natural dignity which made him implicitly obeyed and respected as well as loved by his servants. An old servant of his, Mohun, who had been in the service of the family since the days of Kasi Nath and who had taken care of Grish Chunder in his infancy, was granted a pension equal to his wages and sent to his village home. But the man turned up after a few days, saying that he could not bear to be separated from his dear master and his children. The poor fellow was allowed by Grish Chunder to continue in his service although he was not fit for any work except fondling Grish's young ones and giving Grish himself— in season and out of season—the benefit of his superannuated wisdom! The old man had the misfortune to survive his young master. When Grish's widow and orphans were being removed to Konnagar, he begged hard to be allowed to accompany them and offered to serve them *without pay*—an offer which, for obvious reasons, they were unable to accept, though they were deeply touched by this mark of his devo. ted fidelity. Grish Chunder's coachman, Meerun, a brawny, broad. chested Pathan who hailed from the Purneah district, was also devo. tedly attached to his master and was ready to lay down his life for him and his. As an instance of his fidelity, we may mention that on one occassion, a fiery horse belonging to Grish Chunder bolted with the carriage as soon as the animal had been harnessed to it, without allowing the coachman time to mount his dicky. This happened in a corner of the Howrah maidan which had deep trenches on two sides of it, and the carriage contained Grish Chunder's young hopeful. Finding it impossible to check the course of the unruly beast in any other way, the daring Pathan, without a moment's hesitation, thrust his right hand into its mouth and by pulling out its tongue brought the brute to a dead stop at once, but not before his hand had been severely bitten by the infuriated animal. But for this act of heroic self-devotion on the part of Meerun, the carriage and its young occupant would have, doubtless, been smashed to atoms. The faithful Meerun was, after this accident, laid up for many weeks. He predeceased his master, but as long as he was alive he never forgot that his generous master had once made him a gift of forty rupees to enable him to marry. We may add that Grish Chunder gave, for a like purpose, no less than one hundred rupees to a young Brahmin who superintended the construction of his garden-house at Bellore. Grish Chunder always addressed an old female cook of his, who was of gentle blood, as his "granny," and this so highly flattered the good woman that as long as she lived, she behaved herself in every respect as a member of the family.

As remarked by the late Babu Koylas Chunder Bose, Grish Chunder "had the rare quality of making friends of acquaintances and acquaintances of strangers." " The circle of his friends and acquaintances was so large that it was a positive inconvenience to bear him company either in a walk in the streets, a bathing excursion to the ghats or a run through the Railway station to catch the train. He had so many people to speak to, to make kind enquiries of, that he had often to be reminded that time was running." The fact of the matter is, that Grish Chunder always acted on the principle that civility costs nothing but gains much. So careful was he not to give offence to any one if he could help it, that in his social intercourse with his orthodox and heterodox countrymen he invariably adopted two different styles of greeting. " While he would," says Babu Koylas Chunder, "greet a friend imbued with English ideas by a warm and affectionate shake of the hand, he would bend his neck and fold his hands to one of the orthodox class."

Although politeness is closely allied to morality and could only have arisen after mankind had attained a high degree of moral deli-cacy, it has unfortunately a tendency to lose its ethical spirit and crystallize into a mere form. There is no gainsaying the fact that in modern Europe politeness is very often a synonym for external polish or outward refinement of manners and that a man of many friends has very often no friend at all. Grish Chunder was, however, saved from this disastrous fate by his intense abhorrence of the hollow-ness and lip-friendships which are the bane of modern society. He had a guileless heart, or, as a friend of his has well put it, he always carried his heart upon his sleeve. He had therefore no lack of genuine friends and he grappled such friends to his soul with hoops of steel. The delight which he felt in their company was often marked by—

" Sydneian showers

Of sweet discourse, whose powers

Can crown old winter's head with flowers."

It is not possible to give anything like a complete list of Grish Chunder's personal friends, whose name is legion. Among those, however, with whom he was on terms of intimacy may be named the late Principal Samuel Lobb, the late Maharaja Sir Narendra Krishna Deb Bahadur, the late Maharaja Sir Jotendro Mohun Tagore Bahadur, the late Rajas Issur Chunder and Pertaub Chunder Singh, Raja Sir Sourendro Mohun Tagore Bahadur, the late Kumar Harendra Krishna Deb Bahadur, the late Nawab Abdool Luteef Khan Bahadur, the late Hon'ble Justice Sumbhoo Nath Pundit, the late Babus Bhudeb Mukerjee, Hurrish Chunder Mookerjee, Koylas Chunder Bose, Annada Prasad Banerjee, Kali Prasanna Singh, Anup Chand Mitter, Bhagabati Charan Ghose (Govt. Pleader, Bogra, and the father of the late Mr. N. N. Ghose), Brindaban Bose (of the firm of Alexander Bose & Co.), Sambhu Chunder Mookerjee and Anund Nundun Tagore, the late Drs. Doorga Churn Banerjee, Mohendro Lal Sircar and Chunder Coomar Dey, the late Rai Kanye Lal Dey Bahadur, the late Rai Bunkim Chunder Chatterjee Bahadur, the late Rai Dina Bandhu Mitra Bahadur, the late Babus Romesh Chunder Dutt, Sooresh Chunder Dutt and Debendro Chunder Dutt of Wellington Square, Sree Kissen Gangooly of Bellore and Raj Mohan Bose of Howrah, Rai Raj Kumar Sarvadhikari and Babu Cally Churn Shome.

Grish Chunder was also on the most cordial terms with the Sobhabazar Raj family and the Mookerjee family of Ooterparah generally.

In his speech at the Town Hall meeting in honor of Grish Chunder's memory, Babu Koylas Chunder Bose spoke thus of his charitable disposition:—

"He was a God-fearing man and as such took the greatest delight in promoting works of charity. Though a poor man himself, he shared the little that he earned with those whom he found in need or in distress. It is a fact perhaps not well-known that many a widow and orphan in Bellore was supported by him. It was through his exertions, and by a liberal contribution from his own purse, that the family dwelling house of his friend and coadjutor, the late Hurrish Chunder Mookerjee, was saved from the auctioneer's hammer. He was and will for ever be remembered as the friend of the poor When the last Cyclone had left its devastating effects upon Bellore and the adjacent villages, he would regularly every morning walk miles through the country, distributing relief with his own hands from funds as well his own as those placed at his disposal by the Relief Committee."

Grish Chunder's contributions to divers public charities and testimonials usually ranged from rupees ten to rupees twenty-five each. The latter limit was, however, sometimes exceeded, as when he subscribed rupees fifty towards the founding of a Native Hospital at Howrah—an amount quite out of proportion to his slender income, upon which many hungry mouths were billeted and an appreciable centage of which was swallowed up by the monthly allowances granted by him to some of his female relatives, including his mother to whom he used to pay rupees sixteen a month after his removal to Bellore, while she continued to live with her other two sons. We need hardly say that Grish Chunder's limited pecuniary resources did not permit of his gratifying his charitable feelings to anything like the extent desired by him, in the shape of money gifts. But as Mr. Rockfeller, the great American multimillionaire, told us not long ago, there can be no comparison between the benefactions of the rich and those of the poor. The charity of the rich merely means their parting with a portion of their superfluous wealth, while the charity of the poor means the rendering of personal service, which is of infinitely more value than any mere pecuniary sacrifice. Judged by this standard, Grish Chunder yielded to few of his countrymen in the practice of charity ; for, though he was but a poor man himself, he never failed to raise his voice and wield his pen with all his God-given might, on behalf of the poor and the helpless. Even after he had forsworn, under stringent medical advice, all exercise of the brain, and given up in consequence public speaking and the writing of lead-ing articles for his paper, he continued to write applications and memorials for any body and every body who had a just grievance, whether public or personal, and who sought his help in getting it redressed. In vain did his friends and relations remonstrate with him on the danger he incurred by thus overtaxing his brains. He invariably replied that he had no money to help people with, and he could not therefore find it in his heart to refuse a fellow-creature in distress even the poor service of his pen.

Grish Chunder's strong sympathies with the poor and the help-less naturally led him to advocate the cause of the ryot. But it must not for a moment be supposed that he was antagonistic to the zemin-dars as a class, with many of whom he was on terms of the closest intimacy throughout his life. We quote the following pertinent remarks made on the subject by Babu Koylas Chunder Bose :—

"* * * But his warmest sympathies were with the poor and the helpless ; and the ryot's cause always lay next to his heart. He has been somewhat misunderstood in the matter of his advocacy of the interests of the ryot. It has been somewhere imagined, though without rhyme or reason, that he was inimical to the zemindars as a body and that he considered the Permanent Settlement a great blot in the administration of the country. Nothing could have been a graver mistake than that. He decried the Permanent Settlement as a compact existing only between the Government and the landlord. A really permanent settlement, he said, would be that which would secure to the ryot a perpetuity of interest in the land he occupied. The power of harassing him, of continually enhancing his rent and even of driving him out of home, is the great lever of oppression which the law has placed in the hands of the landlord and which many uneducated, selfish and unscrupulous landlords are ever too ready to use. But the cases of such landlords in these days of the moral and material advancement of the country are rather the excep-tion than the rule, and while Babu Grish Chunder exposed these few in his slashing articles without pity or remorse, he at the same time held up to the admiration of his countrymen the picture of those model zemindars who are the honour of the land, who look upon the ryot as a member of their own family and watch his interests with paternal solicitude." Such a model zemindar was the late Rajah Pertaub Chunder Singh of Paikparah, in noticing whose death Grish Chunder wrote as follows in the *Bengalee* of the 28th July 1866 :—

" He never enhanced ! A world of meaning may be conceived out of that simple word. The loss of such a man is undoubtedly a calamity and the country therefore justly mourns his premature death."

The late Revd. James Long rightly described Grish Chunder's aims, when he said :—

" There is unhappily in Bengal a wide gulf between the educated classes and the masses ; between the zemindar and ryot. Grish Chunder aimed at bridging that gulf, and while the zemindar enjoyed the benefits of the Permanent Settlement, he wished that permanent settlement should be made with the ryot also. His desire in fact was to elevate the ryot without levelling the zemindar."

We feel no little diffidence and hesitation in attempting to describe the attitude of Grish Chunder towards religious creeds and conceptions. We hold that a man's religion is a matter of too subtle and personal a nature to be properly dealt with anywhere else than in his autobiography. The biographer naturally fears to tread upon such holy ground. We cannot, however, begin our brief account of the religion of Grish Chunder better than by describing him, in the words of the late Principal Lobb who intimately knew him, as " one who, though perplexed in faith, continued to remain pure in deeds ; who having given up the *form* still retained the *substance*, not making religious emancipation a stepping-stone to profligacy and vice." Living, as he did, in the full blaze of the culture and enlightenment of the nineteenth century, he deeply imbibed the spirit of free and fearless enquiry which characterized that century from start to finis. The religious dogmas which Grish Chunder had been taught from his earliest infancy to hold in undoubting veneration, loosened their hold upon him, one by one, as his faith in them became gradually unsettled by the influx of Western science and Western thought.

In the early part of the century, Byron had summed up the universal scepticsim of the age in the following couplet, which Grish Chunder was very fond of quoting :—

" Well hast thou said, Athena's wisest son,

All that we know is, nothing can be known."

The same sentiment was differently expressed by another great poet who died towards the close of the century—

" But what am I ?

An infant crying in the night ;

An infant crying for the light ;

And with no language but a cry."

If the sceptical spirit of the century affected even the poets, it profoundly influenced such devout and earnest thinkers as Carlyle and Emerson, who preached—each in his own way—the philosophy of duty with a force and an emphasis which powerfully appealed to all who had lost faith in the old religious dogmas. Grish Chunder, who was a great admirer of both these eminent thinkers, adopted for his motto a saying of Carlyle's—"Work is worship." He was also in the habit of quoting frequently Pope's well-known lines—

" For modes of faith let graceless zealots fight,

His can't be wrong whose life is in the right."

Thus he sought to find that solace in the performance of duty which he had failed to derive from his perplexed faith. The marvellous progress made by Science in recent times has fairly knocked on the head the old anthropomorphic conception of a deity. As an acute Genevese thinker has well put it, " every fresh cosmical conception demands a new religion which corresponds to it." But although Grish Chunder lost his primitive faith in an anthropomorphic divinity, he never ceased to believe in the existence of, and to feel the highest reverence for, a Supreme Power of whose nature and attributes, however, he professed profound ignorance. This feeling of reverence towards the Supreme Ruler of the universe was regarded by him as constituting the essence of all religion, and he did not attach much importance to the form of worship adopted by a particular worshipper. Thus, in an article headed "Action in Bengal" which appeared in the *Bengalee* of the 10th November 1866, he wrote as follows :—

" * * * The Brahmo shuts his eyes and repeats what he, in the smallness of his soul and the confinement of his knowledge, conceives to be the attributes of the Lord. It may be that the real God is endowed with virtues which it is not given to man to fathom. The idolater makes a God of human features, hands, eyes, forehead and feet. The spiritual worshipper prepares a deity of mercy, of justice and the various components of the human soul. We fail to see the difference between the two. Both copy from frail, wicked, sinful man. The

God of Nature may be fundamentally distinct, infinitely superhuman, or organically different from human. The idolater gives his God a multitude of eyes, the spiritual worshipper calls him omniscient. The sense intended to be conveyed by both is the same. Why then these mock heroics against idolatry? We are exhorted to action, to martyrdom, to violence, if not in deed at least in feeling. The hypocrisy and cant of the thing is nauseating, insupportable. In the name of religion we are treated to a puritanical persecution. Is this reform or rebellion? Truth is modest, not blustering. The surest laws of nature work the most silently. Progressive Brahmos will escape much foolishness by thoroughly digesting this great fact. The human mind was never yet won by storm for any good purpose."

Grish Chunder was no "dark idolater of chance," but believed in the existence of a "Power that makes for righteousness"—as Matthew Arnold would put it. Although he never made a parade of his religion, he devoutly prayed to God every morning. A craving for religion is, after all, one of the most powerful instincts of our nature. Even the great founder of the Synthetic Philosophy, after waging a life-long war against religious creeds and dogmas, closed his *Autobiography* with the following significant passage :—"Religious creeds, which in one way or other occupy the sphere that rational interpretation seeks to occupy and fails, and fails the more the more it seeks, I have come to regard with a sympathy based on community of need ; feeling that dissent from them results from inability to accept the solutions offered, joined with the wish that solutions could be found."

Grish Chunder's advocacy of social reform was always tempered by his extreme anxiety lest what was really good in the existing social order should be allowed to perish with what really deserved condemnation, in a headlong and indiscriminating reforming fury. He adhered to this judicious and cautious course even at the risk of being sometimes charged with inconsistency or half-heartedness.

The late Nawab Abdool Luteef Khan Bahadur, in the course of his speech at the Grish memorial meeting, paid the following tribute to the catholicity of Grish Chunder's sympathies :—

"* * * * Moreover his tendencies were truly catholic, and altogether devoid of the petty prejudices of caste or section, and there never was a time when a good thing was on foot for the benefit of any particular class or community, that it did not elicit a hearty word of encouragement from the noble-minded, generous Grish. I am able personally to testify, on behalf of the Mahomedan community, to the many and frequent occasions on which their welfare and advancement have received support and assistance from his able and fertile pen."

CHAPTER XIV.

———: o :———

PERSONAL APPEARANCE AND HABITS—STYLE OF WRITING— MEMORIAL MEETINGS—ULTIMATE FATE OF THE BENGALEE.

Before we proceed to offer a few general remarks on the style and spirit of Grish Chunder's writings and speeches, we may as well describe briefly his personal appearance and habits. Grish Chunder's physique more resembled that of an Afghan than that of a puny inhabitant of the plains of Lower Bengal. He was fully six feet in height and was proportionately stout. His broad chest and brawny limbs betokened great bodily strength and muscular energy. He was a splendid walker and could at one time cover ten miles in about a couple of hours' time with perfect ease. He was of a dark olive complexion and possessed a high intellectual forehead, a Grecian nose and a pair of large, lustrous eyes. The crown of his well-formed head was sparsely covered with hair, thus betraying how heavily he taxed his brains. There was a good-humoured look about his handsome features which inspired confidence even in little children, of whom, indeed, he was exceedingly fond. This was happily described by the late Principal Lobb in the words of Tennyson :—

> "And manhood fused with female grace
> In such a sort, the child would twine
> A trustful hand unasked in thine,
> And find his comfort in thy face."

His office dress consisted of a pair of loose *pyjamahs* and a flowing *chapkan*, with a sheet of linen folded crosswise over his breast. This simple and inexpensive dress, to which of course should be added a shirt and a pair of socks, was generally made of cotton ; it set his fine physique to great advantage.

Grish Chunder was a perfect teetotaller, a good sleeper, a good eater and an early riser. His self-reliant habits made him almost independent of his servants. Even in the depth of winter he bathed in a cold, biting tank, nor did he ever wear a shawl; a quilted silk *chuddur* did duty for a shawl. He never used a punkah at home even at the height of summer, but always fanned himself with a palm-leaf fan.

Franklin says in his *Autobiography*:—"I was brought up in such a perfect inattention to those matters as to be quite indifferent what kind of food was set before me, and so unobservant of it that to this day if I am asked I can scarce tell a few hours after dinner what I dined upon." Dr. Johnson, on the other hand, attached so much importance to a good dinner that a man who was indifferent about it was, in his opinion, not fit to be entrusted with any serious business. Although Grish Chunder was, like Johnson, a lover of good cheer, he resembled Franklin in this respect that his equanimity was never ruffled by a dish being over-done or under done, but he would partake of it with the same apparent relish as if it had been properly done.

Grish Chunder never indulged in any expensive tastes or fancies. His library even was not well-furnished. It reminded one of De Quincey's description of Wordsworth's library.—"The two or three hundred volumes of Wordsworth occupied a little homely, painted bookcase. * * *. They were ill-bound or not bound at all— in boards, sometimes in tatters; many were imperfect as to the number of volumes, mutilated as to the number of pages. * * * " It must, however, be borne in mind that Grish Chunder did not stand much in need of a library of his own, as he could get all the books he wanted from the late "Calcutta Public Library," of which he became a subscriber within a few years of its location, in 1844, in the building now occupied by the Imperial Library.

But there was one luxury which Grish Chunder always delighted to indulge in. When he was only twenty-two years old, he bought a small garden at Ooltadanga in January 1852, and four years later he bought another at Bellore—subsequently making considerable additions to both, as opportunity offered. Nothing gave him greater pleasure than to have an opportunity of—

"Annihilating all that's made
To a green thought in a green shade."

In his enthusiasm for gardening, he bought and studied a number of standard English works on the subject, and only a year or two before his death, he was engaged in bringing out a small compilation entitled "Directions for the rearing of Europe Vegetables." Some twenty-four pages of the brochure had been printed when ill health compelled him to hold it in abeyance.

But it was neither his kitchen-garden nor his orchard that had half so great an attraction for him as his flower-garden. He had such a genuine love for the latter, that he felt reluctant to despoil it of even a single floral charm. His feeling was akin to what has been so beautifully described by one of his great English contemporaries—

> "I never pluck the rose; the violet's head
> Hath shaken with my breath upon its bank
> And not reproach'd me; the ever-sacred cup
> Of the pure lily hath between my hands
> Felt safe, unsoil'd, nor lost one grain of gold."

Turn we now to consider Grish Chunder's style of writing. The remarks made on the subject by the late Babu Koylas Chunder Bose in his speech at the Grish memorial meeting are so apposite, that we gladly avail ourselves of them :—

"His style had a grace, an elegance and a force by which you could at once distinguish it from that of any of his countrymen. Run your eyes over the columns of the *Hindoo Patriot*, the *Recorder* and the *Bengalee*, and the articles written by Grish Chunder would manifest themselves to you as if they were stamped with his own name. They are singularly idiomatic and as such have not yet been rivalled by the writings of any of his countrymen. But his writings were valued chiefly because they were original. He was an original thinker and his thoughts were always brilliant and happy"

We can vouch for the correctness of the above remarks, as we have put the matter to a practical test. We have lately had occasion to wade through a number of bulky old newspaper files and we have not experienced the slightest difficulty in spotting the articles written by Grish Chunder, as they all bear on their face the hall mark of his genius—his rare power of giving a new turn to the commonest of subjects and of expressing the happiest of thoughts in the happiest of words, often coined for the nonce from the inexhaustible mint of his fervid imagination, his brilliant coruscations of wit and humour, his withering sarcasm, his slashing criticism, and the inimitable graces and idiomatic raciness of his nervous diction. One thing has struck us most forcibly. We have found the above characteristics to exist in almost the same perfection in the earliest writings of Grish Chunder on which we have been able to lay our hands, as in his later writings.

"Perhaps the most distinctive characteristic of his writings," says Babu Sambhu Chunder Mookerjee in his article headed "A Great Indian but a Geographical Mistake" from which we have already quoted more than once, "is *dash*, and he made amends for his literary and speculative profusion in this quality by the perfect absence of it in his character and life. There is in his sentences the very rush of the mountain torrent, the hue of the setting sun, and the breath of the sea breeze. One is sure to identify the writer with a lover of sport by flood and field, a young Nimrod, a Walton, a Waterton, a Mansfield Parkyns, above all, a Christopher North, *au fait* at angling, wrestling, boxing, lecturing, abusing, writing prose that passes into poetry, and poetry that passes into cloud and mist, so rich in fancy, so jubliant, so full of animal spirits, so full of broad farce—relieved by occasional touches of tenderness—his writings; but a closer scrutiny will discover the cool Bengali cynic, which he in some measure always was, and oftener assumed, and, above all, the home-loving and home-ridden cockney. For this last he was. He had never travelled, nay, hardly been out of Calcutta, out of home. He was domestic to a fault. Hence his limited knowledge of his country, limited knowledge of the world and things in general, hence his ideas were of books bookish, his sympathies, wide as in all sincerity he professed them to be, untrustworthy and unreal."

It would be ungracious on our part not to acknowledge the high compliment paid to Grish Chunder's prose poetry by Babu Sambhu Chunder; but we are surprised to find that he should have looked for the counterpart of such poetry in Grish Chunder's humdrum daily life. Were not the finest comedies in the French language, or indeed in any language, written by Molière, who was remarkable for his morose disposition in private life? Was not the ballad of *John Gilpin*, the most humorous ballad in the English language, composed by Cowper to while away a fit of despondency? Was not the inimitably humorous character of *Captain Dugald Dalgetty* conceived by Scott whilst he was under the influence of a racking pain? And were not the finest productions of Goldsmith's muse written in a lonely garret? If Grish Chunder was only a home-ridden cockney, we should admire all the more "the power of thought—the magic of the mind" which enabled him to impart to his prose idylls the freedom and the purity of the open air. We must enter our emphatic protest against the remark that Grish Chunder's ideas were of books bookish and that his sympathies were untrustworthy and unreal. We have already had occasion to remark that Grish Chunder was by no means a mere bookworm. It is true that he never sought to gather knowledge by tramping about the country. But he always mixed freely and largely with people of all sorts and conditions in life, and he was thus enabled to obtain a true and minute insight into the state of the country and thus rightly accord his sympathies.

Babu Sambhu Chunder also charges Grish Chunder with want of enterprise and ambition. "He had no enterprise, no personal boldness, no ambition. No salutary discontent with his lot dogged him in his quiet even path or for a moment clouded his unvarying cheerfulness, no high tastes cherished in secret made him miserable, no worthy aspirations urged him day and night to deeds of high emprise."

All this makes fine reading, but does not, after all, mean much. The fact that Grish Chunder rose in the course of sixteen years to the highest position attainable by an uncovenanted officer in the large public office where his lot had been cast, sufficiently shews that he had spared no reasonable efforts to better his position. If it was not given to him to "pluck bright honour from the pale-faced moon," or to partake of any of the loaves and fishes reserved for the covenanted or commissioned grades of the service, or if, in consequence of his having given heavy hostages to fortune in the shape of a large family entirely dependent on him for their daily bread, he did not venture to throw up his appointment and try fresh woods and pastures new, he could not well be charged with want of ambition. He realized too late the mistake he had made in entering Government service as a clerk, and vowed that no son of his should ever repeat the error. As for himself, he cheerfully submitted to the inevitable and did with all his might whatsoever his hand might find to do.

22

"...........To know
That which before us lies in daily life
Is the prime wisdom".

David Hume has said somewhere that it is a far happier thing
for a man to be born with a disposition always to look at the bright
side of things than to be born to a fortune of ten thousand a year.
Grish Chunder was pre-eminently blest with such a disposition.

It is idle to speculate with Babu Sambhu Chunder what splendid
success might have been achieved by Grish Chunder as a great
party-leader, had he been born in England, where his ready tongue
and ready pen would have enabled him to thunder alike in the senate
and through the press.   It is vain also to reflect with Sir Henry
Cotton that " had he lived in India in any other time than the present,
he would undoubtedly have attained the very highest rank."   Even
in the age and in the country in which he was born, he might have,
we believe, made a much greater name for himself than he actually
did.   Judging from the solitary specimens that he has left us of his
power to give an exquisitely humorous account of actual travel, as
displayed in "My first Railway to Rajmehal," of his power to
narrate a serio-comic story, as indicated in "The Borrowed Shawl,"
and of his power to give us an inimitably humorous character-sketch
like "The Omedwar," or a brilliant photograph of social life like
that presented in his short paper on " Female Occupations in Bengal,"
or a still more brilliant biographical sketch, as exemplified in his " Life
of Ram Doolal Dey the Bengalee Millionaire," there can be little
doubt that he was eminently fitted to excel in each of these different
walks of pure literature, and that had he given his genius fuller play
in this direction, he might have permanently enriched Anglo-Indian
literature with many valuable contributions from his genial pen ; for
Grish was not like Hurrish and Kristo Das a mere journalist, but was
a literary artist of no ordinary skill and power.

We have already had occasion to speak of Grish Chunder's marvellous facility in drafting official correspondence. The ease with which
he wrote his leading articles was no less remarkable ; we have often seen
him finish writing a two-column editorial in a couple of hours' time, in
a room crowded with miscellaneous company in whose conversation he
took part every now and then. His power of concentrating his attention

was, indeed, wonderful—allowing even for his slightly defective hearing, the result of an accidental injury caused to one of his ears in early youth. Before putting his pen to paper, he invariably indulged in a few minutes' brown study. But having once settled in his mind how to deal with the subject on which he proposed writing, he found no difficulty in proceeding with it. The words seemed to flow from his pen almost without any effort. He was, however, very fastidious in the composition of lectures or discourses intended to be read before a learned society. Carefully-written sentences and passages were mercilessly scored out and re-written to satisfy his squeamish taste. On our once remarking to him that by so doing he considerably added to the labour involved in the execution of his self-imposed task, he quoted the example of such elegant writers as Lord Macaulay and Oliver Goldsmith and said that an elegant style could only be attained in this way.

Grish Chunder qualified himself for public speaking by an assiduous study of the masterpieces of British eloquence. He never made a set speech in his life, but always spoke impromptu and on the spur of the moment. He could therefore give no help to the reporter, and in those days of imperfect reporting very few reporters could do without such help. The fluency with which Grish Chunder spoke also made it extremely difficult for the reporter to follow him. The few reports that we possess of his speeches give therefore no adequate idea of his oratorical powers—not to speak of his commanding figure, his clear, ringing voice, his graceful action and faultless delivery.

When Grish Chunder completed his scholastic career, it was the aim of every well-educated young Indian who aspired to literary distinction, to acquire a thorough mastery over the English language, so as to be able to carry on all literary work in that language, to the utter neglect of his own vernacular which could then hardly boast of a good literature. The idea of creating a new vernacular literature by bringing a sound Western culture to bear upon it, was of later growth. Grish Chunder used to lament that his ignorance of Sanskrit prevented him from following the glorious example of his intimate friends Dina Bandhu and Bankim, whose contributions to Bengali literature were watched by him with the keenest interest and greeted with the warmest applause. His regret was well-founded; for, with his fervid imagination, his brilliant wit, his exquisitely delicate humour, and his rare descriptive power, he would, doubtless, have been able to contribute to the literature of Bengal something which posterity would not have willingly let die.

Elsewhere will be found full reports of the proceedings of the memorial meetings held in honour of Grish Chunder at the Town Hall of Calcutta and the Canning Institute, Howrah, on the 16th and 29th November 1869, respectively.

At the Town Hall meeting, which was largely and respectably attended and presided over by the late Raja Kali Krishna Bahadur, the late Maharaja Sir Narendra Krishna Bahadur moved the first resolution :—

"That this meeting desires to record its deep sorrow and regret at the death, in the very prime of his life, of Babu Grish Chunder Ghose, who, by his highly independent, manly and virtuous character, by his kind, affable and guileless disposition towards all classes of people with whom he happened to come in contact, by his patriotic exertions for the benefit of his country, and by his natural gifts and ability which were displayed to the highest advantage in all his writings and speeches, won the love and admiration of the community to which he belonged."

The late Babu Koylas Chunder Bose, who was the leading speaker of the evening, seconded the resolution and the late Principal S. Lobb supported it.

The late Babu Peary Chand Mittra then read the following resolution which had been passed by the Council of the Bengal Social Science Association :—

" That this Council has heard with regret of the decease of one of its members, Babu Grish Chunder Ghose, and desires to place upon record its high sense of his zeal and earnestness in the cause of social progress in this country "

The late Nawab Abdool Luteef Khan Bahadur moved the second resolution :—

" That by way of memorial of the lamented deceased, a scholarship in his name be placed at the disposal of the Director of Public Instruction for the benefit of any Anglo or Anglo Vernacular school at which the Memorial Fund Committee may recommend its grant, and that public subscriptions be invited in furtherance of this object."

The late Babu Gopaul Chunder Dutt seconded the resolution and the late Mr. James Wilson supported it.

The third resolution, which related to the formation of a Memorial Fund Committee, was proposed by the late Babu Chunder Nath Bose and seconded by the late Babu Issur Chunder Nundy.

At the Town Hall meeting a letter was also read from the Secretary to the Ooterparah *Hitakari Sabha*, communicating two resolutions passed at a meeting of the *Sabha* held on the 14th November 1869, recording its deepest regret for the untimely death of its late Vice-President and its high sense of the most lively interest always evinced by him in the welfare of the Society, and expressing its willingness to co-operate with the General Committee for the purpose of raising funds in aid of any kind of memorial which the General Committee might agree upon. It may here be mentioned that the Memorial Committee ultimately decided to make over to the Oriental Seminary the whole of the sum collected, with a request that the interest on the money be spent for the purposes of a scholarship to be awarded every year to the best student in the second class. A scholarship of rupees five per mensem, tenable for a year, is accordingly awarded every year to the best student in the second class of the Seminary.

At a meeting of the Bethune Society held on the 25th November 1869, the late Rev. K. M. Banerjee, who occupied the chair, referred to the death of Grish Chunder in the following terms in his speech :—

" The third was a very melancholy subject. They had lost by death their very able Secretary to the Section on Literature and Philosophy, the late Babu Grish Chunder Ghose. In him the Society had lost a very valuable member, who had rendered to it important services by his lectures and speeches, and who had always evinced a warm interest in its welfare.   His death was, no doubt, universally regretted, as the public meeting held at the Town Hall did amply testify.   He was a true patriot, because he was always the friend of the poor, the friend of the ryot.   He fought for their cause with great ability and independence and never succumbed to any kind of influence which might have been brought to bear upon him to deter him from his great object.   Week after week, he brought forward their case before the public in some shape or other, in that ably conducted paper—*The Bengalee.*   He would even reprove his friends when he found them lukewarm in their sympathy with the poor.   He (the Chairman) would therefore desire to record the deep regret of the Society at the death of one of their most useful members, who was, at the same time, in his relations with the public, an honest worker in the cause of the amelioration of the poor.''

At the Canning Institute meeting the following resolution was moved by the late Mr. S. H. Robinson, seconded by the late Dr. R. N. Burgess, and supported by the late Revd. Mr. James Long, who was the leading speaker of the evening :—

" That this meeting desires to record its deep sense of the loss sustained by the death of their late Vice-President Babu Grish Chunder Ghose, and their grateful remembrance of the many valuable services he has rendered to the Society.''

It was further resolved to move the Howrah Municipality in view to the Bellore Road being made to bear the name of Grish Chunder in honour of his memory—a request which was readily complied with by the Municipality.   The proposition was carried by acclamation.

After the death of Grish Chunder, the late Babu Becha Ram Chatterjee managed to hold up the *Bengalee* for some eight or nine years, with the material and gratuitous help of a number of well-known scholars, among whom may be named the late Babus Chunder Nath Bose, Raj Krishna Mookerjee, Tara Prasad Chatterjee, Koylas Chunder Bose and Sree Nath Ghose.   Finding himself unable, however, to cope with the increasing difficulty of maintaining the paper, Babu Becha Ram Chatterjee sold at last to Babu Surendra Nath Banerjee the good-will and the Press of the *Bengalee*. The transaction is thus described in the *Early History and Growth of Calcutta* by Raja Binay Krishna Deb :—" In or about 1878, Babu Surendra Nath Banerjee purchased the good-will and every thing in connection with the *Bengalee*. There arose some dispute in connection with the above transaction, but at the happy intervention of the late Maharaj-Kumar Neel Krishna Bahadur, the elder brother of the writer, the matter came to a happy settlement."

The mantle of Grish Chunder could not have fallen upon worthier shoulders than those of the illustrious patriot whose name is familiar as a household word throughout the length and breadth of this vast peninsula and who has not only fully maintained all the best traditions of the paper, but has also given it a daily currency since the 1st February 1900. May he long be spared to accomplish his glorious mission !

GRISH'S LETTERS.

.

Calcutta, 7th January 1855.

My dearest brother,

I hasten to allay your anxiety concerning mother. She is quite well now. Shezdada, sick of having nothing to communicate to you in the melancholy way, must have added some varnish to his version of mother's illness. Perhaps too a latent wish to enjoy a magnificent *shrad* influenced his pen, and the vision of such a festivity whetted his wit. Mother was really ill, but not to the extent that would have justified the hope of enjoying a *shrad*. She had fever in the first instance and copious stools followed. Satcorry was asked to come, but he came a day after the fair, as his way is. So we called in a Bengalee Kubiraj who had graduated also in the Bengalee class of the Medical College, and in two or three days' time mother was all right. I am delighted to hear that we have such a close prospect of seeing you ; but I fear you are destined for Midnapore, in which case we can't see you. I hope however that you will be thus gradually approaching us. There is a vacancy at Midnapore. Radhanauth Gangooly, who was there, has been transferred to Beerbhoom. My father-in-law says that the Board of Revenue has promised to let the Collector of the former station have an intelligent Deputy Collector if he really stands in need of the services of such a person.

Before starting for your new destination let us know, pray, what that is, that we may not be on the thorns of suspense longer than can be helped. Tell uncle and aunt that Chonoo and Promoda have come to our place since yesterday. They are quite well. I am really very sorry for your peas and cabbages. What expense have you incurred on their account ? I would advise your hypothecating the dear vegetables to our good friend Bissonauth Baboo, to whom my complements of the season, pray. We are all very well and prosperous here and the children, barring a few instances of cough and cold, are doing capitally. Write to me about my dear Bhoomoney. Give her my New Year kiss and blessing. Have you given her the dolls I sent per Mr. Borh ? I dare say they are curiosities in your quarter—at least that one with the spring. Hope you have not spoilt it by turning the key on the wrong side.

I promised to give you a detailed version of the Wars of the Roses in our family. Here it is, though I am sorry I lack the ability of either Hume or Mackintosh to give zest to my descriptions.

•   •

23

II.

My dearest brother,

I have just received your note of the 1st current, and believe me it has removed a load of anxiety from our minds. The papers reported that the Sonthals were mustering in great force at Midnapore, and you can easily imagine our distress at the bare idea of such a gathering when some of our dearest friends upon earth were travelling in that vicinity with no, or only an insignificant, escort. Thank heaven you are all safe and sound and ere this reaches you, you will probably have been installed in snug quarters at Balasore. How did you relish the journey ? I dare say it must have taxed your powers of sufferance to no little extent. Patter! patter! The heavens looked as if they were in no hurry to conclude their cataract scene and begin giving us a bit of genuine sunshine. I dare say the rains gave you an endless deal of trouble. But never mind, after pain comes pleasure. We have nice weather here today and before the same is the case with you there at Balasore. How is Bhoobun deary? Hope the pains of the journey have not affected her constitution, poor little thing ! You will be glad to learn that my brother's wife has been safely delivered of a fine, handsome, healthy boy. The child is as fair almost as its mother, with very regular features. Pray to God that he may live ! Give father, uncle and aunt my *pronam.* Tell them that all is going on right here since their departure. The Jhoolun Festival is fast approaching and we are preparing for the jubilee. But your absence and that of the rest of the family has necessarily thrown a damper on our pleasures. We hope however, when the hour arrives, to muster sufficient spirits to go through the festivities *secundum artem.* Mother is very glad to hear of your safe arrival at Midnapore. There was a report in Town which got also into one of the daily papers, that Jogesh Ghose, the Deputy Magistrate, with his wife and children, had been cut down by the Sonthals. Mother naturally was extremely uneasy on your account, but your flying note has dispelled all fears on that head. Did you hear nothing of the Sonthals at Midnapore ? Mother is quite pleased with the manner in which you have noticed her *goor-tantool* supply. She desires me to convey to you her regret that she could not give you a larger quantity. She hopes, however, as soon as any bearers from here think of returning to their country, to remit you a further stock of the above very exquisite edible. Write to us as often and as much as you can. Tell father that I have been as yet unable to dispose of his garrie and horses. I sent the former with a good horse to Mendes' auction of Friday last, but nobody would bid higher for the turnout than Rs. 100 (one hundred rupees). I have therefore thought proper to make the concern over to Soorjee Bysack of our office, who will pay me a sum of Rs. 120 for it in three monthly instalments. I shall take a proper written acknowledgment from him as soon as he is able to get ready a stable and take the garrie from my hands. A Mahomedan chap came to me the other day and offered as much as Rs. 47 for the good horse, but though I consented to the bargain and the fellow promised to bring me the money, I have not seen or heard anything of him for the last three days. I have also received an offer of Rs. 10 for the white horse, but I have stuck out for Rs. 15.

III.

My dearest brother,

You are a shocking bad economist, for you are fast losing sight of the very judicious maxim, "Take care of your pence and the pounds will take care of themselves." I have calculated that you have needlessly helped the Post Office to a revenue of four annas when the thing conld have been settled for six pice. Why don't you write on mail paper instead of on that superb stiff paper whose composition comes within an ace of parchment? Have you got no store of the former? if so, tell me, I shall provide you with some. I am really delighted to hear that your superior (I can't spell his name, excuse me) is such an excellent man as you describe him to be. I was sure you would pull well with him—for who ever failed to like you? Stick to him and if he be a sharp young man he will no doubt get a berth in the Presidency and as a matter of course he will move heaven and earth to get you along with him. So the Sonthals are a mere stalking horse in the imaginations of old women and young cravens. I thought so. The Dhangurs are too contemptible a race to give much cause for alarm or anxiety to British subjects. I envy you your travelling reminiscences and wayside pictures. The Neil Ghiries must have put you into raptures. Oh! how I should like to have such a sight! Bye and bye the Collector will probably invite you to go about on a shooting excursion with him on that fine range. Take care, don't show your ignorance in the use of firearms, for according to English notions every gentleman is invariably a good rider and some-thing more.　　　*　　　　*　　　　*

I am grieved to hear that Bhoobun has not taken the separation from us all, in good part. Give the dear creature as much company as you can, and then she will get over old associations in contracting new ones. Mother gives you her blessing and desires me to ask what sort of fare you have down there. She knows that you cannot eat bad things, and she is therefore anxious to know whether the rice and fish and milk and ghee and sweetmeats that are available at Balasore do come up to the standard of Calcutta. Poor Dada's child died on the 9th day after birth. There is really a curse upon our house with regard to male children. Benoo and Bidhoo and Chundie and Obin are all well.　　　*　　　　*　　　　*

IV.

My dearest brother,

The Post Office has been again interposing its dilatory influence between your letter and myself. Yours of the 8th instant reached me only yesterday. What does Mr. Riddle deserve for his serious delay? Oughtn't he to be impeached for high crimes and misdemeanours in having put Grish Chunder Ghose of Simlah out of his brother's letter for three days beyond time? Indeed the Post Office, like Doctorjee, is callous in respect to the feelings of the parties whose patronage supports it. It makes no consideration for the anxieties of separated friends. It acts on the supposition that the world is as matter-of-fact as its runners and dawk bearers, who are as much interested about the things they carry as either the railway or the electric telegraph. Indeed when we were together we could not, for the life of us, understand why people should be everlastingly complaining about postal matters. Our separation has exposed the magnitude of the evils against which people so justly complained and still complain. But let that pass. No use complaining against what cannot be helped. You carp at my domestic economy. Why, my dear brother, I can afford to sport an additional two pice on an envelope. The enclosure then is so snug and the exterior looks so neat and tidy that you must excuse my sacrificing a little to my taste and notions of decency. An extra half anna is nothing to me, residing in the bosom of my family with my expenses all in order. But it must necessarily be ruinous (considering the principle) to your slender finances. Do you therefore continue to wear gauze, and broadcloth shall be my covering. Such a great difference exists between metropolitan and mofussil ways of living. Issur Chunder Mitter has been posted to Dinagepore, a most abominable place. So you must thank your stars that you have steered clear of such nasty holes. Balasore, they say, is much superior to Calcutta in point of climate and I don't wonder therefore that your health keeps so well. I am exceedingly glad to hear that my Bhoomonie is learning English. Who is the teacher, pray? I fancy it's yourself. Don't get tired of the task but keep on, and I dare say when Bhoobun returns to us in September 1856 we shall have the satisfaction of greeting her in our adopted language.

I really have not heard the particulars of the quarrel between Koylas Dutt and Heysham. But the latter, you know, is a very unruly fellow not quite amenable to superior authority. Hence Koylas' hatred for him. Their wars are however now restrained by an armistice pending Mr. Bidwell's return from the Sonthal expedition. What does Mr. Heysham mean by serving people with notices signed by himself, calling upon people to deposit their ground rents at the Treasury of the Calcutta Collectorate within a stated time and signifying to them the consequences of their refusal to meet his call? I hear he has succeeded in frightening all Calcutta and even we have hastened to make the necessary payment at the earnest request of Trilochun Mittre. Now I question Mr. Heysham's authority for frightening Her Majesty's lieges this way, and were it not that the Calcutta Collectorate is at Calcutta and not at Alipore, many would have raised the question and contested the Collector's right to impose a fresh tax upon landholders in the shape of carriage hire and other items to the advantage of the Government purse. I am exceedingly obliged to your Bissonauth Baboo for his kind opinion of myself. I indeed long for the day on which I shall come in contact with him *vis à vis*. I dare say I shall like him vastly. Really, my dear brother, there is nothing on earth equal to a high-principled intelligent, young man who can be *sincere* in *every* respect and with whom your mind can hold converse in all matters that come under the cognizance of human beings. I hope this friend of yours answers to the description I have given above. Is he a married man and are his children with him? Tell me, my dear Nadada, what are the amusements of Balasore? Is it *cutcherry* from day to day and *doll bhat* from morn to even, or is your mofussil existence chequered by brighter passages? Have you any parties or picnics, excursions into the hills, &c. &c? What are the current tomashas, Jattras or dances, concerts or theatres? Bye the bye, have you received a letter lately from Bhuggobutty Churn

Ghose of Bograh ? He wrote to me that he will bore you with one. He is coming down to Bailoor during the holidays. Were you here we could have made most agreeable parties at his place and once more regaled ourselves with the hearty hospitality of our friend Sree Kissen Gangooly and the Bailoorites. So kid soup is the culminating delicacy in your little parties ? I am right glad to hear that it is so, for under that circumstance you can give as many dinners as there are days in the week without becoming victimized to any great pecuniary extent, and as you live a mile from the city there is but little chance of many people attending at your parties. Indeed you should be very particular in the choice of your guests. Your position demands, and I believe your own notions of propriety will suggest to you, that you should keep yourself as free from familiar social intercourse with the greater portion of your acquaintances at Balasore as possible. What sort of a place is this residence of yours ? From its isolated position I suspect it is a garden-house and just such a one (surrounded by groves and lofty trees) as father likes to have. Tell the dear old gentleman that I have been compelled to plaster anew, at an expense of some six or seven rupees, my garden *atchalla*. Every portion of the old plastering had fallen off, exposing hideous gaps in the wall. This time I believe it is all right, as the mistry who did the job was completely up to such things, not a charlatan in his profession like the last rascal. There are small cracks visible now as the wall is getting dry, but they are not serious ones and may be remedied by an application of cow-dung, a process which the *mallee*, under my direction, is now going through. In another ten days I hope to have the room in possessable order and duly whitewashed. Kindly ask father if I may have some of the old barren trees just at the entrance of the garden cut down to make room for the mango, leechee and other valuable grafts which the mallee has procured under my orders from trees of established repute. I like jungle scenery myself, but think it preferable to have new fruit-bearing trees to a batch of superannuated old stunted trunks. The jungle in front of the *atchalla* I shall keep inviolable, for that will keep me from the public gaze—but the seven or eight old mango and jack trees that greet your sight just as you enter the garden, I intend demo- lishing to make room for younger blood. The rascal of a mistry has been putting off rendering up my garrie from day to day. He complains of the want of sunshine which he says prevents him from applying varnish, every thing else being complete. I have given the fellow another three days' time, by the end of which I have signified to him my resolution to have the garrie in whatever state it may then be. Mr. Lavalette has written to me to say that owing to certain losses which he has lately incurred by the failure of an auction at which he had put several articles for sale, he was compelled to defer payment of the monies due from him until November next. I have again written to him through Hurro Chunder Mittre, who resides in that locality, asking him to pay at least a portion of the money immediately. I have not yet received a reply. But I will continue dunning him until all the money is safe in my cash box. Your organ has not yet, I believe, been sold. I have asked Mr. Lavalette to write to me full particulars regarding its destiny—he not having returned any answers to my previous queries on that head. Father's things are all right. I open his almirah once every two days. I could not do so however for some five or six days after the Jhoolun festival, owing to some of Dada's lanterns and other articles having been heaped up in the room whilst Dada's room was undergoing repair. Would you believe it? the first day I opened the almirah after the room had been cleared, I discovered the rascally white ants at work. They however could not do any material damage, as the discovery was very timely. I thought of procuring the poison which has been administered to the record shelves of our office to fortify them against the inroads of the white sappers and miners, but many advised me not to do so, lest the poison should affect the articles in the cabinet. I have therefore administered only a sufficient dose of turpentine to the shelves and air them regularly.   *   *   *

We are all right here and the children, without exception, are singularly healthy. Poor Bama is however suffering a great deal from her eye. Satcorry operated upon it whilst the cataract was in an unripe state, and the upshot has been that the organ is swollen prodigiously, bringing on excruciating pain, headache and fever. Satcorry appears to be frightened at the course things have taken. But he puts the best face on it and is now treating with the advice and under the directions of Dr. Webb. Ma desires me to convey to you her blessing. She cannot believe that father will again take the trouble to accompany her to Poorie after he had once satisfied his curiosity concerning that far-famed place. I do not see any reason why he should go on to Juggurnauth at such an out-of-the-way season. I think the wisest plan for him would be to come down to Calcutta in time for the holidays, and after the Juggodhatri Poojah accompany mother to yours and thence to Poorie. Ask him with my *pronam,* to take the latter course, which is recommended by all our friends here. Kurreembux has not certainly been a loser by the bargain about the white horse—he has, according to his own confession, profited by the transaction to the extent of one rupee. I have therefore forborne bestowing upon him the gratuity ordered by you. If, as you say, you have entertained three Mohurirs at Rs. 10 each and a Sheristadar at Rs. 20, thus consuming the entire Rs. 50, granted you for Establishment, how then have you dealt by Chand Sing and Gangaram Sing, and that other Sing whom my father-in-law thrust upon you? You certainly don't pay them from your own pocket, do you? Beware of such extravagance. So Mr. Brown is really anxious to be transferred to Balasore—or is it merely a feint, to escape from the odium of being driven from an independent charge to a subordinate place owing to incapacity, that he has been using? For my part, I should be glad to see you stationed at Bhodruck which is a much healthier place than Balasore, they say, and where you can reign supreme. "Better to reign in hell than serve in heaven." What do you mean by constantly writing that you send out Bhoobun into the fields every evening? You really don't let the poor girl soak her feet in the filthy water with which the fields at this season of the year must necessarily be covered? or have the rains left you?

V.

Calcutta, 1st October 1855—6 P.M.

My dearest brother,

          I have been rather late in taking up your letter of the 23rd ultimo for reply. I was in expectation of conveying to you the news of father's safe arrival. But up to this moment he has not arrived yet. I fancy the rains have detained him. Brother has received your note of the 27th ultimo and informed me of its contents. You want Macpherson's Procedure, don't you ? I shall of course look out for a copy and send it over per Kanny Sing, when he leaves this. Dada's Blackstone is at your service.

2nd October 1855—6 P.M.

Father arrived here this morning, He was detained a whole night at Ooloobaria owing to boisterous weather. Hence the delay in coming to Calcutta. He wrote to you, he says, from Midnapore and sent you also some ginger and dall. Have you received his note and the consignments ? We have nice accounts indeed of the manner in which you contrive to keep body and soul together in that dirty corner of yours. You have hitherto been amusing us wtth *couleur de rose* representations of your comforts. Father says that you keep lent all the week round, the fish of your place heing worse than dog's meat. Fah ! throw up your magistracy, brother, and come down to Calcutta for rare pillaos and kallias, hilsa fish and mango fish—*khursela, rooee* and *parsia*. Oh you unfortunate man, oh ! you monk of Balasore, there you have no good fare, but only a bubble to subsist upon—the bubble reputation. Yet I dare say God will reward you in the end and compensate you for these harassing privations by making a great man of you. This hope should sustain you through *kristomoog* dall and vegetable curry, and reconcile you to your destiny. I, for my part, would have revolted against the bill of fare and gone to any expense to keep myself from the gastronomic condition of a Hindoo widow I We had a first-rate feast at Dada's expense at Goluck Bysack's (of our office) garden. The affair cost brother some fifteen rupees—an expense which has played the devil with his equanimity and led to his vowing never again to have anything to do with such frolic. There have been rare doings in Calcutta since I last wrote to you. The Baliaghatta bridge, over which we have passed many a time, came down with a tremendous crash, sending to their long home and in a frightfully mutilated condition some twenty to twenty-five unfortunate people and hideously wounding a great many others. The bridge was being macadamised. A heavy roller with a dozen yoke of oxen was the immediate cause of the break down. The suspension chains suapped at both ends, and down came bridge, roller, oxen, ghatries, men, women and children at one swoop, confusion worse confounded. This stupendous tragedy I have to relieve by the narration of a comic event that occurred here a few days back.   •   *   *

Father will leave this after the Juggodhatrie Poojah, in company with mother, who intends, after her trip to Juggurnauth, to stay with you until September next when she will accompany you to Calcutta. How is Bhoomany doing ? Has she completely got rid of her cold ? You ask for a graphic account of the children. I am really unable to put in the necessary degree of salt that will please your taste. Will it be sufficient for you to know that Beeny is as rough and manly as ever, Mokhoo as fair and half-worded, Chun as thin and precocious, Money as black, Beedy as sickly, Satcorry as stout and wrong-headed ? Only my Oby has changed since you last saw him. He has learned to stand, articulate a few broken words, and masticate any hard substance. Peroo is the same thin, demure, quiet, engaging lad that you left him, Brojo as shameless and mischievous as a monkey, Bhooto fast trying to imitate his immediate superior. There now, will that answer your expectation—or do you seek more full and detailed information concerning the rising Ghoses ?   Has father's absence any way inconvenienced you ?   The bearers who brought the old gentleman home return tomorrow with supplies for your starving garrison.   Dada has written to you separately per the bearers in question.   Thank you for your sermon on the poor fund.   By the blessing of God I have many twopice to spend upon the poor without spoiling the neatness of my despatches by putting them in a wrapper of note paper.   You have really the [wit] to construct a mountain out of a molehill

      *   *   *   *

VI.

Calcutta, 16th October 1855.

My dearest brother,

      What, in the name of all the saints in the calendar, keeps you from replying to our letters ?   The whole family is uneasy on your account.   It is nearly a fortnight since I wrote to you—and no answer yet !   Surely the Post Office could not have been the cause of all this.   Do send us a letter, pray, and pour balm upon the fears and anxieties of many an expectant friend.   Your holidays have doubtless com. menced.   How mean you to kill your useless time ?   Write me a history of Balasore and I will engage to puff it in the columns of the " Patriot."   Do you receive your copy regularly ? and do you *read* it ?   Now be sincere for once and tell me the truth as to my latter query ?

       *   *   *   *   *

We are in the vertex of the Doorga Poojah festival.   Our holidays date from today and end on Thursday week

     *   *

VII.

Calcutta, 21st October 1855.

My dearest brother,

      Your letter of the 15th current reached us on the 19th.   It has dispelled a host of dark anticipations and ugly imaginings.   Your unusual delay in answering my last naturally led to a sea of anxiety.   We would not have relished the Poojah, I assure you, but for Nakakamohasye's Bengalee letter which reached us on the morning of the Suptoomie Poojah day.   It confirmed too surely the reason which I had mentally suspected as having influenced your premeditated delay in answering my note.   You were simpleton enough to think that the Poojah would be at a stand-still for want of your remittance.   So you rather let us groan under the most excruciating thoughts than write an empty-handed letterr   Dada had been dreaming that Russic had returned from Balasore with a rueful and woe-begone countenance, and when questioned as to how you were doing, returned no answer but quietly took his seat at the further end of the Bytuckkhana ; that Sustibur followed with the same dismal expression of the face and slipt into the room like a blasted spirit. Bama had been dreaming some equally horrid dreams—and fancy to what a pass we were brought down as every succeeding day passed away and the Dâk had no letters for us from Balasore. Really, my dear brother, you acted very foolishly in supposing that we were hard up for money. Whilst I am your agent you may with-hold your remittances for an entire year, until you have paid off your debts, and I will engage to defray every necessary expense the family here may wish you to incur for the honor of the "auld" house. I have duly received your Treasury draft for a hundred and forty rupees from which (when cashed) I will provide the assignments made by you. But you must really excuse my not proceeding to purchase either a gold watch or chain until I have paid off the debt you incurred when leaving this for Balasore. There is already a sum of nearly 15 rupees due to your creditor on account of interest which I am going to send her. Now it is one thing giving away a charity of Rupees 4 or 5 a month to a near relative, and another paying the same sum as interest. In the one case the gift is attended with the necessary honor and the prescribed quota of virtue ; in the other, the payment takes the nature of an ordinary pecuniary transaction. Therefore think not, my dearest brother, that you may, on considerations of charity, postpone liquidating your debt to aunt, giving her the interest of her money regularly—for that, in point of fact, is the only thing she cares for. I should like to see you get rid of your incumbrances as fast as possible. What is the expense of your living at Balasore ? It can't exceed one hundred rupees, at all events. The remaining hundred of your salary you must remit to me monthly, and as you have no expenses in Calcutta now which are likely to surmount the remittance you have already sent me, I propose to devote the full amount of your future remittances for four or five months to the payment of your debts. What say you to this arrangement ? I have not been put to the least inconvenience, whatsoever, by the want of a watch and a guard, let me assure you.

You will be glad to learn however that I have already provided myself with a shawl turban, and a capital one it is, for 18 rupees.   *   *   *

What you call "the inestimable benefits of parental care" is a thing we have had for so long a time that I believe both Dada and myself could willingly afford to spare it to you. You are in the jungles and you therefore need more emergently a guiding hand to extricate you from the mazes of life than ourselves. Take them both, father and mother, if you wish it, and we will jog on very jollily in their absence. But I fear you are angry with us for having ever wished for father's return to Calcutta. Such a thing never entered our brains, I assure you, but uncle here was so importunate that I should write for father's return that I could not help putting in a line that way just to humour him. Father has not wronged you in the matter of the *kochoorie* and *nimkee* which you get up at home for lunch. On the contrary he has been shaming the girls here on the score of their incapacity and raising to the skies your wife's excellence in *cuisiné* affairs. But he damned the fish of your tanks, the sweetmeats of your confectionery shops, and the *chaool* and *daool* of your bazars—and he damned them all with a vengeance. But he is returning nevertheless to the scene of your " *medd*," as Russic Pundit would put it. He can't abide in Calcutta. He won't be able to abide in Balasore. God has given him a quicksilver spirit, and now that his blood is up with a taste for travelling, he will, I conceive, tramp about the country like a "Wandering Willie," here and there, to the no small detriment of your purse. Your Bissonauth Babu is now in Calcutta. We invited him to the Poojah. But unfortunately he looked in whilst I was away. He waited for me upwards of two hours, I was told. I am very, very sorry indeed not to have seen him. Dada says he is a most excellent body—the very pink of gentlemanliness and very good—well worthy of acting as your mentor in a strange country. I intend preparing a feast for him and inviting him thereto, not to lose such a happy opportunity of cultivating the friendship of so good and charming a person. The Poojah went off very gloomily on account of the weather. It rained incessantly almost, giving a tearful aspect to every pleasure and thus destroying their intensity. Luckily we had no *jattra* or *kubbee* this year, or there would have been a sad and useless waste of money. The old gentlemen were for saddling us with some such fuss, but our good sense and resolution enabled us to politely stave off their importunities. Our Poojah was darkened further by some family *disagremens* which have not yet fully disappeared.

*   *   *   *   *

VIII.

Calcutta, Simlah, 8th November 1855.

My dearest Brother,

The Post Office is learning to mend its ways. Your plan of writing across the superscription of your letters the dates on which you post them has succeeded amazingly in quickening the pace of the Dâk runners. Stick to it and we shall never again miss your letters at the proper hour. As to kicking up a row at the Post Office, I consider such a proceeding at present useless. Hereafter I may think of such a thing. I have been very late this time in answering your letter. Excuse me, my dear brother, for the apparent neglect. The fact is, I am just at present quite swamped with office work. Mr. Sturmer, that lean and hungry-looking fellow—the sworn enemy to Native progress—has fallen ill, and the doctors have advised him to take a change of air. He has obtained four months' leave to visit the Upper Provinces and Hurris, in supersession of all the other auditors, has been appointed to take charge of his duties. I have been pitchforked to Hurris' place with the additional responsibility, which Hurris never had, of supervising the audit of my former disbursement—the Benares—which has been made over to a raw young fellow, Mr. Gordon, who understands nothing of the work. We were asked to make our own arrangements with Mr. Sturmer regarding the remuneration for the additional labor imposed upon us by these transfers. But we generously declined touching a pice of his money. I am however the most unfortunate, having now a vast amount of work before me in the Presidency Circle, swollen up like a July torrent by the accession of a host of regiments on account of the Sonthal insurrection—over and above the labor imposed on me by Major Champneys' plan of getting me to overlook Mr. Gordon's work also. The upshot is, I am bewildered with work which, I fear, I shall not be able to get through ever by devoting my spare hours at home to the task.

I am very glad that you have at last turned your thoughts to domestic economy. Your arrangements for paying off your debts are unexceptionable and I shall give effect to them to the best of my power. You think and write (excuse me) a great deal of nonsense about the watch and guard which you borrowed from me. You will oblige me vastly by dropping every thought on that subject. Between brothers such things should be considered as matters of course and not form subjects of homilies and straining of courtesies as if the obligation was too vast for patient bearance. I shall really have an affray with you if you be so eternally harping on the theme— which your Act IV or your still more refined Affray Bill will scarcely have the power to prevent. Your present of the Pugree I decline to accept, seeing that you are so hoplessly in debt and that you must first be just before you can be liberal. When your income increases I expect a more costly present and one that shall be more durable, vizt., a maintenance. Mother is very anxious to see you, but you have suc-ceeded in dissuading her from proceeding to your place so early as she had determined. Father is wroth at your negligence in making arrangements for the return to us of the palkee which Bissonauth Baboo had borrowed of you for the purpose of bringing his family down to Calcutta. The Baboo has been unnecessarily put to an expense of five or six rupees in sending back the palkee to Balasore and father has been deprived of the means of proceeding to your station again, which he must now do by purchasing or hiring (which comes almost to the same thing) a palkee. He is afraid lest the paucity of wisdom exhibited in this small affair may lead you to difficulties and hence his further anxiety to be by your side as soon as possible. We invited Bissonauth Baboo to sup at our place on Saturday last, but he excused himself on the ground of feeling feverish. He has promised however to see us before leaving for Balasore. I have purchased for you a copy of the Premsaugor for Re. 1-12 annas. The book is printed in the Naugree character. I could not procure any published in Oordoo. I shall send you the volume through Bissonauth Baboo, as also a pair of clothes for yourself and another for Bhoobun. How is the dear creature? We are glad to learn from uncle's Bengallee letter that she is learning English at a steam pace, very good news indeed! The *dolies* you called for in your note have been sent through a cousin of my *mallee's* who is going home. By the same opportunity you will be furnished with a *haman dista* to break your *dal* with, a store of *teelkootas*, and a consignment of *patkholas* for your wife. Don't however let her have an immoderate quantity of the latter article. You remember how last year she nearly managed to give you the slip and all for this same *patkhola*. Then she was at Calcutta and between Satcorry and Seboo we contrived to frustrate her tragic inten-tions. Now you are comparatively in the jungles with scarcely a grown-up son of Esculapius within hail of your quarters—so that in the event of there being any hitch in the proper digestion of the clay things you must be thrown upon your own resources to bring about a natural state in the stomach. Be forewarned therefore and you shall be forearmed. What of the Commissioner? Are his drums within hearing and his flags and ensigns within sight? Let me know full particulars, pray, in your usual happy way, of the grand event—for an event it certainly shall be in your humdrum Mofussil existence—almost as grand and important as the arrival of a new Governor-General or the display of a review on the esplanade of Fort William. So you are still in the agonies of a sinner awaiting doomsday? But you will profit by the delay and let me hear in March next that you have come off with flying colors from the presence of your Judge. I am sure you will baffle the skill of your scrutinizers.

   *   *   *   *

The *Citizen* has increased its rates—and I think it will come very dear to you to subscribe to a copy of that paper even in partnership with somebody else. Why don't you get up the plan of a Library and reading room for your station and by becoming its Secy. help yourself to the daily newspapers at a small cost to yourself?   *   *

You have hoped against hope for once. I am leading a bachelor life still. My period of tribulation will not terminate until after a week hence. My family is how-ever quite well—as also the rest of the rising generation of Ghose House. The children about whom you express such an anxiety have done nothing out of the usual course of things to warrant or furnish matter for any detailed history.   *   *   *

You doubtless have seen from the *Patriot's* Register of News that Mr. Galiffe, late Superintendent of Police, has got the Canal Collectorship. The papers mention that a Deputy Collector will be nominated to act as his Assistant. Why don't you try for the place? You must move heaven and earth to get yourself transferred to the metropolis; for, if you become a Prince at Balasore it is nothing to us, whereas any little appointment of note here will put you in the way of serving your friends and ennobling your family. Don't cease dunning Mr. Grote on the subject. Talking of Mr. Grote, I was the other day standing back to back with him at the Town Hall. The community of Calcutta had assembled there for the purpose of voting a memorial to Sir Lawrence Peel. The meeting was a rather boisterous one, the principal actors in the scene being Ram Gopal Ghose and Mr. Peterson. The latter proposed a statue which the former denounced as a folly, proposing in its stead a picture and scholarship endowment. The two motions were put to the vote, but Peterson's superior eloquence attracted the mob of Europeans present to his side. Ram Gopal, though in all his glory and having right on his side, nevertheless failed. Mr. Grote however, with characteristic energy and sense of propriety, raised his hand as often as Ram Gopal's motion was put to the vote. At last when the demagogue eloquence of Mr. Peterson carried the day, Mr. Grote, unable to contain his indignation, burst into a soliloquy which I overheard, being alongside of him at the time—"Nonsense! a statue! They will never be able to collect money for such a thing, nonsense, nonsense!" and he left the Town Hall in very great apparent disgust.

Father is quite uneasy here. The want of a *garrie* has vexed him sorely. He cannot go to the auctions, he cannot go to the *Sahibbarries*. Can human misfortune proceed further? He wants an excitement and the *Jattra fureur* has made us lose many a goodly rupee. We had Kartick Ghose in the compound last Saturday night to humour the old gentleman. We had another *Jattra* about a month ago to satisfy the same appetite. The garden no longer pleases him because you have taken prisoners his playmates. And in his bewilder n t he will one of these days give us the slip and post to Balasore. He already fancies you are playing the prodigal and he cannot bear to see your money wasted in gratuities to this man and that. He will probably be with you in another month.

*   *

IX.

Calcutta, the 12th December 1855.

My dearest Brother,

I could not keep my promise of writing you a one-sheet letter before this, owing to a dearth of mail paper. I have procured however a sufficient quantity of this very necessary article and will not be again guilty of perjury. The pressure of work of which I complained to you in my last, has a little subsided owing to my having got somewhat familiar with my new duties, although I am yet compelled to devote a portion of my leisure at home to the harassing business. I could not, in my last, do justice to many things which I had it in my mind to bring prominently before you. Bissonauth Baboo, for instance, had only a passing notice from my pen, though I much longed to ring his praises in a more prolonged key. He is indeed a jewel of a man and his manners, at once frank and gentlemanlike, are calculated to attract the esteem of those who have the good fortune to come in contact with him. I dare say he has not received from us the welcome which his merits entitled him to, and you will therefore be good enough to excuse us to him, supplying in your own person the deficiency which, I am well aware, we have been guilty of. We invited the Baboo more than once to come and have a friendly supper with us, but he as often excused himself on the plea of ill-health—and sick he certainly was—for father when he went to see him found him quite broken down and going upon crutches. Yet you will please tell him in my name that we naturally felt ourselves disappointed by his excuses and some-what sore at being unable to do him the rites of hospitality in the time-honored way. We could not give him even a stirrup-cup—if I way use the expression—for when he last saw us he had taken good care to provide himself with a potent excuse for refusing ever so single a sweetmeat that we could otherwise offer him in the way of *misteemookh*, by just half an hour ago dining to his fill at Baboo Peary Chand Mittre's place. We had accordingly only the meagre satisfaction of giving him a glass of water and a *pawn*. When however he again comes to Calcutta—which, I hope, will be next year—we will not let him off so easily. Tell him that he must prepare himself to tender compound interest for what he has on the last occasion robbed us of.

*   *   *

I am really very sorry to hear that the fates have again placed in your hands the wheel of Mr. Ixion and the stone of Mynheer Sysiphus. Why, my dear Nadada, you seem to be pursued by the harpies from the moment you entered upon busy life. There was firstly that accursed Boothby (may the Furies play at bat and ball with his sinful soul) who would give you no holidays and make you work from 8 A. M. to 7 P. M. Then there came the deluge at the Collectorate and after a merciful Providence had sent you an Ark in the shape of the Board's Office whereon to rest after your grievous ducking, lo! an unkind angel tears you away from friends and home and deposits your already too well-battered brains and person in a Biscay of work and labour at Balasore. Really you have seen life—and I only wish you may not long to see the end of it.

    *   *   *

    I am glad that you are getting provident. Your kitchen garden bears sufficient evidence of your ant-like foresight. But will you succeed in raising cabbages and turnips and peas and radishes ?—that's the question. The cabbages in my Wooltadanga garden (for I have now got two gardens, and I defy you to guess where the second is) are coming out very splendid. The gardener is a very *pucka* man and I wish you could have one like him to look after your vegetables. I have cut down a whole lot of old trees enough to serve us for fuel for a year. The garden looks more spacious, and when I have planted out the mango and litchee grafts which my man has procured from trees of established repute, it will look admirable indeed. But I am keeping you in suspense about the second garden of which by this time you have strained your ingenuity in attempting to find out the locality. Know then, my dearest Brother, that I have actually become owner and occupier by purchase of a plot of land measuring 3 biggahs and 9 cottahs, with a tank of water and several fruit trees thereon, lying and situate at Bailoor within the jurisdiction of Howrah, bounded and abutted—there is no use giving you a copy of the indentures. You will naturally ask what in the name of wonder made me go to Bailoor for a pleasure garden ? The story is soon told. When I was at Bhuggobutty's during the Doorga Poojah vacation I bethought me of going over inspecting the garden which eldest uncle, you may remember, had for the last six months been talking of as a beautiful place and so forth. Myself, Sreekissen, Bhuggobutty and one or two others sallied out in quest of the property and succeeded in discovering it. Its position, only a few paces from the Bazar, on the public highway and at a small distance only from the River, at once caught my desire and I resolved to purchase it. On my return to Calcutta I set about the matter in right earnest and effected the bargain for a hundred and fifty rupees. And a burgain it undoubtedly was—as there are a hundred Mango trees, about 40 Jack, 30 Cocoanut, 3 Golapjam trees and a respectable-sized Bamboo tope, lots of apple trees, &c. &c., upon the ground, the wood whereof, if cut down and sold in the Bazar, would any time fetch the price I paid for the garden. There is an adjoining piece of ground, measuring some four or five biggahs, which I am also about to purchase and then I shall have a respectable-looking place. If the bridge be erected at Hatkhola Ghaut, as Mr. Rendal has proposed, you may rest assured I shall be a made man. I intend building a Garden House in my new property fit to accommodate a zenana. But that won't be in a hurry. I must wait till I have made some money. At Xmas I shall give a grand feast at Bailoor in repayment of the numerous ones which we have discussed at the expense of our good friends of the locality. Oh ! how we shall miss you ! I could wish you had the wings of the eagle to fly over and enjoy yourself. But when you come home next year we hope to entertain you to our heart's fill. Till then you must like the lark be content to gaze from a distance at the water you long to drink but which you cannot reach. You ask to know whether my Obie has got a complete row of teeth. I am glad I can answer in the affirmative. The little thing is getting as mischievous as its father. Chundie had been ailing off and on for the last few days. But she is all right now after having helped Satcorry to a two-rupees fee. Benoo, Bedoo and all the other boys and girls are quite well. You enquire why you don't get the *Patriot* regularly. Ask Bhooloo Baboo ; he posts the paper.   *   *   *   *

X.

Calcutta, 19th January 1856.

My dearest brothe

I did not reply to your last at the usual time, as I was in expectation of conveying to you the news of your transfer, from the official Gazette. I have, however, been disappointed. Today's Gazette is silent on the subject. I have written however to Koylas to send me due notice of the joyful event as soon as he happens to learn anything about it in the course of his official readings. I have some news to communicate to you. Father is bent upon the "grand pilgrimage," as you call it, and has sermoned mother into a similar state of mind. They will leave this as soon as your reply is received. Father thinks that his honor is concerned in the matter as the people of Balasore must be thinking poorly of his religion after his sudden disappearance from the station without stepping over to Poorie to have a peep at the Great God. I in vain hinted to him the possibility of the people of Balasore being too much engaged with their own affairs to devote that earnest consideration to his, which his morbid imagination seems to give them credit for doing. Further, that even if the good men and women of the place had such a marvellous taste for talking about the conduct and religion of a stray sojourner amongst them, now absent however, he had very little to suffer from their opinions, inasmuch as your transfer to a station nearer to Calcutta will remove the possibility of his coming *vis à vis* with his busy critics a thousand chances off. But you know the old man—when he has set his heart upon anything, not all the Gods and little fishes can reason him out of it. So look up. You may expect guests at the very moment probably, at which you are packing up for Calcutta. Mr. Heysham has at last got a Deputyship. He is very lucky in having been posted to Calcutta and the 24 Pergunnahs. I hear that Govind Persaud Pundit has been charged with the Calcutta and 24 Pergunnahs collections—in which case I don't see what work there is for Mr. Heysham. Our office has been removed to the Commercial Buildings, otherwise I would have called at the Board's Office to learn tidings of your transfer.

*   *

XI.

Calcutta, 30th January 1856.

My dearest brother,

I called on Mr. Rodrigues of the Board's Office yesterday. He told me that he had received a letter from you, taxing him for not having replied to two other letters of yours which you had despatched previously. At his request I have to inform you that the two previous letters in question have miscarried, thanks to the arrangements in the Post Office. He has received your last letter, but its answer is delayed owing to his having not as yet been able to create an opportunity for asking Mr. Grote upon the subject of your transfer. Another Lackerstein-like gentleman who was talking to Mr. R., told me however that Jadub Chunder Chatterjee, the Deputy Collector of Burdwan, has applied for pension and that his son Shama Churn Chatterjee, who is now the Sheristadar of the Commissioner's Court at Burdwan, is a candidate for his father's place. But Mr. Grote has purposely kept back the latter's nomination roll in order to get you to Burdwan. I believe therefore you are fairl y booked. Trilochun Mitter, who was here on Sunday last, told us that Koylas Dutt had mentioned to him in the course of conversation that you were about to be transferred to Burdwan. Whence the latter had derived his information Trilochun could not enquire. But I believe he must have heard from the right quarter. At all events there are as many chances of mother Kally eating our sweetmeat as there are of her not being so fortunate. That would indeed be a day for us when you come to Burdwan. I am already busy building a thousand castles in the air in anticipation of the joyful event. What an infinity of *Kababs* and *Kalias* shall I discuss at your expense—my mouth really waters just to think of it.

My Chundie, thanks to mother Chundie, is getting better, and I have sent the whole brood to Konnuggur for a fortnight's change of air. When you come to Burdwan I believe I shall billet them upon you for a longer period. By this time father must have reached your place. Keep me informed of his movements privately.

The *Phœnix* is a tri-weekly paper and its price is, I hear, 3 Rs. a month, rather too much for these cheap literature times! The *Patriot* did not light upon you like an angel of news that it is, because Bhooloo thought you were coming to Calcutta, so there was no use sending you the paper any longer. It shall however be now regularly forwarded to you until countermanded. How are your peas and cabbages coming on ? those in my garden have grown magnificently. You will perhaps be delighted to learn that I have purchased—I have just fearfully cut my hand, so can't continue writing except in a scrawling way—for which beg your pardon—another 4 Biggahs at Bailoor which gives me 7½ Biggahs altogether. When you come to Calcutta I will shew you the property which is very beautifully situated indeed. Good bye. I can't proceed any further with this bad ent.   *   *   *

XII.

Calcutta, *19th February 1856.*

My dearest brother,

Don't take it amiss that I did not answer your letters earlier. I was bothering every soul who I could think had the faintest chance of knowing any-thing about you, for information about your transfer. I called two several times on Mr. Rodrigues. But that gentleman had rendered himself invisible. I called again, he was not to be found. Well, thought I, if Rodrigues is so fond of going home before 4 P.M.—for I assure you I called a little after that hour all three times—I must bid adieu to all hopes of seeing his beautiful figure until such time as the repairs being finished we could return to our snug quarters near the Board's Office. But that is not likely to occur soon. So I got hold of a clerk very much resembling Mr. Rodrigues and sitting alongside of him—and on the third day of my trip to the Board asked him to give me news concerning your probable movements. But he at once and most unmercifully knocked down the fine castles I had built in my mind by telling me that the story of your transfer was a myth—that there were a hundred applicants in the field already and that though Mr. Grote had used every endeavour to get you over to Burdwan, Mr. Ricketts proved your evil genius and the resolution come to was that one of the senior Deputy Collectors should step into the vacancy. I wish to God that my informant has hoaxed me and that the result will falsify the news he has inflicted on me. Mother is quite in despair at the turn affairs seem to have taken and she accuses you bitterly of having raised her to a pitch of ecstasy only to hurl her to the lowest depths of despondency. The prospect of promotion which is before you in the event of your continuing at Balasore alone reconciles us to the dreary fact that your transfer to a locality nearer home is postponed *sine die*—and since it can't be helped, why then grapes are *indeed sour*! Nobody can stop your coming to Calcutta during the next Doorgah Poojah holidays—and they occur only six months hence. We lay that flattering unction to our soul and endeavour to stifle every grief by its continued application.

*　　*　　*　　*　　*

Benoo here is about to get married—she has abjured all pretensions to the masculine gender, dresses like a female and does not attack you tooth and nail if addressed in the feminine gender. Bhobany Dutt's brother has been proposed as her bridegroom. Has father returned from Juggurnauth and relieved you from the predicament of cooking for yourself and performing the menial occupations of the household for want of servants? Why indeed, my dearest brother, you have not the shadow of a right to pay father's pilgrimage expenses from your individual pocket. I have just as good a claim to the thing as I have to my father's property and shall stick out as litigiously for the one as I would for the other—wherefore no use quarrelling, give up the point at once like a good boy. We will go shares. That's the only concession I can make to you.

*　　*　　*　　*　　*

XIII.

Calcutta, 8th March 1856.

My dearest brother,

Your letter of the 3rd Instant reached me only yesterday. Of course I got it in the office where I had no such commodity as mail paper and postage stamp. They could not be begged, borrowed, nor stolen. So I was *malgre moi meme*, as the French say, compelled to violate the rule you had chalked out for my observance. I have lost no time however in laying hold of opportunity by the ears—and the demurrage this time is not long enough to breed a grievance. The news of your illness had really struck me of a heap—and uncle's letter to Bhooloo was like water to the lark in the dry state of my mind. I am glad you have recovered so soon, as the length of the furlongh solicited by you and sanctioned by the Board had led me to rate your sickness considerably more serious than what you now affirm it to have been.

Mother heard nothing about the matter as I would on no account pain her tender sensibilities by mentioning the news to her. The poor woman had been dreaming a whole lot of dreams concerning you and accordingly her mind was in the best condition to magnify a molehill into a mountain. I have now however told her all about your late illness which she sincerely deplores.

     *   *   *   *   *

Don't despair of coming to Burdwan yet. The vacancy there has not yet been filled up. Shama Churn Chatterjea, the new Deputy Collector who was your rival, has been already posted to Sylhet. Mr. Ricketts—who was the only member of the Board antagonistic to your transfer to Burdwan in preference to your seniors who have applied for the indulgence—has been appointed Financial Commissioner, so that Mr. Grote's hands are now free to act in your favour. Write to him again, dun him. I hear Rodrigues has been appointed Mr. Ricketts' Head Clerk on 300 a month. The knave did not certainly deserve this piece of good fortune. I have an emissary in the Board's Office who will give me the first news regarding you that turns up in that eventful Department. I saw Koylas Bose lately, but he has heard nothing of the rumours in which we have such all-absorbing interest. So you start for Cuttack at the end of March? [Mother] cautions you against any sort of exposure or irregular [diet]. She in particular entreats you to abjure *urhur dall*. I wish you success and hope you will astonish your examiners by the correctness of your answers. Will Samuells have anything to do with the scrutiny? He is a very clever man, but should you find him hypercritical just remind him of the construction of Act 21 of 1841 which spoiled his reputation in the Sudder Court in the reign of Judge Colvin. We have nothing of interest stirring in Calcutta just now except that Lord Canning has relieved Lord Dalhousie and the latter has sneaked away to England. There was an attempt made to present Lord Dalhousie with an address, but nobody, with the exception of a few placemen, would sign such a document and the Secretary accordingly had recourse to the infallible expedient of sending the parchment round with begging letters to the public offices in which, as in duty bound, it speedily got filled up. The new Governor-General has as yet done nothing to indicate his presence amongst us. He appears to be very fond of his horses and carriages which are being brought out of England with scarcely less care and ceremony than what attended his Lordship's passage out. When does father intend coming to Calcutta? Give him my *pronam* and advise him to look sharp, as many of our friends and relations are whetting their appetite in expectation of the *prosaud* which, as a matter of course, he is supposed to be coming laden with. Mother is determined to go to Juggurnauth in July next—notwithstanding father's gentle warning regarding the inconvenience of such a pilgrimage.

     *   *   *

XIV.

Calcutta, 12th March 1856.

My dear father,

You will be good enough to come down to Calcutta at once. That man Hurro Chunder Mittre has *sold* me. The villain has embezzled some six hundred rupees of the Government revenue. He has been served with a Perwannah to deposit the money in the Collectorate within 5 days. Of course the money is not forthcoming. The rascal came to my office this afternoon and with a rueful face declared his inability to pay the amount as his brother Dinoo had spent it. He further stated that if you had been in Calcutta the matter would have been easily adjusted by your sending for Dinoo Mittre and getting him to sign over his right and title to the house and gardens at Bansbaria and selling the property. As there is little hope of my brother's getting transferred to Burdwan, for the Deputy Collector of that station has not been allowed the pension he had applied for, but only a month's leave in its stead, I think you had better come down.

      *   *   *

XV.

Calcutta, 24th March 1856.

My dearest Brother,

You are too good and I am too bad. That is the only way in which I can account for my remissness to profit by your very *very* kind and generous and brotherly offer. I am one of those that have a most morbid sensibility in matters of money— or insensibility—if you please. I would not, for the empire of the Cæsars, drag another into the predicament in which it has pleased Providence to place me. When I shall be in want, who but you, my dearest brother, will feed and clothe me and mine ? But as long as these hands are capable of earning me my bread—yea more—excuse me if I do not grasp an accommodation which, I know, it will cost you many a fatiguing day to place at my disposal. You are turned a very fine casuist, my dear, and the *rai* that you have written out in justification of your making the offer and my accepting it, let me assure you, would have made the noodles of the Sudder Court stare in wonder and amazement at the good sense and legal acumen of a native judge. But what in the regions of the law and under the atmosphere of the *Cutcherries* would have appeared extremely pertinent and ingenuous, is the very reverse in the domains of King Conscience who keeps a much too nicer pair of scales than Justice in the Courts cares to furnish herself with. Thank you therefore, my dearest brother, for the aid you would most willingly afford. But I would prefer putting it by as a *Corps de Reserve*—to be used on a rainy day. Father, you will be glad to learn, safely reached home yesterday and my delay in answering your letter of the 17th current has been caused by my desire to squeeze into my reply the news of father's arrival. The rascal Hurro Chunder Mitter was at our place yesterday and father has sufficiently frightened him, I believe. The defalcation, my father-in-law after an inspection of the accounts tells me, amounts to Rs. 556—from which will be deducted a sum of Rs. 100 and upwards on account of arrears of commission due. Don't be any way uneasy about the loss. I might have been robbed of a much larger sum by a successful burglary. Father has a great influence upon the Mittre devil and who knows but he may screw the last anna out of him. He hopes to do as much, as the fellow has a house and gardens at Bansbaria. Tell aunt that Chonoo has been delivered of a fine boy. Mother and child are both well.   *   *   *   *

We are all well here with the exception of those graceless valetudinarians, Obey and Chundie—who have again fallen ill.

*   *   *

XVI.

Calcutta, 7th April 1856.

My dearest brother,

You must by this time have reached Cuttack. I hope the journey did not in any way injure either your health or spirits. Who, my dear brother, could have believed two years ago, that you, who could not proceed from the outside to the inside apartments of the *auld* house without the escort of another grown-up person, would have to travel 3 mortal days by yourself over a wild and far off country, bivouacking in paddy fields, under the crests of mountains or in the deep gloom of the forest? Really you are realising the romance of life whilst we unambitious souls will rot in the hole in which we first saw heaven's light. But will you explain to me one mystery connected with your late trip? How in the name of *Pákráj* did you manage to cook your dinners? Or was it Chand Sing that did that job for you? How have you passed through the furnace?

I have ascertained at the Board's Office that your application for a transfer to Burdwan has been favourably received so far that your prayer will be taken into consideration on a vacancy occurring. I hear that the Deputy Collector of Burdwan will retire at the expiration of his extended leave. Then will be the time for you to strain every nerve and use every interest for getting transferred. *   *   *

XVII.

Calcutta, 14th April 1856.

My dearest Brother,

Your letter without date, posted on the 11th Instant, reached me yesterday afternoon. I am really glad to learn that you have boarded your former health and retaken it in style. That's right. Nothing so horrid as a sick person. My Obinas, thank heaven, is now quite well again, tho' the imp cost me four rupees in the shape of fee to our good neighbour Siboo. I will tell you how I got into the perhaps avoid-able expense. The urchin was fasted into a very devil and at night he became so unmanageable that I was thro' sheer fright compelled to send for the doctor in order to exercise him. Having once come, of course the son of Esculapius must needs come again—Rs. 4. Q. E. D. Now for *your* Doctor. How the devil did he come to charge *you* for his visit and to so large a figure as sixteen rupees with a jolly boat of Rs. 4 for his follower. I thought you were privileged to get medical advice from your Civil Surgeon *muflaise*. *   *   *   *

You can't get to Burdwan now—that's flat. Bhooloo's brother-in-law Khetter was telling me that he had copied a letter of the Board's in which Jadub Chunder Chatterjea, the Deputy Collector of Burdwan, was informed that his applica-tion for pension should not be entertained—but a month's leave was allowed him at the expiration of which period the Board will again consider his fitness or otherwise for pensionary support. I hear however that the Deputy Collector of Nuddea has retired on pension, leaving a vacancy in that District. Mr. Grote has truly got the Nuddea Commissionership. Now is the time for you, my boy. Apply at once for Nuddea officially. Write to Mr. Grote privately. Make interest with Shalk—hang me, I can never bring myself to spell that name correctly—and Samuells—and here's a fine opportunity for you to taste of the bracing waters and fine cream of Krishnagar. Don't be too long doing what I advise you. Grote must bring you under his own eye in order the more effectually to serve you. Who, think you, will be Senior Secretary to the Board? Guess it, man—why your old friend A. R. Young. Use your cue and opportunities and you are a made man. Now for a little talk about myself. Excuse the *ego*—for I know, you hate that just as much as I do myself. I am done for ; that whining knave Hurro Chunder Mitter has almost ruined me. You know how, at father's most earnest and pressing solicitation, I consented to be that man's security.

＊   ＊   ＊   ＊   ＊

XVIII.

Calcutta, 22nd June 1850.

My dearest brother,

What, in the name of all the saints in the calendar and all the devils in Pandemonium. could have put into your little head the magnificent conceit that your letters to home are classed with the various bores in the universe ? Really, my dearest brother, you wrong both myself as well as your anxious relatives in Calcutta by giving voice to the opinion that you are one of the least interesting creatures whose progress through life is matter of supine nonchalance to us all. You probably have the plea of my occasional tardiness in taking up your letters for reply to cast into my teeth. But when I tell you that such is my way and that my official correspondence very often falls as much as three weeks into arrears. you will doubtless excuse my remissness to now and then answer your letters with punctuality and despatch.

＊   ＊   ＊   ＊   ＊

But you yourself are not quite the saint in respect to speedy letter-writing that you would fain bully yourself into being allowed credit for. Why, man, we have had our patience at times put to the last degree of tension before we are favored with one of your twenty-line epistles. But I do not wish to afflict you with any more of this disagreeable *tu quoque*. I satisfy myself with giving only the cue of a whole bundle of similar invective which you can at your leisure amuse yourself with disentangling. Now to business. Pray don't send any more remittances unless you choose to give me a charter for a Bank. All your debts have been cleared and a large sum is standing at your credit in my books. I shall send you an account current when next I write to you.   ＊   ＊   ＊   ＊   ＊

XIX.

Konnugur, 27th July 1856.

My dearest brother,

I lose no time in taking up your letter of the 24th current, for reply. You are getting awfully thin in the matter of your communications. Perhaps that's one reason why you have been so punctual in your reply. That is at least one great object gained. I would not for the world lose such an advantage, to secure an additional dozen lines. Don't think before you write. But let the words spontaneously flow from your pen. I myself am aware in my own person of the procrastinating tendency of thinking. The blue devils are a clog to our activity and mar despatch. Obin is all right again. I am just now on a visit to the dear family. I have news for you, my father-in-law has just had a boy—and tho' the little darling has been ushered in rather early, from its mother's womb, she being just in the 8th month of her interesting situation, yet it exhibits every show of health. May God grant it long life! Well I say you have not yet told us for certain whether you intend coming up to Calcutta during the Doorga Poojah holidays. I may as well let you know that this year the Moha-Maee runs but a slender chance of being idolised in our house. The Jhoolun is about to be knocked on the head. You doubtless wonder what resolution could have possibly effected such a striking change in our habits and feelings. Wonder on. Wonder on—the world is full of wonders, and why should not Ghose House have its mysteries? Shall I invoke the muse and give you with the aid of the supernatural inspiration the reasons which have operated to render such sad havoc in our shows and our ceremonies?   *   *   *   *   *

XX.

Calcutta, 17th September 1856.

My dearest Brother,

There I don't agree with you. You do not give me longer stuff than I do you. I admit you occupy a larger space. But that is owing to the clever habit you have of putting three words to the line—whilst I, with greater condensation of calligraphy, carry out to the letter the principle of *multum in parvo*. I could weekly inundate you with sentiments. But as I abhor sentimentalism and dread paper speculation more than the hydrophobia, I have in this matter adopted the doctrine of " do to others as you would be done by." I can nevertheless amuse you with *tableau vivant* of men and manners if you wish it—though your time is, I fear, more seriously and perhaps usefully occupied for you to desire such triflings. *Apropos* of literary executions—what, in the name of the muses, is the character of the movement you have been organizing in that *Kiskinda Moolook* of yours? Literature in Balasore! You might as well talk of astronomy amongst the cannibals! I wonder if more than half a dozen of your people (with the exception of yourself, our friend Bissonauth Baboo—to whom my sincere compliments—and the *Sahib logues*) can read English with any degree of fluency. But send us a copy of your prospectus. We will see if we can make anything out of it.

So we have *not* been inundated. The thing was impossible. The bores were rather troublesome, it is true, but the river at its highest rose only to the level of the road, soaking only the Strand. I hear that the surrounding country, Nuddea and Santipore especially, have suffered dreadfully. They are completely under water. Father says that you had better postpone your visit to Cuttack—seeing that the rivers have overflowed and considerable danger exists in crossing those in your route.

* * * * *

XXI.

Calcutta, 12th Jany. 1857.

My dearest brother,

What sunshine is to the Laplander, what a sail is to the shipwrecked mariner, what water is to the parched lips of the traveller in Arabian deserts, what the failing of an Indian dynasty was to Lord Dalhousie, what a Lottery prize is to the pauper, what a new beauty is to the voluptuary, even such has your letter of the 7th Instant proved to me. I feel like the porter who has just discharged a crushing load, like the sleeping man who has awoke from a nightmare, like the felon at the gallows who has been hailed with a reprieve. If every break in your correspondence be succeeded by a similar delight, I shall indeed be very ungrateful to the sensations that now possess me if I grumbled at your delay. But on the principle that extremes are injurious, I vote that you give us a weekly supply of thoughts instead of straining our anxiety to the screwing point in order to come down to us with an unexpected clap of good news.

From the tenor of your letter it seems that mine of the 24th has missed you. I therein told you how our preparations for a splendid garden party were upset by the sudden and serious illness of our cousin Burdidee (Luckhie). She was attacked with cholera in its most virulent shape and had well nigh given up the ghost and given *us* a *ghost !* They were compelled to bring her downstairs in order to remove her to the river, but the cold raw night operated as a reason with the healthy for not exposing themselves for the sake of the dying; otherwise, sure enough the removal would have been effected and death, as a matter of course, followed. Thanks however to this intervention, the tragedy did not proceed to that extent, for the delay induced us to try the effects of the far-famed snuff. Happily the medicine took ground and before twenty-four hours had elapsed the patient's pulse returned. In another day she was past all danger. But the garden party could not take place on Christmas day notwithstanding such favorable turn. We had it therefore on the Sunday immediately following. The party consisted of upwards of 40 men—the feasting was on a magnificent scale and the old voluptuary Kristo Bose of Goa Baugan, who formed one of the party, obtruded upon us a set of dancing girls. Roop Chand *Puckhy* regaled us with his vocal performances likewise, and altogether such a gala was kicked up as had not been witnessed in Wooltadanga for many years. The affair cost me upwards of 45 rupees, but the money was well spent, considering the amount of pleasure it purchased. I know you will turn up your nose and read me a lecture. But, my dearest brother, people that move in society cannot help incurring these expenses now and then. On the sheer principle,

do to others as you would be done by, I believe I can set up an excuse for my extrava-
g ance—and then only it comes perhaps once in four years. We missed you grievously,
let me assure you. Oh! for the day when you shall have been transferred to some
place near Calcutta! We are doing very well. My Bhoomony is looking handsomer
and handsomer every day. Why don't you write a line concerning her ?   •

· XXII.

Calcutta, 9th June 1857.

My dearest Brother,

  I was an the point of writing to you about the unusual delay made by you
in answering my last letter when yours of the 4th came to hand. I did not answer
father's note because, thought I, brother's replies were quite enough.

  The English in Calcutta are in a prodigious funk on account of the massacres
at Meerut and Delhi. A few days ago, the ladies and gentlemen residing at Ballygunge started from their beds at midnight and, dressed in all manner of garments, were
deporting themselves from their homes in search of life, when lo! the unusual and
alarming sounds that had placed before their distracted imaginations visions of
murderous Native Infantry with their bloody swords uplifted in the act of striking
down the *Ferangee logue,* turned out to be the festive glee and pyrotechnic wonders of
a bridegroom's party proceeding to the joyful business of marriage. Calcutta is quite
safe—although the magnates of Chowringhee don't think so. But the state of the
country in the North West is really alarming. Do you take me for such a gull as to
be deluded by a special constable's bamboo stick and paper warrant into swearing to
leave my family and friends in the hour of danger for the purpose of swelling the
throng of stupid Volunteers who would as soon (from want of skill) fire upon friends
as upon foes. No! no! I am a wiser man than to do such a piece of folly. Have you
heard anything about my poor father-in-law? The estimable gentleman had nigh
lost his appointment for an unguarded word. I mention the incident in order that you
may profit by it. He was one day coming down by Railway from Connuggur when he
chanced to be the only native in a second class carriage the inmates of which were
entirely Europeans. There were one Mr. Church Jr.—a merchant—a Captain Mathe-
son—Mr. Judge the Attorney and one or two Indigo planters in the compartment.
The rascals drew my poor father-in-law into conversation on the subject of the mutiny
and by dint of hard abuse of every thing native managed to get the honest gentleman
out of temper—so that in the heat of a bantering discussion he gave vent to some
badinage at the expense of the English people. This conversation was formed into
a basis for charging the Depy. Collector of Alipore with "high crimes and misdemeanours" etc. and the sneaking scoundrels who brought the charge after having maliciously
provoked the expressions on which it was based, went in a body to Mr. Beadon the
Home Secy, to lay it before the Governor-General, and to the Judge of Hooghly who, at
their instance, strongly supported it. The upshot was, my poor father-in-law, than
whom a more loyal subject perhaps breathes not, was hauled up before the Home
Secy. But his explanations, though saving him from dismissal, nevertheless could not

stay a most insulting wig in the shape of an official despatch. After this who can be sure of anything in this ephemeral world! When mother goes up to Poorie you will oblige me by placing 50 Rs. at her disposal on my account and I will credit you with the sum in my books. Tell her that her father's *Thakoor Mohasye* has asked me to procure for his use a silk *Namaboli* from Juggurnauth. The man promised to deposit its price with me. But I suppose he won't do so if he can help it.

*   *   *   *

XXIII.

Calcutta, 9th July 1857.

My dearest Brother,

So the story of the disbanded men is all humbug. I am glad that it is so, on your account. The panic here has subsided, tho' the redoubtable Volunteers still patrol the streets at night and annoy honest men who fall in their way. Dreadful news that from Cawnpore. You may have read it all in the *Phœnix*. The *Friend of India* has got a thundering wig from the Home Office. He is losing many subscribers who are all transferring their patronage to the opposition shop—the *Hindoo Patriot*. Hurris expects to realise this year a profit of some six hundred rupees.

*   *   *   *

XXIV.

Calcutta, 29th July 1857.

My dearest Brother.

I am very sorry to learn from yours of the 27th Instant that father has had a return of the old complaint. Tell him by no means to disturb himself. He is doubt-less very snug and comfortable in that beautiful little station of yours which every returning pilgrim from Poorie has been describing to me as a very Eden of ease and elegance. But I believe the *couleur de rose* owed its existence materially, I may say wholly, to the open hospitality which you seem by all accounts to have kept up for the benefit of the holy travellers. Prawn Dutt's brother is in ecstasies regarding your Bungalow which he values at a rental of 500 Rupees a month according to Calcutta nerricks. Issur Singh, whom you very kindly supplied with one of your own palkees when his became unserviceable, raises your humanity and your condescension to the heavens, and even Cally Bose, your old friend of Collectorate associations, has been extemporising a homily on the excellence of your sweetmeats which tempted him to a severe illness, he says.

*   *

XXV.

Calcutta, 2nd August 1857.

My dearest Brother,

The times are getting very troublous. Troops will parade our streets and the Volunteers will have no end of watching bye and bye. The ensuing Mohurrum is looked up to as a bomb or a shell the bursting whereof is a never-ending source of anxiety. But I believe the panic is a senseless one with the Barrackpore corps disarmed and the Body Guard—though somewhat shaky—mustering only 200 sabres. Poor Col. Goldie of ours is reported to have been killed at Futteghur where he was on leave. If the news be true we have indeed lost an invaluable friend. May ten thousand thunders burst over the rascally mutineers. Indeed there is no knowing how soon staunch soldiers may shoot their officers and mingle amongst the mass of ruthless savages! I hope there is no cause for apprehension at your little station.

Well and we are going to have the *Jhoolun* after a great deal of manœuvres and counter-manœuvres. Father, it appears, has been writing to uncle here that he will pay the whole expense of the festival (minus *our* respective quotas) privately into uncle's hands. And of course uncle has no objection to the arrangement. So we have been played out of our decision by the old gentleman The Pharisees will perhaps try to look as glum as a procession of mourners—and you know glumness is a deuced infectious disease. Jhoolun therefore will be to us the sort of merriment which the author of the *Night Thoughts* enjoyed when dancing a minuet before the barrel of an Irish Captain's horsepistol. But I don't care My Chundie has been laid up with a burning fever—so I fancy I shall not be able to amuse myself with Kartick Ghose's *Jattra.*

I have this morning learnt from Koylas that you have at last obtained the long-expected and well-deserved promotion. Try and save money—for if the privations you already suffer and are likely to still further undergo are not to render you independent after a few years, I don't see the rhyme of your continuing to torture yourself.   *   *   *   *   *   *   *

XXVI.

Calcutta, 5th Jany. 1858.

My dearest Brother,

I had proceeded on a tour into Baraset and the adjoining villages. Of course it was a pleasure tour, at the expense of another. Hence this delay in acknowledging your favor of the 26th ult.

You can guess what a merry jovial life I am now leading, from the fact, that during the last three New Year holidays I was altogether a diner-out. New Year's day we had our Garden picnic (subscription)—consisting of self, Dada, Koylas, Cally Churn Shome and Mohender—very select. Bill of fare—in the morning *loochie,* cauliflower curry, sweetmeats, cocoanuts and oranges. Dinner—rice, mutton chops, cutlet, kalia, dall with goat's meat—eggs roasted—snipe, and mango-pickle – capital meal—very—a real New Year's treat. I wish you were here to be one of the company. Just the thing you would have relished. Better luck next time. On the 2nd January went to Bamoonmoora, three miles further off Baraset, in a fine spring-cushioned palkee garrie—company—Kristo Bose, Gopal Mitter, Issur Chuckerbutty and a few others—arrived at 3 P.M. Bill of fare—pillao, and various curries. Went in the evening to Badoo and thence to Mohesshurpore—returned to Badoo—had a jolly good tiffin at night and pure excellent date-juice—slept there. In the morning returned to Bamoonmoora—bathed in a garden tank neck deep all round—learnt to swim—no end of cocoanuts—drank date-juice again, plantains, oranges &c. Dined on rice, all manner of curries, goat's flesh &c. At 2 P.M. started for Calcutta—jumped down near Shambazar bridge—strolled into Wooltadanga garden—returned home by 7 P.M.—tiffed—went to bed and slept like a buffalo! My story is ended and the *noty* tree has become bare. Why *noty* hast become bare? etc. Now for news. A very fatal occurrence took place yesterday. You knew of course Shib Narain Deb—the brother of Wopen—such a nice gentlemanly fellow he was. It appears that he had purchased at a public sale certain Tosa Khana jewels. Somebody told him that he had not done right in doing so. The idea haunted him and he foolishly work ed himself up to the belief that Sreenarain Bysack, his immediate superior, was conspiring with the 2nd son of Rajah Radha Kant, to ruin him—he left a written statement to that effect and at about 1 P.M. deliberately put a loaded pistol into his mouth and shot himself dead! Poor fellow! he deserved a better destiny!

Appendix B.

——:O:——

Memorial Notices etc.

The Bengalee: Saturday, 25th September 1869.

The late Baboo Grish Chunder Ghosh.

We dip our pen in our heart's blood to record the death in the very prime of his life of one of the ablest and foremost among our countrymen—the founder and editor of this paper—Baboo Grish Chunder Ghose. The country has lost in him a noble specimen of humanity which it is rare to meet in these days. A more honest, conscientious and patriotic Hindu gentleman perhaps never came across our path. It was impossible to see him and not to be inspired with admiration for the unaffected simplicity and blandness with which his countenance was marked. He belonged to no clique or coterie of Young Bengal and Old Bengal who have the misfortune to be so often and so numerously divided, and yet he was a favorite with all. In his social inter-course with his own countrymen whether of the most orthodox or the most heterodox kind, his behaviour was the most correct. He never in his life either by deed or by word offended any body's feelings or flattered any body's prejudices. His manners were as pleasing as they were consistent with gentlemanly etiquette. While he would greet a friend imbued with English ideas by a warm and affectionate shake of the hand, he would bend his neck and fold his hands to one of the orthodox class. The circle of his friends and acquaintances was so large that it was a positive inconvenience to bear him company either in a walk in the streets, a bathing excursion to the ghats or a run through the Railway station to catch the train. He had so many people to speak to, to make kind enquiries of, that, he had often to be reminded that time was running. It was impossible to know him once and to pass him by. He pleased every body as he himself seemed to be pleased with all. He was a born gentleman. He disarmed malice of its sting by his open straight forward nature, aud while he could scarcely make an enemy he was sure to make a friend even on the most slight acquaintance. The principle of his life was to love and not to hate.

His private career was exemplary. Unlike most of his enlightened countrymen he never allowed the insidious cup to touch his lips ; and yet he was a most jolly companion ever ready with an inexhaustible fund of jokes, anecdotes and stories to brighten the faces of the circle in which he happened to be placed. His public character was alike noble and independent. His speeches and his writings were never influenced by party prejudices or sectional interests. He was a warm advocate for the emancipation of the ryot and while he fought for his cause with discriminate zeal and surpassing ability he never allowed his understanding to be biassed against well mean-ing and considerate zemindars. His mind was so well-balanced that he could never be accused of undue partiality to any classes of interests. His editorship of the " Ben-galee " has been one of uniform manliness and independence. Though prevented by illness and the pressure of official duties from writing much of late, he never allowed a moment of leisure or comfort to pass without inditing something new or original : his chief merit was that he could give to the happiest of thoughts the happiest of words. His style was singularly classic and chaste—such as has never been eqalled by that of any other Bengalee gentleman. To fluency of pen he added the uncom-mon qualification of fluency of speech. He was a ready speaker and never in his life delivered a set speech. An article in the " Calcutta Review " evidently from the pen of Colonel Malleson, thus bears testimony to his wonderful ability in this respect :—" The lecturer, Baboo Grish Chunder Ghosh, the Editor of one of the best native papers in this part of India, is well known as a speaker for the brilliancy and fertility of his ideas which he gives utterance to with a fluency which many English speakers might well covet."

But the " Bengalee " did not monopolize his pen. His contributions to the " Bengal Recorder," a weekly paper started by one of his elder brothers who now holds a high position in the Government service and who is also well known for his literary ability, were innumerable and much applauded. The then Editor of the " Friend of India," Mr. Marshman, never lost an opportunity of commending the style and spirit of these writings. Circumstances however over which the brothers had no control obliged them to abandon for a time their literary undertaking, but again the ardent spirit broke forth, and Baboo Grish Chunder on his own account started a new paper and christened it the " Hindoo Patriot." For a series of years he conducted it in a most able and independent manner, when the late Baboo Hurrish Chunder Mookerjea came to his aid as a Lieutenant. The genius and energy of Hurrish soon proved him to be a worthy compeer when Baboo Grish Chunder con-ferred on him the Captainship of his own accord, contenting himself with occasional displays of wit and strength of mind which could not be mistaken. During the time of the mutiny when men of the blood and scalp school were denouncing wholesale vengeance upon " pandies," and " niggers," Baboo Grish Chunder was invited to contribute to a periodical started under the auspices of a few patriotic Hindu gentle-men under the name of the " Calcutta Monthly Review." His articles on race antagonism were most telling, and such was the indignation of the English Press upon him that a member of it seriously proposed to give him a sound thrashing, perhaps in ignorance of the fact that the man was full six feet high with a proportionate breadth of stature and firmness of limbs. But that breadth of stature and that firmness of limb which might have resisted or baffled any human force, melted like wax before fire at the touch of the dart flung by the hand of the inexorable tyrant—Death. And as we think of his cruel act, our tears begin to flow and moisten the paper on which we write.

The pen equally refuses to record the details of this hurried end. On the night of Monday, the 13th September, he complained of feverishness and of an acute pain all over his body. The pain gradually increased but not to such an extent as to cause alarm in his family. On Friday morning he felt himself so well that his medical attendant advised him to take some light food. In the night however he had fever which the Doctor said the next day was nothing. On Saturday night he was delirious. Another Doctor was therefore sent for. This gentleman came early Sunday morning. In the evening he called again and said in answer to enquiring and anxious friends : " The case is very serious, the patient ought to be looked after very carefully. But there is hope yet." It was believed by all that Baboo Grish Chunder would recover as there was not any change in his countenance. But this hope was doomed to disappointment. On the following morning at 2½ A. M. he breathed his last in his garden-house at Bellore. This malancholy event has moved the whole native community, and called forth one sincere outburst of grief. The inhabitants of Bellore in a body attended the Ghat, and when his ashes were consigned to the river, they mournfully retraced their steps, lamenting that Bellore was again destined to be enveloped in the gloom from which Baboo Grish Chunder had by his indomitable energy extricated her.

A biography of Baboo Grish Chunder Ghose will be a fitting memorial of him and we trust the task will be taken in hand by some one of his numerous friends well acquainted with his life. For ourselves and for the present purpose, we can only give a brief summary.

He was born in Calcutta in his paternal abode at Simla in June 1829. He was the youngest son of the late Baboo Ramdhone Ghose, son of Cossinath Ghose, the friend and contemporary of the well-known Ramdoolal Dey whose life Baboo Grish Chunder himself had written in an excellent paper of about 80 pages. In his Childhood he was as quick and inoffensive as in his riper years. He was sent to school by his parents at the age of nine, and he completed his school career even at sixteen. The Oriental Seminary was his *alma mater*. When in the higher classes, he was a great favorite of the proprietor of the school Baboo Gourmohun Auddy and of the Head Master, Mr. Herman Geffroy, a teacher of great ability and classical learning. Mr. Geffroy liked him much for his English composition and would always give him subjects for practice in English poetry. Once he wrote some excellent verses the subject being given to him from a classical poet. We even now remember the first two lines of one of these pieces .

> "Once on a time in a rosy bower,
> "Young Cupid plucked a blooming flower."

For mathematics he had scarcely any taste and was therefore never at the head of his class. At the annual distribution of prizes which then came on with great eclat at the Town Hall, he either got the second or the third prize. After the close of his school career, he obtained a small berth in the Financial Department on Rs. 15 a month, but he soon displayed such aptitude for business that he was promoted to a place of Rs. 50. Through the interest of a friend by the name of Templeton he got a higher berth in the Military Auditor-General's Office and he there continued till the end of his life, having risen to the highest post (registrarship) which an Uncovenanted assistant, Native or European, could hope to attain. He and Hurrish Chunder Mookerjea were fellow workers and were appreciated in an equal degree by their Covenanted heads. On the death of Hurrish who was the senior of the two, Grish Chunder succeeded to his place and in time was placed at the head of the office. It is a matter worthy of note that these two noble sons of Bengal, who would have undoubtedly shone in any other sphere of business, should have been united in a common bondage and tied to the desk. The little leisure they could find from their official duties was devoted to literary pursuits. Baboo Grish Chunder was very fond of societies and clubs. He was the President of the Canning Institute, Howrah. What could not have men like Hurrish and Grish Chunder done had their time been their own. Their country yet owes much more to them than to any one else and should therefore find some fitting memorial for their commemoration.

The Indian Daily News: September 21, 1869,

We record this morning with regret the death of another native man of mark, one whose sympathies with, and earnest labours on behalf of, the masses of his countrymen, have been rarely equalled. We refer to Baboo Greesh Chunder Ghose, the able and honest editor of the *Bengalee*, who expired yesterday morning at about 3 o'clock, to the great grief of his friends. And in that term must be included more than his countrymen; for those of our own race, who knew the Baboo, also held him in high esteem. His public life was manly and straightforward, and the probity of his private life is said to have exceeded the sterling worth of his public character. Such men are rare, and we are not surprised to learn that he will be missed from amongst his friends. It is no secret that we held him to be at the head of his contemporaries in the Anglo-Bengalee press. Many of them were content to advocate sectional interests. He had wider sympathies and more noble aims, and we have often read his manly and trenchant articles with undisguised admiration. There was no pettishness or double-dealing in him: and with more men of his stamp, we should not despair of the future of India. It has not been difficult for some time past to trace in the *Bengalee* the master hand "conspicuous by its absence." There are many men left amongst his countrymen who are far more pretentious; but we fear there are not many more able or more conscientious than Greesh Chunder Ghose. He may well be deplored by his friends, for it will be long ere they find a successor to fill his place.

In Memoriam.

(*The Reflector.*)

Baboo Greesh Chunder Ghose, the able and distinguished editor of the *Bengalee* is dead; and with him has set the last sun in the horizon of Anglo-Bengallee journalism. Born of a family not less truly illustrious than any in Lower Bengal, and the youngest of a trio of brothers alike distinguished for all the best qualites of the head and the heart, Greesh Chunder received a thorough English education, such as seldom falls to the lot of most native youths, in the *Oriental Seminary*, in the palmiest days of that veteran educational institution, which is the grand fabric of single-handed energy and perseverence of Baboo Gour Mohun Auddy. Having left school, the Baboo entered the arena of public life, and commenced it at the lowest round of the ladder of *keeranee-dom*,—the *neplus ultra* of the end and aim of the educated natives of this country. Day by day, by sheer dint of sterling ability, energy and application, he rose alike in his own position and in the esteem and affection of his superiors, until on the transfer of Mr. R. H. Hollingberry into the Financial Department, he became the Registrar of the office of the Controller-General of Military Accounts, then known as the Military Auditor-General's Office. While honorably discharging his duties in this honorable post, death put a stop to his career, not only to the infinite sorrow of his numerous relatives and friends but also to the greatest possible regret of all who personally knew him or knew him not. Thus departed from among us a scholar and a gentleman, of whom we have attempted to give a sketch above. The suddenness of the news of his demise—which we must confess has come upon us with the force of a thunderbolt—has given such complete predominance to our *heart* over our *head*, that we regret we cannot do more justice to the lamented deceased. As an Anglo-Bengalee journalist, Baboo Greesh Chunder was decidedly the foremost man of his time. Such was his innate love of journalism and his mental activity, that while yet a student, he, assisted by a galaxy of brothers and cousins (who were also his school-mates) established, what may be called, a system of Manuscript News Papers in the *Seminary*. These contained essays and dissertations on literary subjects and other important subjects of the day, and written out by himself and his fellow students and circulated amongst his friends in his *Alma Mater*. Shortly after the close of his School career, he started the *Bengal Recorder*, which, after conducting it for upwards of two years, he was obliged to give up for reasons which do not interest the general reader. But an active life like his was not to remain idle for any length of time. He projected and brought into light the *Hindoo Patriot*, the able Anglo-Bengallee journal, which, say what its spiteful traducers will, is at once a power in the realm, and an honor to the educated Natives of Bengal. Having reared and nurtured his dear little bantling, with the tenderest paternal care and solicitude, during the first few years of its existence, he made it over to his excellent friend and *co-laborateur*, the illustrious Boboo Hurrish Chunder Mookerjee, whose career as a journalist is too well-known to need any elaborate tribute here. He then, in conjunction with a few friends, started the *Bengalee*, the editorial chair of which he filled until the pleasure of the Almighty called him away from his sublunary career.

Perhaps we would be playing *Hamlet* without the prince, if we omit to mention, that Baboo Greesh Chunder never was, nor cared to be, a stipendiary writer. His mind was too large for pound-shilling-pence journalism. He wrote for the good of his country and countrymen. He wrote in the conscientious discharge of, what he thought, a duty. How far he succeeded in this let our readers judge for themselves. We gladly extract the following from the columns of our contemporary the *Indian Daily News*, and need hardly say, that we endorse every word of this honorable tribute to the memory of one, of whom it may emphatically be said, that " take him for all in all, and you shall not look upon his like again."

" We record this morning with regret..
....to fill his place."

The Hindoo Patriot, dated 27th Sept. 1869.

The late Baboo Grish Chunder Ghose.

There is a blight upon Bengal. Its best men are falling under the fell Scythe of Death like so many blades of grass. Beginning with Rajah Issur Chunder Sing we have within the last eight years lost such foremost men, each a host in himself, as Baboo Hurrish Chunder Mookerjea, Baboo Romapersad Roy, Rajah Pertap Chunder Sing, Rajah Sir Radhakant Bahadur, the Hon'ble Sumbhoo Nauth Pandit, Baboo Ram Gopal Ghose, the Hon'ble Prossunno Coomer Tagore, Baboo Huru Chunder Ghose, Rajah Sutt Shurn Ghosal, and lastly Baboo Grish Chunder Ghose. Whether in intellectual attainments, legal knowledge, judicial talents, practical ability, social influence, public spirit, princely munificence or devoted patriotism, the great departed we have named above were each in his own way equally conspicuous, and it is sad to contemplate how few there are among the rising generation fit to take their place. Happily there are still a few left of the glorious band, who have made Bengal what it is now, and may Heaven bless them with long life! But it behoves the rising generation to remember that the destinies of their country are in their hands, that if they fail to follow up the work which their grand-fathers and fathers have begun, not only will it be their lasting shame, but the good that has already been effected will be lost. The times are now most favourable for the cause of progress, and may our countrymen prove equal to it.

The native gentleman, whose premature death has cast a gloom over a large circle of friends and admirers, was one of the early fathers of the Indo-English Press. Coming from a family, which has been noted for commercial success in the past and love of literature in the present, Baboo Grish Chunder Ghosh was one of the fairest specimens of old system of English education in this country. Singularly enough some of the best native writers in English in Bengal were little indebted to the Government Colleges for instruction. Like his friend and colleague, the lamented Hurrish Chunder Mookerjea, the foundation of Grish Chunder's education was laid in a private seminary under native management. It was the privilege of the spirited proprietor of the Oriental Seminary, the late Baboo Gour Mohun Auddy to send forth to the world almost at the same time a bevy of young men, whose minds had been cultured under his own fostering care and the intelligent and scholarly direction of George Jeoffroy. One of the little band annotated the essays of Bacon, another after earning an unsullied name in the Sudder Bar was honored, for the first time in the history of English rule in India, with a seat on the bench of the High Court, the third is now one of the most distinguished uncovenanted native officers in the service of Government, the fourth carried away the Auckland Prize, which was open to the pupils of both the Hindu College and the Oriental Seminary, and the last though not the least, the subject of this notice, was an early and distinguished laborer in the Native Press. The last three were brothers and formed a sort of literary triumvirate for the advancement of indigenous thought and literature. In the palmy days of the *Hindu Intelligencer*, which was edited by Baboo Kasipersad Ghose once a votary of the Muses, now an indefatigable trier of conservancy cases, they started the *Bengal Recorder*, and conducted it with considerable success, in which the late Hurrish

Chunder, whose literary talents were then just budding forth, was assigned the humble place of "correspondent." About the time the well known charter campaign was meditated by the leaders of native society, an enterprising native gentleman of the banker caste Babu Madhusudun Roy conceived the idea of starting the *Hindoo Patriot*. He was acquainted with the Ghose brothers and invited them to undertake its editorial management. They readily consented, but they or rather Grish Chunder recommended him to Babu Hurrish Chunder Mookerjea. We have the authority of this gentleman for stating that it was Hurrish Chunder who gave to the paper the name "*Hindoo Patriot*" so dear to us, and was elected its first responsible editor. It is superfluous for us to say that the hard intellectuality, rare power of reasoning, and a thorough knowledge of local politics, which Hurrish Chunder possessed pre-eminently qualified him for the chief-ship of the only native political organ of the day, and Grish Chunder who watched with interest and admiration the rapid development of his friend's intellect cheerfully served under him. Grish Chunder's *forte* lay in descriptive and sensational writing, brilliant, dashing, witty and sometimes humorous, falling on his victims like sledge-hammer, or to be more precise with the force of 84—pounder. During the Mutinies he chiefly wrote for this paper those scathing and crushing articles against the Volunteers, which provoked the vengeance of these mighty sons of Mars upon the devoted head of the editor. Grish Chunder was never strong in practical politics, but in his own line he was unrivalled. His power of word-painting, of clothing the commonest ideas in gorgeous and glittering costume, radiant with flashes of wit and humor, and occasionally of originality, was equally conspicuous in the pages of the *Calcutta Monthly Review* and the *Bengalee*, of which he was the founder and editor. Latterly he took to public speaking, and the same qualities which distinguished his writings also distinguished his speeches. As a speaker he first attracted notice in the Hall of the Dalhousie Institute, when it resounded with the eloquence of Dr. Duff and Sir Mordaunt Wells. He was also a public lecturer, and his lecture on the Life of Ramdoolal Dey, though overcolored on many points, is a most favorable specimen of his style and spirit. Grish Chunder latterly removed from Calcutta and located himself in Bellore, where by his genial manners and frank and affable disposition he soon became a general favorite. He founded the Bellore School, which he nursed with a truly fatherly care, and the students were so much attached to him that when they heard of his death they wept for him as if they had lost a common father. He was also a member of the Howrah Municipal Committee, and though he could not like his contemporaries elsewhere stem the tide of Municipal recklessness and extravagance he never failed to do his own duty. He began life as a clerk on Rs. 15 a month and rose to the highest place open to an uncovenanted assistant in the office ; but in the whole course of his service, though placed over many, he never gave offence to a single individual. Indeed as a man and member of society he never came in contact with a brother man to whom he did not at once endear himself. His fault, if we may so call it, was of an opposite character, he was too good, too soft, too obliging for this rough and hard world, and as a journalist he had sometimes to suffer for it, for it did happen now and then that what he said to-day for the sake of a friend he unsaid the next day for the sake of another, but whatever he said or did came from the over-flowing goodness of his heart. Frank, generous, bold, and truly patriotic he was equally admired in private and in public. Possessed of a fine and sturdy make, or as a friend beautifully expresses it, of Affghan proportions and strength, and singularly free from Young Bengal vices, we never for a moment dreamt that he would pass away in the very prime of life—he was only 40 years old. May his ashes rest in peace!

The Indian Mirror, dated 24th September 1869.

With deep and unfeigned regret we have to record the death of Babu Greesh Chunder Ghose, the able and accomplished Editor of the *Bengalee.* Suffering from ill-health for about the last twelve-month, brought about probably by intense mental application, he had a recent attack of typhoid fever, and while, the best hopes of his recovery began to be entertained, suddenly suffered a relapse; and late on last Sunday night, he expired in his favourite residence at Bellore. The deceased gentle. man was one of the few Bengalees whom natives and Europeans feel equally desirous to honour. Educated in the Oriental Seminary, in early age he gave great indications of ability. He was the friend and efficient *co-laborateur* of the late Hurrish Chunder, the apostle of enlightened patriotism in India. Like Hurrish, his best opportunities were devoted to the elevation and welfare of his countrymen, to the exposure of injustice and oppression, to the spread of such principles as he honestly believed, were good and great. Like Hurrish Chunder, he had a great command over the English language, ready on all occasions with his pen and speech; bold, undaunted, hardworking and energetic. Like Hurrish, he rose from small beginnings to a distinguished position, like him died at the exceedingly early age of 37, though unlike his illustrious friend, he led a pure and temperate private life. The drudgery of a Government Office could not repress his spirit, nor did his duties to a large family prevent him from doing what he owed to his country. He it was who first started the *Hindoo Patriot*; he frequently contributed to the *Calcutta Review* and was connected with almost every English Newspaper started in Bengal by our countrymen. Though often differing in views and principles we always held him in high esteem, and now that he has departed from us for ever, and gone home to a better world, we convey through these lines our feeble and melancholy testimony to his great worth. He worked well and has died honorably. May Heaven grant peace to his soul, and blessing to his disconsolate family and children!

The National Paper, dated 22nd September 1869.

The " Bengalee " has sustained a severe loss in the death of its able and talented Editor, Babu Grish Chunder Ghose, which sad event took place on the morning of the 20th instant at 3 A.M. at his place in Bellore. We need scarcely say that all who knew him and came in contact with him, will deeply mourn his untimely demise. Bold and public-spirited from his early age, there was scarcely an Indo-English Journal established before the dark days of the Mutiny in which he had not a chief hand. He was a regular contributor to the *Hindoo Intelligencer,* then edited by Babu Kashi Persaud Ghose. He was the Joint-Editor with his brother Babu Sree Nauth Ghose, of the *Bengal Recorder,* another weekly paper, established only a few years before the *Hindoo*

Patriot was ushered into existence. The *Hindoo Patriot* was first brought into the field by him. He was a regular contributor to that paper in the time of Babu Hurrish Chunder Mookerjea. After the death of Hurrish the paper was again held up by him, jointly with another gentleman who is now in the staff of the *Patriot*. For some reason or other, he broke off his connection with this paper, and sought to make the *Bengalee* its successful rival. He watched with eager anxiety its interest to his last days. In him we have lost a veteran Indo-English journalist, and an ardent sympathiser with all national movements. It may be said here, that he was one of the few supporters of the National Gathering when the project was first conceived. He observed with great delight its subsequent progress, and always used to observe to us, that in time the movement will be a source of great Power to the people. He was usually very frank and gave praise where praise was due, and censure where it richly deserved. He could never close his sympathy with party interests, and we may justly say of him, that the like of him we shall rarely see again.

সোমপ্রকাশ। ১২ আখিন সোমবার।

কি দুঃখের বিষয়? বঙ্গভূমি দারুণ শোকের আর একটী আঘাত প্রাপ্ত হইলেন। বাঙ্গালী সংবাদ পত্রের সম্পাদক বাবু গিরিশ চন্দ্র ঘোষ দেহত্যাগ করিয়াছেন। তিনি বহুগুণের আধার ছিলেন। তাঁহার তুল্য সাধু সদাশয় লোক সচরাচর জন্মগ্রহণ করেন না। ইংরাজী ভাষায় তাঁহার বিলক্ষণ বিদ্যা ছিল। তাঁহার মত সুলেখক পাওয়া ভার। তাঁহার লেখার একটী বিশেষ গুণ এই ছিল, তিনি কোন পক্ষে পক্ষপাতী হইয়া স্বমত ব্যক্ত করিতেন না। তিনি যে সমাজে জন্মগ্রহণ করিয়াছিলেন, তাহার বিদ্বেষী হইয়া কখন কৃতঘ্নতার পরিচয় প্রদান করেন নাই। যাহাতে সমাজের সর্ব্বাঙ্গীন উন্নতিলাভ হয়, তাঁহার সে অকপট চেষ্টা ছিল। অতএব এরূপ লোকের বিয়োগ যে হিন্দুসমাজের হিতাকাঙ্ক্ষী ব্যক্তিদিগের হৃদয় শল্য হইবে তাহার সন্দেহ নাই।

এড়ুকেশন গেজেট। ৯ই আখিন ১২৭৬, ইং ২৪শে সেপ্টেম্বর ১৮৬৯।

"আমরা অতিশয় দুঃখিত চিত্তে প্রকাশ করিতেছি যে, "বেঙ্গলি" নামক ইংরাজী সাপ্তাহিক সংবাদ পত্রের সম্পাদক বাবু গিরিশ চন্দ্র ঘোষ জ্বরবিকার রোগে গতাসু হইয়াছেন। গিরিশ বাবু ইংরাজিতে কৃতবিদ্য, সুলেখক এবং বাগ্মী ছিলেন। তাঁহার স্বভাবও অতিশয় ঋজু ও অমায়িক ছিল। গিরিশ বাবুর নির্ম্মল চরিত্রে কোন কলঙ্ক ছিলনা। এ দেশে ইংরাজী লেখা পড়ার প্রাদুর্ভাব হওয়াতে যেরূপ ফল সমস্ত প্রসূত হইতেছে, তন্মধ্যে গিরিশ বাবু এরূপ ছিলেন যে, তাঁহাকে হিন্দু এবং ইংরাজ উভয়েই আত্মগৌরবের স্থল স্বরূপে নির্দ্দেশন করিতে পারিতেন। অল্প বয়সে ইঁহার মৃত্যু বঙ্গভূমির দুর্ভাগ্য—আমাদিগের মাতৃভূমি একটী প্রকৃত রত্ন-হারা হইলেন।"

The Bengalee, Friday October 1, 1869.

We take the following from the *Dacca News*.

" It is with much pain we record the death of the late editor of the *Bengalee* —Babu Greesh Chunder Ghose. By far the foremost of his Anglo-Bengalee contemporaries, the Babu united in a happy medium the manliness of an honest journalist with the complacency of a mild Hindoo. We have for some time past missed his telling articles in the paper which he raised by his talent to be the leading Native journal of the Metropolis."

The Hindu Reformer.

With deep regret do we record the death of Baboo Greesh Chunder Ghose the able editor of the *Bengalee*, who expired this life at 3 o'clock on the morning of, the 20th September last. The following notice of his death from the " Indian Daily News " will show in what esteem he was held by both the native and European community on that side of India; ane though his name may not be so conspicuously known here (Bombay) as those of some of his countrymen of Bramho-Somaj note, his death cannot but be felt as a national loss.

The Bengalee, Saturday 22nd October 1869.

We have much pleasure in giving prominent insertion of the following from Colonel Malleson, Guardian of His Highness the Maharaja of Mysore regarding the late Babu Grish Chunder Ghose:

To the Editor of the Bengalee.

Sir,—I have read with deepest concern your account of the last days of my valued friend, Babu Grish Chunder Ghose. My official connection with the deceased commenced early in 1856, and from that time till 1863 I enjoyed constant, indeed almost daily, opportunities of noticing the valuable qualities by which he was characterised. I never knew a more upright man, one possessing to a higher degree the qualities of manliness, independence, and love of virtue. He possessed, too, great abilities, and a resolution proof against all difficulties. It may not be generally known that unaided save by a grammar and a dictionary, he had mastered all the intricacies of the French language; and although, from the want of opportunity of conversation, he could not speak, nor even pronounce it, there was not a book in that language which he was unable to read.

It was a pleasure to me for many years of my official life to be associated with such a man; and afterwards, when I was transferred to other duties, to keep up the acquaintance with him. Beyond the sphere of his own relations there are none, I am sure, who regret his loss more than I do. Among his countrymen his name, I trust, will still live; and I earnestly hope to hear that some testimonial will be raised to mark the career of one, of whom they have the highest reason to be proud. I shall be glad to aid such a movement by a donation of Rs. 100.

<table>
<tr><td>Mysore,
6th October 1869.</td><td>}</td><td>I remain, Sir,
Yours obediently,
G. B. Malleson.</td></tr>
</table>

The Bengalee, October 30, 1869.

We have much pleasure in publishing the following from Major Osborn :—

To the Editor of the Bengalee.

Sir,—From the tenor of Lieutenant-Colonel Malleson's letter in your issue of of the 23rd instant, I infer that there is some plan afoot to raise a subscription, either with a view to provide for the family of the late Babu Grish Chunder Ghose, or of erecting some tribute to his memory. As one who admired the abilities, and respected the fine and independent character of the late Babu, I beg to be permitted to contribute fifty rupees to further either of the above objects.

<table>
<tr><td>Calcutta,
25th October 1869.</td><td>}</td><td>Yours faithfully,
Edward Osborn.</td></tr>
</table>

Supplement to The Bengalee.

Calcutta, Saturday, November 27, 1869.

The Public Meeting in Honor of the late Grish Chunder Ghose.

Agreeably to the announcement in the papers, a crowded and respectably attended meeting in honor of the late Baboo Grish Chunder Ghose came off at the Town Hall on the afternoon of Tuesday, the 16th November 1869. Among others we observed the following gentlemen :—Raja Kali Krishna Bahadoor, Raja Narendra Krishna Bahadoor, Hon'ble Dwarka Nath Mitter, Revd. J. Long, Revd. C. H. A. Dall, Dr. Salzer, H. Beverley Esq. James Wilson Esq. J. B. Roberts Esq. S. Lobb Esq. M.A., P. Creagh Esq., James Mackenzie Esq., J. Remfrey Esq., R. Wilson Esq., C. T. Davis Esq , Maulvi Abdool Luteef Khan Bahadoor, Kumar Harendra Krishna Bahadoor, Dr. Juggobundo Bose, Baboos Digumber Mitter, Peary Chand Mittra, Doorga Churn Law, Sham Chund Mitter, Hurray Kristo Addy, Roma Nath Laha, Keeshub Chunder Sen, Issur Chunder Ghosal, Mooraleydhur Sen, Debendro Chunder Dutt, Brindabun Bose, Kristo Das Pal, Pran Kissen Mookerjee, Cally Prosono Dutt, Hem Chunder Banerjee, Rajendra Lal Mitter, Kunjo Lal Banerjee, Kannye Lal Dey, Rajendro Dutt, Anundo Nundon Tagore, Calley Churn Ghose, Koylas Chunder Bose, Doorga Prosad Mookerjee, Rajendra Missry, Joy Kristo Gangooly, Amarendra Nath Chatterjee, Bhyrab Chunder Banerjee, Kissory Chand Mitter, Kamhika Nath Chatterjee, &c. &c.&c.

Rajah Kali Krishna Bahadoor was called to the chair, and he spoke as follows.

" Gentlemen,—We are assembled here this day to testify our deep sense of orrow for the untimely death of our friend, Baboo Grish Chunder Ghose, Editor of *The Bengalee.* The deceased belonged to a respectable family, and I knew him to be a man of exemplary moral character and of great intelligence. By means of the press, with which he had been connected for many years together, Baboo Grish Chunder advocated the cause of our country with great ability and independence, and there was scarcely a good undertaking in which he did not take an active part. The memory of such a man deserves to be preserved. I leave it to my countrymen to lay before the meeting, more in detail, the claims of the deceased to a suitable public recognition of his valuable services to the country, and of his many private virtues. I have been requested to take the chair on this melancholy occasion, and though I consider myself undeserving of the compliment so kindly paid to me, I am constrained to respond to the wish of the meeting. With the few remarks I have made regarding our late lamented friend, I beg to open the business of the day. The notice under which this meeting has been convened runs thus :—

" The friends and admirers of the late Baboo Grish Chunder Ghose having expressed a desire to meet in public with a view to join their regret with that of the country at large for the loss which has been sustained by his sudden and untimely death, and also to consider and agree upon a suitable memorial to mark the public recognition of his many virtues, a general meeting, in furtherance of the object, will be held at the Town Hall, on Tuesday, the 16th November 1869, precisely at 4 P.M. Raja Kali Krishna Bahadoor &c. &c.

Letters of apology from the Hon'ble Mr. Justice Phear, Baron Dowleans, and several other gentlemen regretting their inability to attend the meeting were here read.

The following is Mr. Justice Phear's letter :—

To Babu Koylas Chunder Bose.

My dear Sir,—I am obliged to you for your note, which only reached me last evening, and I regret that I am unable to attend the public meeting at the Town Hall to which you invite me.

I do not feel sure that there has not been manifest among us lately a disposition to render public testimonials too common : but I have certainly known no one whose services more thoroughly deserved recognition at the hands of his countrymen than do those of the late Baboo Grish Chunder Ghose. He was an able, conscientious worker in the cause of social reform –independent in spirit and earnest of purpose. Bengal has too few citizens of this sort and can ill spare one in the prime of life.

Yours very truly,

J. B. Phear.

The following letter from the Secretary to the Ooterparah *Hitakari Sabha* was also read :—

To the Secratary to the Committee formed for the purpose of convening a meeting to commemorate the death of Baboo Grish Chunder Ghose.

Sir,—I am desired by the Business Committee of the Ooterparah *Hitakari Sabha* to forward to you the accompanying resolutions passed at the monthly meeting of the said Sabha held on the 14th current with reference to the late Baboo Grish Chunder Ghose, and to request that with the permission of the General Committee you will have the goodness to read the Resolutions at the meeting to be held at the Town Hall on the 16th idem and to inform the assembly that it is the sincere desire of the Sabha as expressed in one of the accompanying Resolutions to act conjointly with the General Committee of Calcutta in furthering and promoting the object of the intended meeting.

I remain,
Your most obedient Servant,

Ooterparah,　　　⎫
The 14th Nov. 1869.　⎬
　　　　　　　　　⎭

Peary Mohun Banerjee.
Honorary Secretary.

Resolutions.

1. That the Hitakari Sabha at Ooterparah expresses its deepest regret for the untimely death of its late Vice-President, Baboo Grish Chunder Ghose and entertains a high sense of the most lively interest always evinced by him in the welfare of the Society.

2. That the Sabha undertakes to act in conjunction with the General Committee for the purpose of raising funds in this part of the country in aid of any kind of memorial which the said General Committee would agree upon in commemoration of the death of Baboo Grish Chunder Ghose and in recognition of the manifold services done by him to this country at large.

Peary Mohun Banerjee,

The 14th November. 1869.　　　　　　　　　　　　*Honorary Secretary.*

Rajah Narendra Krishna Bahadoor then moved the 1st Resolution :—

" That this meeting desires to record its deep sorrow and regret at the death, in the very prime of life, of Baboo Grish Chunder Ghosh, who by his highly independent, manly and virtuous character, by his kind, affable and guileless disposition towards all classes of people with whom he happened to come in contact, by his patriotic exertions for the benefit of his country, and by his natural gifts and ability which were displayed to the highest advantage in all his writings and speeches, won the love and admiration of all community to which he belonged."

The Rajah Said :—" Gentlemen,—

" In rising to move the Resolution I have been requested to submit to the meeting, I would only say a few words. A few words only because with all that I can say, I fear I shall not be able to do justice to the subject before us. The sad and melancholy event—the untimely death of Baboo Grish Chunder Ghose, which has brought us here is a source of the deepest regret and heart-rending sorrow, but we are cheered with the thought that we meet to do honour to departed worth. With talents of a high order, he had a patriotic soul and a generous heart and a high moral character. I could say much in illustration of these qualities, but I would leave it to speakers better able to describe him. He was a good and virtuous man and he devoted all his energies to the good of his country. In him we saw the true picture drawn by the poet that

"An honest man is the noblest work of God."

Babu Koylas Chunder Bose in rising to second the Resolution addressed the meeting as follows :—

"Rajah Kali Krishna and Gentlemen,

I am afraid I shall hardly be able to take a part in the proceedings of this meeting in a manner at all becoming the importance of the subject we are here met to consider; first, because the lamented deceased whose virtues we desire to commemorate was a dear and a loving friend—our friendship having commenced in years of child-hood and having never known until death a break or separation. You will therefore readily excuse my feelings when I say that this meeting, instead of affording me consolation at this public recognition of his many eminent virtues, really heightens my grief by making me the more painfully alive to the reality of the sad event of which for the peace of my mind, I would seek to remain in blissful oblivion. But it is impossible now to attain that state of mind in the midst of this strong demonstration of sympathy and sorrow for one who was the glory of his friends and the honor of his country. The cruel fact stares me in the face and chokes up the words in my mouth as they struggle for utterance. But yet I have a duty to discharge, and how-ever feebly and imperfectly I may be able to do it, I shall claim your indulgence for a few minutes. This meeting, Sir, graced as it is by representatives from every class of the community, from titled dignitaries to the humblest clerks in a public office, has a significance which it is impossible to overlook. It indicates in a most unmis-takable manner that Hindu Society, instead of being convulsed and torn as it used to be in days gone by, by sectional prejudices, party feelings, caste pride, pride of wealth and birth, is leavened into a common brotherhood animated by the kindliest and best of feelings for every individual member of the community. Aristocratic feelings, I am glad to observe, are at so heavy a discount. It is one of the most pleasing and hopeful signs of the age. It is undoubtedly the work of that great leveller of human distinctions and vanities—Education—which brings on a common level the wealthiest and the poorest of the land. This meeting, therefore, I repeat has a significance indicating true social and moral progress in the land. We can estimate the extent of that progress almost numerically by counting the number of Rajahs, zemindars and millionaires who have joined this demonstration to honor the memory of a private individual who was neither favored by wealth nor rank and yet has left a lasting impress of his goodness upon their minds. By honoring him they have honored themselves.

The Resolution which was moved by the Hon'ble Rajah who has preceded me, and which I am desired to second, clearly sets forth the salient points in my departed friend's character. It says, that to a highly independent, manly and virtuous character, he joind a kind, affable and guileless disposition, with natural gifts and ability which were displayed to the highest advantage in all his writings and speeches. But there is one word in the Resolution which above all others gives a just and correct estimate of Baboo Grish Chunder Ghose's character. Who that has known Baboo Grish Chunder even for a day will not bear his willing testimony that he was a "guileless" man? Such a man is rarely to be met with in these days of external polish and outward refinement of manners. Baboo Grish Chunder always carried his heart upon his sleeve, and never said a word or did a thing which that heart did not approve of, or of which he had reason to be sorry. He had many earthly trials, had many domestic misfortunes, had been impoverished by the expenses of lawsuits which were forced upon him, and yet his conduct throughout was straight-forward and honest. His moral character in all respects was exemplary. He was a god-fearing man and as such took the greatest delight in promoting works of charity. Though a poor man himself, he shared the little that he earned with those whom he found in need or in distress. It is a fact perhaps not well known that many a widow and orphan in Bellore was supported by him. It was through his exertions, and by a liberal contribution from his own purse, that the family dwelling-house of his friend and co-adjutor, the late Hurrish Chunder Mookerjea, was saved from the auctioneer's hammer. He was and will for ever be remembered as the friend of the poor. When the last cyclone had left its devastating effects upon Bellore and the adjacent villages, he would regularly every morning walk miles through the country, distributing relief with his own hands from funds as well his own as those placed at his disposal by the Relief Committee.

But the most prominent trait in his character was his blandness and affability towards all with whom he happened to come in contact. He in his life was never known to have given anybody offence. He was incapable of it. On the contrary he had the rare quality of making friends of acquaintances and acquaintances of strangers. He a had smile and a nod for every one that came across his path. But his warmest sympathies were with the poor and the helpless; and the ryot's cause lay next to his heart. He has been somewhat mis-understood in the matter of his advocacy of the interest of the ryot. It has been somewhere imagined though without rhyme or reason that he was inimical to the Zemindars as a body and that he considered the Permanent Settlement a great blot in the administration of the country. Nothing could have been a graver mistake than that. He decried the Permanent Settlement as a compact existing only between the Government and the landlord. A really permanent settlement, he said, would be that which would secure to the ryot a perpetuity of interest in the land he occupied. The power of harassing him, of continually enhancing his rent and even of driving him out of home is the great lever of oppression which the law has placed in the hands of the landlord, and which many uneducated, selfish and unscrupulous landlords are ever ready to use. But the cases of such landlords in these days of the moral and material advaucement of the country are rather the exception than the rule, and while Baboo Grish Chunder exposed these few in his slashing articles without pity or remorse, he at the same time held up to the admiration of his countrymen the picture of those model Zemindars who are the honor of the land, who look upon the ryot as a member of their own family and watch his interest with paternal solicitude. Baboo Grish Chunder Ghose was himself the model of a man. His intellectual gifts and moral susceptibility were so nicely balanced, that he had neither the eccentricity of a genius nor the whine and cant of a bigot. Blessed with a fervid imagination which was tempered by a sound understanding, he was able to wield his pen with the hand of a master. He wrote strongly, because he felt strongly; but there was no venom in what he wrote. He was incapable of harbouring ill feeling or malice against any body. He had indeed the slashing faculty in some abundance, but it was more acquired than natural. It was the result of a vast amount of reading of novels and current literature. His style had a grace, an elegance and a force by which one could at once distinguish it from that of any of his countrymen. Run your eyes over the columns of the *Hindu Patriot*, the *Recorder*, and the *Bengalee*, and the articles written by Grish Chunder would manifest themselves to you as if they were stamped with his own name. They are singularly idiomatic, and as such have not yet been rivalled by the writings of any of his countrymen. But his writings were valued chiefly because they were original. He was an original thinker, and his thoughts were always brilliant and happy. There are now many young men amongst us whom he himself educated in his style of writing and in his ways of thinking, and who now humbly tread in his footsteps in the hope of being able one day to rival their great master. He was in fact a gratuitous teacher to many who have benefited by his lessons. His last days however were chiefly devoted to the moral and material welfare of the little village of Bellore in which he had latterly taken up his residence. By the dint of his industry and perseverance he raised the Bellore school from the status of a patshalla to that of a first class institution, qualifying pupils for the Entrance Examination. The Bellore roads and communications which were only before village pathways were turned by him, in his capacity of Municipal Commissioner of Howrah, almost into bowling greens. The Howrah Institute, where men like Sir Richard Temple, Dr. Mouat and others have delivered some valuable and interesting addresses was founded and fostered by him; and in his death the Institute has lost a clever and efficient President.

Thus then, whether as a man of honor, principle and virtue, of warm and patriotic feelings, of unaffected simplicity and blandness of manners, of a heart overflowing with the milk of human kindness, of high moral courage, of sound understanding, clear thinking, fine writing and independent action, the country has sustained in his death a loss which it is not easy to repair. The great principle of his life was to serve his country for his country's good. It is a national misfortune that he should have been cut off so soon. It is too trying for me to proceed any further. It only seems to me too strange that the poet should have anticipated the words in which I should mourn the loss of my friend.

> Oh friend! for ever loved, for ever dear!
> What fruitless tears have bathed thy honour'd bier!
> What sighs re-echo'd to thy parting breath,
> While thou wast struggling in the pangs of death!
> Could tears retard the tyrant in his course;
> Could sighs avert his dart's relentless force;
> Could youth and virtue claim a short delay;
> Or beauty charm the spectre from his prey;

Thou still had'st lived, to bless my aching sight,
Thy comrade's honour, and thy friend's delight.
If yet thy gentle spirit hover nigh
The spot, where now thy mouldering ashes lie,
Here wilt thou read recorded on my heart,
A grief too deep to trust the sculptor's art.

S. Lobb Esq., M.A. Supported the Resolution.   He said :—

" Mr. Chairman and Gentlemen,

Had I not been specially requested to say a few words on the present occasion,
I should have preferred to remain a simple listener.   For I knew so well him in honour
of whom we are here assembled to-day, that silence might seem, on my part, to be the
best tribute of respect.

Greesh Chunder Ghose, as you are all aware, was a man of high intellectual
attainments and gifted with no common oratorical powers.   But he was something more
than a clever writer and a fluent speaker—for he was a good husband, a good father
and a good citizen.   If I were asked to describe the character of this worthy man, I
believe I could find no better words than those in which Tennyson addresses his lost
friend—words which the manly form and courteous demeanour of Greesh Chunder
Ghose often brought to my recollection during his lifetime, and which have more than
once occurred to me of late while reflecting upon his melancholy death—

High nature amorous of the good,
But touched with no ascetic gloom ;
And passion pure in snowy bloom
Thro' all the years of April blood ;
And manhood fused with female grace
In such a sort, the child would twine
A trustful hand unasked in thine,
And find his comfort in thy face.

I consider the example of such a man as highly valuable, in an age like the
present, to very many amongst us as well Europeans as Asiatics.   For he was one who,
though perplexed in faith, continued to remain pure in deeds ; who having given up
the *form* still retained the *substance*, not making religious emancipation a stepping-
stone to profligacy and vice.

In conclusion let me remind you that though our friend is no more, yet in a
certain sense, he is with us still—his memory being ever present to purify our thoughts
and ennoble our actions.

And is he dead, whose glorious mind
Lifts thine on high ?
To live in hearts we leave behind
Is not to die.

The Resolution was carried unanimously.

Moulvie Abdool Luteef Khan Bahadoor said ·—

Mr. Chairman and gentlemen,

It affords me real gratification in being able to move the second Resolution, and I do so with the greater pleasure that in fulfilling an obligation sacred to friendship, I discharge a duty which is imposed upon every man, who feels that his life and actions are fraught with lessons of good or evil to the generation that will take his place on earth after him :—Most fitting, do I think, it is, that the name and memory of Greesh Chunder Ghose should be preserved and placed with never fading interest before the minds of the educated youth of this country ; for Greesh from his boyhood upwards was a model for young people to be guided in their daily walk and conversation by it, and to be sustained in the midst of trials and difficulties by the genuine spirit of resignation and cheerfulness which diffused a charm throughout his company and conversation :—There is scarcely a man here who in some one instance or another is unable to furnish evidence of the enlightened and intelligent interest taken by him in the education of his countrymen, while the promptitude and earnestness with which he entered into every scheme, and to the best of his means and opportunities aided and advanced every project, calculated to lead to their intellectual and moral progress, point him out as one of the foremost of their benefactors :—Moreover his tendencies were truly catholic, and altogether devoid of the petty prejudices of caste or section, and there never was a time when a good thing was on foot for the benefit of any particular class or community, that it did not elicit a hearty word of encouragement from the noble-minded generous Greesh :—I am able personally to testify on behalf of the Mahomedan Community to the many and frequent occasion on which their welfare and advancement have received support and assistance from his able and fertile pen :—His needless for me to describe the qualities aud virtues of one, who while alive, was reckoned by almost every one here present, as a personal friend :—I therefore conclude by moving the second Resolution, viz.,

II. "That by way of memorial of the lamented deceased, a scholarship in his name be placed at the disposal of the Director of Public Instruction for the benefit of any Anglo or Anglo Vernacular school to which the memorial fund committee may recommend its grant, and that public subscriptions be invited in furtherance of this object."

Baboo Gopaul Chunder Dutt seconded the resolution with great pleasure. He said it scarcely requires any argument from him to enforce it. It carries with it its own force. It truly embodies the sense of the friends and admirers of the lamented deceased in fixing upon the most fitting memorial of the career of one whose name it is intended to preserve. It is well known that every available moment of leisure of the late Baboo Grish Chunder's time was devoted directly or indirectly to the cause of education. It would be very difficult for the speaker to specify all the acts of his dear friend in connection with education, as they were of a straggling character and spread over a vast surface. But he would point out one institution which will ever remain as a monument of glory to the memory of his friend. He alluded to the Bellore school which from an obscure village patshalla had risen to the position of one of the most

flourishing schools on the banks of the Hooghly. The speaker had the honor of visiting the school on several occasions examining the classes, and he must say that the
character and quality of the education it imparted reflected infinite credit to the ability,
industry and zeal of its chief promoter.

He fully endorsed the opinion that in honoring such a man they honored
themselves.

Mr. Wilson in supporting the Resolution said—He had not the pleasure of
intimate personal acquaintance with the late Baboo G. C. Ghose ; but he knew him
from his writings and had long admired him for the independence of his thoughts and
the liberality of his views. He was not a man devoted to sectional interests. His
sympathies were wide, embracing all classes of his countrymen, for he knew that the
good of the people in general was that of his country, the aim of a patriot being the
good of all. From what I know of him he was an example to the youth of his country ;
and if I were asked to point out a character that they would do well to follow, I should
not point out to them the millionaires of the country, though I neither undervalue
wealth nor the influence which legitimately belongs to it. I should not point out your
philosophers nor poets ; for excellent as poetry and philosophy may be, they are not
to be compared to that manliness of character which constitutes a nation, and of which
the late Grish Chunder was a conspicuous example. Not having had a personal
acquaintance with him, I am not in a position to speak as I could wish, but I always
read his papers with great interest, because of the earnestness of purpose and fervent
love of truth manifest in them. It seemed to me that the Baboo was an ardent lover
of the truth, with great faith in it, and where he was convinced of the truth he would
follow it regardless of where it might lead him. It was this which gave such independence to his writings. What he thought right he would express. But he did it with
a kindliness of manner which those who knew him affirm to have been so marked a
characteristic in all the relations of this life. Those who knew him best were most
ready to bear testimony to his worth, and they might apply to him the words of
Shakespeare in reference to Brutus :

> His life was gentle ; and the elements
> So mixed up in him, that nature might stand up,
> And say to all the world, ' There was a man.'

The Resolution was put to the vote and carried *nem. con.*

Babu Chunder Nath Bose, in moving the third Resolution, said that he was
not quite sure that he was not guilty of some degree of presumption in taking a
prominent part in the proceedings of the evening, when there were so many present
of more advanced age and maturer experience than himself. But the fact of the lamented deceased having been a friend of every body without distinction of age was fully
sufficient to justify his (the speakers') appearance on that occasion. He had not the
good fortune to enjoy the friendship of Baboo Grish Chunder for a long time, but, said
he, during the short time that he knew him as a friend he had been impressed with as
high an esteem for the noble character of the lamented deceased as any gentleman
present in the hall. The virtues of the deceased, both public and private, were so
many that he thought that if twenty such sets of speakers as had appeared that

evening were to recount them there would be no end of the narration. Baboo Koylas Chunder Bose had given the meeting something like a history of the career of Baboo Grish Chunder; but what he (C. N. Bose) desired to point out was *first*, that the career of Grish Chunder was the career of a *private* gentleman, and, *secondly*, that the acts which composed that career were to be praised not so much for their intrinsic merit as for the peculiarly silent and unostentatious manner in which they were done. He presumed that many who were present in the hall did not know that Grish Chunder was a great advocate of *female education*—that the widow, the unfortunate widow whom he had left behind to mourn his death to the end of her life, was an educated woman—that the poor girls whom his death had rendered fatherless were educated and accomplished girls. That Baboo Grish Chunder did not, like some mock reformers, make any noise as an advocate of female education, was no proof that he lacked moral courage. Baboo Grish Chunder was perhaps of opinion that the cause of female education in the present state of the native society was more likely to be served by dealing with the family in a private manner than with the nation in a public way. Besides he thought that Grish Chunder was not an enthusiast, but a calm and circumspect philanthropist. As a genuine Bengalee, Baboo Grish Chunder entertained great respect for the time-honored institutions and traditions of his native land, and it was just possible that much natural ardour of his mind might have been softened by a grateful regard for the feelings of those around him. He was too good a man to educate his daughter in a manner that would have displeased his father. He was too well assured of the cause of progress in Bengal to think of impelling it in a manner that would have produced great though temporary social disruption.

The assembly consisting as it did of representatives of all classes and communities appeared to him (the speaker) to be of great significance, and the value of that significance was enhanced beyond all calculation by the fact of its having met to do honor to the memory of a *private* individual—an individual whose only fault was that he was a little too afraid of publicity.

Baboo Chunder Nath Bose then moved the third Resolution which ran as follows :—

III. That a committee consisting of the gentlemen named below (with power to add to their member) be formed for the purpose of carrying out the above Resolution :—

Raja Kali Krishna Bahadoor.	Baboo Durga Churn Law.
„ Komul Krishna.	W. C. Bonnerjee Esq.
„ Narendra Krishna.	Baboo Hurray Kristo Addy.
„ Rajendra Narain Deb,	„ Obhoy Churn Goho.
Hon'ble Dwarka Nath Mitter.	„ Peary Mohun Banerjee.
Baboo Digumber Mitter.	„ Digumber Biswas.
„ Peary Chand Mitter.	„ Ram Chunder Mitter.
Moulvie Abdool Luteef Khan Bahadoor.	„ Rajendra Lala Mitter,
Kumar Harendra Krishna Bahadoor.	„ Keshub Chunder Sen.
S. Lobb Esq. M A.	„ Tara Prasad Chatterjee.
Major A E. Osborn.	„ Anund Nundun Tagore.

Revd. J Long.

J. B. Roberts Esq.

James Wilson Esq.

James Mackenzie Esq.

Baboo Bijoy Kissen Mookerjee.

Baboo Cally Churn Shome.

  „   Kristo Das Pal.

  „   Kannye Lall Dey.

  „   Sree Kissen Gangolly.

  „   Issur Chunder Nundy.

  „   Roma Nauth Laha.

Koylas Chunder Bose.
and Bacha Ram Chatterjee. } Members and Joint Secretaries.

Babu Issur Chunder Nundy in seconding the above Resolution said :—

The late Baboo Grish Chunder Ghose for whom we meet this evening was no ordinary man in our community. Virtues he had numerous, both private and public. He was a good citizen, a faithful friend and affectionate father. He unceasingly laboured to do good to his country and advocated its cause with a vigor and vehemence almost uncommon. He was distinguished by an independence of thought and speech that is rarely found among us, and that could hardly be expected even from him, situated as he was. The death of such a man is most assuredly a loss; and a loss of this nature is to be highly regretted.

The Resolution having been declared as passed. Baboo Grish Chunder Mitter proposed that the thanks of the meeting were due to Rajah Kali Krishna for his able conduct in the chair. The proposition was carried by acclamation.

———— :o: ————

The Bengalee, October 25, 1869.

At the meeting of the Canning Institute held in the hall of St. Thomas' School, Howrah, on the 29th Ultimo it was proposed by Mr. S. H. Robinson, seconded by Dr. R. N. Burgess, and carried :—" That this meeting desires to record their deep sense of the loss sustained by the death of their late Vice-President Baboo Grish Chunder Ghose, and their grateful remembrance of the many valuable services he has rendered to the Society."

The Rev. J. Long in support of the resolution observed that he knew the Baboo well, and the great point he admired in him was his breadth of view, his sympathy for all classes of his countrymen, and more especially the Ryot of Bengal. For him he felt strongly : he knew his debased social condition, and he used his journal, the "Bengalee," as a medium for bringing the subject to public notice. Any one that read that journal would remember those various pointed and spirit-stirring articles he wrote on the subject ; and he thought it would be only a just tribute to the memory of the deceased were they collected and brought out in the form of a pamphlet. There is unhappily in Bengal a wide gulf between the educated classes and the masses ; between the zemindar and ryot. Grish Chunder aimed at bridging that gulf, and while the zemindar enjoyed the benefits of the permanent settlement, he wished that permanent settlement should be made with the ryot also. His desire in fact was to elevate the ryot without levelling the zemindar.

His opinion on this point coincided with the real and permanent interest of the zemindars, whose rent would be more secure and better paid by a well-to-do and improving peasantry.

The cause of the nation would be also advanced ; no nation has ever become great with one class raised on the ruins of another. The history of Venice, of Poland, of Prussia and of Ireland shew this most clearly. England itself is a noble instance of the harmonious action of different classes that make up the nation. France is the opposite.

In England the great question of the day is to educate and elevate the masses and to give security of tenure to the agricultural classes.

He most fervently hoped that many might be raised up among the educated classes and landed proprietors in Bengal to follow this course. With united action on the point, how the face of Bengal might be altered and the *chasa lok*, now objects of contempt, might become

<blockquote>" A bold peasantry, their country's pride."</blockquote>

The President, G. E. Macgill, Esqr. C. S., joined in the expression of regret which had fallen from the members for the loss of the excellent and amiable Grish Chunder Ghose, and would have much pleasure in proposing to the Municipal Commissioners to perpetuate his memory in Bellore by naming after him the road near to which his favorite residence had been situated.

The Bengalee, Dec. 18, 1869.

The present session of the Bethune Society commenced on the 25th ultimo, when the Vice President, the Reverend K. M. Bannerjee, who occupied the chair paid the following tribute to the memory of the late Baboo Grish Chunder Ghose :—

" The third was a very melancholy subject. They had lost by death their very able Secretary to the Section on Literature and Philosophy, the late Baboo Grish Chunder Ghose. In him the Society had lost a very valuable member, who had rendered to it important services by his lectures and speeches, and who had always evinced a warm interest in its welfare. His death was no doubt universally regretted, as the public meeting held at the Town Hall did amply testify. He was a true patriot, because he was always the friend of the ryot. He fought for their cause with great ability and independence. and never succumbed to any kind of influence which might have been brought to bear upon him to deter him from his great object. Week after week, he brought forward their case before the public in some shape or other, in that ably conducted paper—*The Bengalee*. He would even reprove his friends when he found them lukewarm in their sympathy with the poor. He (the chairman) would therefore desire to record the deep regret of the society at the death of one of their most useful members, who was, at the same time, in his relations with public, an honest worker in the cause of the amelioration of the poor."

The proposition was carried by acclamation.

Appendix C.

—— · o · ——

Principal Lobb's Letters to Grish.

I.

Chinsura, June 5, 1867.

Dear Sir,

I enclose you stamps to the amount of 4 annas. Should business or plea
sure ever lead your steps this way I shall be happy to see you at the College. Thanks
for your very flattering Review of my Analysis. Do you follow the Index discussion
in the Friday Review! I certainly think Catholic has the best of it this week. One
point in the Friday Reviewer's argument strikes me as rather anomalous. He considers
Catholics *uncharitable* because they class Protestants with Turks, heretics and infidels :
the Reviewer apparently considers charity to consist in an alliance between Protestants
and Catholics against the objectionable Turks, heretics, and infidels. Between the
charity of " a Catholic " and that of " the Reviewer " there is but a minute difference.
The former dooms to religious loss Turks, heretics, infidels, and Protestants. The latter
would confine the penalty to Turks, heretics and infidels.

Now as Turks, heretics and infidels comprise far the larger portion of
mankind, and stand in need of religious benefits quite as much as the rest of their
fellow-creatures, it is difficult to discover any important difference between the two
kinds of charity above noticed.

I think you might make a few good articles for the Bengalee if you took
up the Turk view of the question in opposition to the Catholic aud Presbyterian views.
I expect Mr. Harrison is the Catholic, and if so the Rev. Lal Beharee Dey will find
rather a tough customer.

Would you like an article or two introducing to the readers of the Bengalee
Comte's Classification of the Sciences? In these days of social disintegration as
most of us have our pet theories and schemes Comtism is mine, and I regard the Philosophy of Comte as one day destined to supersede all others : it is aggressive certainly, but not intolerant—and I should much like to see your countrymen giving it a fair
consideration, not judging it by what they may read in Mill or Herbert Spencer or
others, but by what they may learn from their own perusal of Comte's very words. I
don't accept the system in its integrity, but even in outline it appears to me better than
any other theory which is now-a days propounded for men's acceptance. To Hindoos
I think its study would be most valuable, as it would enable them to apprecate correctly the grandeur of their past history, while teaching them that the future altho'
built upon the past must derive its stability from elements peculiar to itself. But I
am trangressing the limits of a letter. The subject is a vast one.

Your sincerely
S. Lobb.

II.

The College Chinsura, Aug. 28, 1867.

Dear Greesh Chunder,

My letter enclosing the cheque was dated August 18th and addressed to you as usual at the Military Pay Examiner's Office. I am obliged to you for stopping payment at Thacker's. I have written to them about it, and when I hear will order them to pay you Rs. 20 without any cheque at all. This will be safest.

I am not surprised at the charge of atheism you allude to. It is the stock accusation against Positivism and though not altogether a correct one has some show of reason. The fact is Comte regards all metaphysical problems as insoluble, and takes up a position of perfect neutrality towards them. He says we can neither affirm nor deny in these cases, but that there is a large arena of thought where we can affirm that this area is positive science, and that from the ensemble of the positive sciences we can constitute a positive philosophy. In accordance with his views he maintains that society in future must be founded on a purely human basis. Theological ideas afford no sure foundation for any social or political construction, they are but treacherous quicksands upon which we build only to find the beautiful fabric we have reared disappear. The Atheist says there is no God, asserts the enternity of matter, and thus pretends to give a solution of the problems which metaphysics attempts to solve. Comte says I neither affirm nor deny the existence of a God. I know nothing about the enternity or non-enternity of matter, but I can trace the laws of phenomena, and I can by the knowledge thus acquired obtain a power over the circumstances in which I find myself placed, which no metaphysical speculation could ever confer. All such speculation is simply barren, the fruit, if any, resembles the apples that grow by the shores of the Dead Sea, imposing to the view but when opened hollow and withered.

All the great Aryan races, the vanguard of humanity are now in the last crisis of the metaphysical stage. Comte says that by a law of nature they are passing into the positive stage, each must work out for itself the peculiar type which its final organisation may assume, but each may benefit by the experience and co-operation of the rest. We are all members of one great body, viz., Humanity. Comte has spoken out boldly and put his views into definite shape, but pretty nearly the same conclusion has been arrived at by Hegel and the Pantheistic school, except that with them it is confused by admixture with metaphysical speculations which do no manner of good.

Yours sincerely

S. Lobb.

I am busy just now bringing out a second edition of my Analysis, considerably enlarged. In my Preface I intend to attack the present system rather strongly. I wish to organise some lectures here in the cold season. Would you give us one?

If you really think there is any thing in Comte's argument I should like you to read the 2nd vol. of H. Martineau's Translation. It is not common in India but might be got at the Metcalfe I should think.

III.

Chinsurah, Sept. 8. 1867.

Dear Greesh Chunder,

I observe some spiteful remarks on you and me in the last number of the Friday Review. I don't intend to fall foul of the Friday Reviewer myself, and do not admire his personalities and consider that he has conducted the argument with a Catholic in the most unwarrantable and unseemly manner.

He calls upon me explicity to avow myself about the worship of Positivism, and puts his language in the most offensive form. Of course I should take no notice of such remarks, nor am I willing to be prominently brought forward in such discussions, as whatever my private opinions may be I never give the least expression to them in my teaching. An educated man is able to judge for himself on these matters —if any one asked my advice and opinion I should give it but should never dream of thrusting my conclusions upon a learner, nor of dragging them forward on any occasion unnecessarily.

In the prefaces to my Analysis I have strongly objected to the teaching of what is called philosophy in our colleges, for the simple reason that it trenches so much on subjects which a young man cannot decide and which should certainly not be introduced till he has taken the first degree. For men who have passed through a good preliminary training and who are battling with the stern problems of practical life it is most important that all the great questions which now agitate society should be thoroughly examined, but for young and untried men this task is a most'dangerous one. If you agree with me I think you could not do better than advocate the excision of philosophy from the curriculum of university studies, and the substitution for it of some more definite and less dangerous subject.

I send you a letter, which though in no way alluding to the Friday Review, is intended to answer an objection therein expressed. If you think it is too strong or dangerous or uncalled for don't insert it but I have tried to be guarded in my language and not to give offence to any body but the ideal metaphysician and as he is an abstraction I do not fear wounding his dignity. What a pity it is that these matters cannot be discussed temperately without indulging in useless personalities. After all I think you are better in this respect in India than we in England.

The Friday Reviewer I expect has founded his attack on me upon a short note which I inserted in the preface to my Analysis of the moral feelings.

Yours sincerely
S. Lobb.

IV.

September 15. 1867.

Dear Greesh Chunder,

I fancy that the notices of Positivism I sent you are now exhausted. The part hitherto touched upon is purely scientific and what has been given is a mere sketch. I think it requires elaboration. With a view to expand and explain I have written the accompanying notice, and will endeavour to supply you with more from time to time. I do not pretend to penetrate myself into all the depths of science, but you can depend on the accuracy of what I now send as it is a free version into English of the arguments of M. Littre a distinguished French Positivist, and a man eminent in science. He does not accept the whole of Comte's scheme and therefore according to the Friday is an intellectual abortion, but he accepts quite enough to invalidate the claims either of theology or metaphysics to preside over the future construction of society. All that is necessary is to perceive that theological ideas for any constructive purposes are worn out both in Asia and Europe, while metaphysical ideas were never anything more than simply destructive. Granting this there only remains one and that a human basis on which to construct society, and this basis has this inestimable advantage that each nation and family can build upon it according to its peculiar needs. Positivism does not proclaim all men hopelessly wrong, but sees the germs of good everywhere and believes that the good is destined to increase, tho' never finally to obliterate all traces of evil. The world would be but a kind of Cross Elysium if there were no struggle for existence.

Yours sincerely
S. Lobb.

Tell me if you like the articles to stop.

V.

Chinsurah Sept. 24. 1867.

Dear Greesh Chunder,

Many thanks for your kind letter. I am glad to know that Positivism is gaining some attention in India, as I feel certain the system is thoroughly well adapted to satisfy the intellectual needs of a very large class. Brahmoism is very well but unstable, and if I may coin a word unnational. What is required is a system which can be grafted upon Hinduism, which Hindus can make their own and which by espousing they will not be obliged to sacrifice and of their national customs or traditions —in a word a system which is *national*. I enclose a letter which you can insert, if you like, when you have room. Perhaps it had better be reserved till the material you now have is exhausted, it will serve to keep the subject before the minds of those who are interested in it for another week. I will take some books to Madras and while there work you out a few more notices. If I give Comte's own works it will of course take but little trouble, the labour is in moulding one's own thoughts so as to do justice to another man's ideas.

I will let you know more about the Lectures hereafter.

Yours sincerely
S. Lobb.

VI.

Chinsurah Sept. 29. 1867.

Dear Greesh Chunder,

I send you another contribution on Positivism and the last I shall be able to send before I return from Madras. While away I will do what I can in writing upon the subject, and will let you have the result of my labours after the holidays. You are I think quite right in the view you take of Positivism. it affords men who are emancipated from the old beliefs a resting place and does not demand that any violent innovation should be made in the belief of the people—the change will come about gradually, and in the meantime those who believe they have a firm footing can do their utmost to render it still more secure.

Thanks for your very flattering defence of me. I don't think the article in the Friday was written by Lal Behary—the paper seemed to me much better conducted while it was in his hands than it is at present.

Trusting that you will enjoy the approaching vacation.

I remain,

Yours sincerely

S. Lobb.

VII.

Chinsurah Oct. 22. 1867.

Dear Greesh Chunder,

Will you kindly insert in the Bengalee for 4 successive weeks, the following advertisement :—

NOW READY,

The second edition of the Analysis of Abercrombie on the Intellectual Powers, with notes and questions.

To be had of Messrs Thacker Spink and Co. Calcutta.

I hope you have received a copy of the Analysis, as I ordered one to be forwarded to you.

I am sorry that I have no more articles on Positivism ready at present. For some time to come I shall be very busy with the College examinations, so cannot promise to do much.

Has any definite decision been arrived at about the Radhakant memorial ?

I hope you received my letter about Krishna Kamal Bhattacharjee's explanation, written just before I left for False Point.

Your remarks on Brahmoism last week seemed to me very pertinent. The system is not a bad one in many respects, and those who sincerely accept it are to be honored : but it has no coherence, and the recent split is an evidence that it affords no solid basis for a permanent organisation. Logically it is compatible with as many different systems as there are different individuals, and practically it is useless as it defers the solution of the most important questions to a Future Life. I never could understand why a Brahmo should give up caste and other social distinctions. I should have thought these might have been easily grafted upon a system of Deism.

Yours sincerely

S. Lobb.

VIII.

Chinsurah Oct. 25. 1867.

Dear Greesh Chunder,

Many thanks for the " Friday Review." The writer is not quite so abusive as of yore, though his insinuation about endeavouring to hide the Atheism of Comte in a *not very honorable manner* is quite unfounded. In what I have written for your paper, no attempt has been made to conceal any thing. It was candidly admitted that there was a show of reason in confounding Atheism with Positivism. Positivism say the theologians is Atheism, the essence of the two is the same; well then to be, consistent the theologians should be prepared to assert that Positivism is Atheism, if not the two are not co-extensive and their essence cannot be the same.

Of course so far as the term Atheist has a disreputable signification, it is an unpleasant one to be applied to an individual, but as merely connoting certain speculative opinions I see no more objection to be called an Atheist than to be called a Presbyterian or Baptist.

If in spite of all explanations men will insist upon confounding Positivism and Atheism there is an end of it—they will not be persuaded and must be left to the calm enjoyment of their own theory on the subject.

As regards the approximation of Positivism to Fetichism, this is no matter of reproach, in as much as Comte entertains a very exalted veiw of the social and even intellectual value of Fetichism, and could be shown by numerous passages from his works.

Though we call one stage higher than another, this does not indicate that there is any kind of moral or intellectual degradation in the lower stages. We do not say that youth is a more degraded state than manhood, far from it in many respects it is a much nobler state, but taken all in all the state of manhood is an advance upon the state of youth. As with the individual so with the race.

The remarks made by the writer about its being necessary to pass through monotheism in order to reach Positivism are utterly at variance with Comte's sentiments, as your friend Professor Krishna Kamal can doubtless tell you. Would Krishna Kamal mind expanding the remarks I have here made and putting them into the form of a letter addressed to you, adding ofcourse his own observations?

Any notices on Positivism that may appear in the papers I shall feel much indebted to you, if you would forward to me. Has the Hindoo Patriot at all troubled upon the subject?

Yours sincerely
S. Lobb.

IX.

October 28. 1867.

Dear Greesh Chunder,

I send you another contribution on Positivism. I am afraid you will find it rather badly written. But I think that with care it may be decyphered.

Kindly send me 2 extra numbers of the Bengalee for Saturday October 26th.

So the Friday is extinct and Lal Behary's appointment cancelled. Is there a strong feeling against the appointment among Orthodox Hindoos? I should have thought with his great knowledge of English that Lal Behary would have made an excellent Head Master, while his religion would have been harmless, as an honorable man would not infringe the implied compact that existed between himself and the Government, and one who knows his countrymen so well as Lal Behari would know that any proselytism among his pupils would be not only mischievous but also useless.

As regards the employment of reverend gentlemen in the Educational Department, the question has two aspects. There is the ordinary view that all such gentlemen are soldiers of the cross ready to spread their tenets both by persuasion and by force. But there is another view. In *all* the churches there are men chafing under the intellectual thraldom imposed upon them, who would be glad to escape from their ungenial work and who if employed in the Educational Department might be thoroughly trusted. These men would bring a special aptitude to their work, and a love for it which is sadly wanting in some of the present occupants of our professorial chairs. The only objection which I can see to the emplying of such men, arises from the suspicion with which all ecclesiastics may be regarded by the native community, owing to the discredit which some over-zealous missionarie have brought upon the whole class to which they belong.

Yours sincerely
S. Lobb.

X.

Chinsurah Nov. 17. 1867.

Dear Greesh Chunder,

I send you another and tolerably large contribution on Positivism. This with the one you already have will I suppose keep you going for some time.

As you don't seem very timid as to what you insert, I have come out rather strong in the concluding section. I have done so because in one of your letters you seemed to think the system a repulsive one to your countrymen on account of the science. Of course any thing that you like to omit or even modify I leave to your judgment entirely.

The article on miracles in the last number of the Bengalee is very well done. It puts the case very neatly. What I think requires to be clearly brought out is that when events now occur which would have been termed miraculous in former ages, we instinctively refer them to some natural operation, and our interpretations, as in the case of table-turning, spirit-rapping &c. &c., may not always be satisfactory, but we feel assured that these phenomena may and will be accounted for at some time upon a natural hypothesis. There is a danger now-a-days of rejecting all evidence when any unaccountable phenomena are concerned, instead of accepting the facts and suspending our judgement till some consistent theory can be established.

Yours sincerely
S. Lobb.

XI.

Chinsurah Nov. 24. 1867.

Dear Greesh Chunder,

I send you an extract from the new edition of Lewes's History of Philosophy, containing an estimate of the Positive Religion; I have added a very few observations of my own. The passage quoted will I think be interesting to many.

If you insert it do not make it one of the series on Positivism, but let it appear as an independent article, and if you have no objection after you have exhausted the materials already supplied.

I have not forgotten your promise to give us a lecture here, and shall put your name down on the list. I propose to commence the series in January (the first to be delivered on 18th Jan.) and to terminate it in April. What month would suit you best ?

How does the "Canning Institute " prosper ? Did you see that the Hindoo Patriot made me out a Roman Catholic ? Who could have given the Editor such a piece of information I cannot in the least imagine. I have written to contradict the statement.

Yours sincerely
S. Lobb.

XII.

Dear Greesh,

I send you a few remarks on Professor Krishna Kamal's article in the last number of the Bengalee. My remarks are short as I have not much time to spare just now The subject, however, is one which admits of much discussion and explanation.

Objections may be brought against Comte's ideal, but in bringing objections it should always be remembered that *it is* an ideal. Would Prof. K. K. B. for instance have a religious ideal do otherwise than advise men to be *thoroughly honest, virtuous, sober, sedate, manly and dignified.* From a religious or ideal point of view they ought to be such, and when men are found who are not such, religion should try its best to make them such. Comte never expected his system to be rigorously enforced ; he always trusted for its acceptance merely to the formation of a strong public opinion, and when that opinion was strongest he was well aware that it could never be quite universal. Hence the *practical* power supplements and diminishes the rigour of the *theoretical* power.

The real difficulty is this—is it probable from what we know of human nature that public opinion will ever be so organised as to accept by simple force of persuasion the ideal which Comte has furnished as an ideal to which it is desirable that our practice should conform.

I have received a letter from the Editor of the National, and he consents to my printing Mr. Macdonald's articles with the reply. No names are to be mentioned. Will you kindly communicate with Baboo Nobo Gopal Mitra on the subject ?

Yours sincerely
S. Lobb.

You have paid me a great compliment in your Review. I think you have hit the points on which stress ought to be laid. Your demolition of the analogy between the Creator and the Sower is not bad.

XIII.

Dec. 7. 1867.

Dear Greesh Chunder,

I send you herewith another contribution on Positivism. This with what you already have will I think last until my return to Chinsurah at the end of this month. Mr. Nesfield tells me that he intends taking in your paper. I enclose Mr. Congreve's last letter to me which you might like to see, please return it when read. I did not think the 3rd article on miracles so good as the first two, which were really excellent. Whenever you introduce the Divine Power, you necessarily introduce miraculous agency, and if we assume the miracle of creation I can see no good reason why we should not allow the possibility of any other miracle. Either supernatural agency is an hypothesis employed to veil our ignorance, or it is a true cause. If the former is the case, it should be altogether dismissed when its artificial nature is manifest; but if the latter is the correct view, I do not see how we can object to the general principle of miracles though we may for good reason reject this or that particular miracle. I do not think the difficulty is surmounted by withdrawing special cases from the Divine influence, and limiting that influence to the creation of some whole or complete organisation. Once introduce the action of Divine Power and you cannot consistently limit it to any particular sphere, it must be universal and it must operate in a way which reason cannot comprehend. The objection that "with God all things are possible" seems to me a perfectly valid one against those who assume the existence of a supernatural power, but also bind that power down to work merely in accordance with certain pre-conceived notions of their own minds. The more the matter is considered, the more I think it will become clear that we must either frankly accept one of the many theologies, or, altogether setting aside the supernatural, build our altars, like the Athenians of old, to the *unknown* God. We may recognise the mystery of existence without attempting to penetrate those secrets which have been for ever hidden from our view.

What does the native community think of the appointment of Dr. Robson? He seems to me a more direct violation of the standard rule, than even the appointment of Lal Behary Dey. The Educational Department is certainly being turned into a refuge for the destitute. Another somewhat peculiar appointment is that of Mr. Hordern to be Director of Public Instruction in Burmah—that gentleman since his entry into our Department having been generally conspicuous by his absence.

I leave Chinsurah tomorrow in the afternoon and shall return in about a fortnight when I hope to supply you with some more articles on Positivism. Perhaps, however the subject is getting stale and you may require your columns for more pressing and generally interesting matter. If so, do not hesitate to let me know.

Yours sincerley

S. Lobb.

P. S. I have put my observations on Miracles into the form of a letter, which you can correct if you like.

XIV.

Chinsurah Feb. 19. 1868.

Dear Greesh Chunder,

If we will have Bishops to lecture at our institutes and preside at our meetings we must not be astonished if they treat us to a bit of their mind. It is their business and they are not likely to let such opportunities escape them. But still if they speak their mind freely they must of course expect voters and seconders of thanks to be frank also—and herein they offer an advantage to their adversaries, which I see from your letter *you* have been very ready to avail yourself of. I admire your pluck in standing up so manfully for an unfashionable and unpopular system. The colours of triumph are reserved now-a-days for the Keshubs and the young enthusiasts who, as I said to Koylas once, pretend to be intimately acquainted with the designs of their God, while they cannot agree among themselves on the fundamental doctrines of their creed. These men while they despise Christianity (which the Missionaries and others don't seem to see) have really adopted a faith which is but Christianity cut away from its essential basis, viz. revelation. It is this similarity which excites the hopes of Anglican Bishops and Scotch Presbyters that they may one day see a Christian Church in India. I should think you could enlighten them as to the mistake which they commit.

I don't agree with Bishop Colenso about the study of Hebrew. Any man of ordinary common sense can extract from an English Bible all that is necessary to be learnt. It is not on record that the inquisitive Zulu who converted the African Bishop was deeply read in Hebrew or any other dead language. The English proletariat with a knowledge merely of the mother tongue has long ago arrived at the conclusions which Colenso is now laboriously and learnedly impressing upon the middle and upper classes. Colenso manages to reconcile himself, and conscientiously so no doubt, to remaining in the Church of England, but I think it would be better for his fame and for the world at large were he to give up his Bishopric and preach to men a new gospel founded on a wider and more substantial basis than the Anglican Prayer Book.

Your country I believe has a noble mission to fulfil in the future, and that mission is an intellectual and spiritual one. There is much danger in the present state of things that men here should be led away by visionary dreams of commercial activity and political aggrandisement. The problems of commerce and politics must I think be worked out by the West, but Bengal can accomplish a revolution most important to the interests of humanity if she concentrates her attention upon man's spiritual future. We are too much fettered in Europe to work out the religious problem with success. The conclusions which your educated country-men reach will be unbiassed and when they govern the actions of any large body of men will not fail to communicate an impetus to the whole race. I am glad to hear you have gained so distinguished an adherent to the cause of Positivism as the Hon. Dwarka Nath Mittra. Such a man is worth a thousand of the raw recruits of Brahmoism— the beardless youths who can read the secret decrees of heaven before they have mastered the elements of arithmetic.

Yours sincerely

S. Lobb.

XV.

Chinsurah April 1. 1868.

Dear Creesh,

Please only send me one copy of the Bengalee in future unless I specially order more.

I read your proceedings at the Canning Institute. I must tell you candidly I think these *sermons* which the Hon. Justice is constantly delivering are in very bad taste and calculated to do no good. Your speech was interesting, and Sir Richard Temple's was a model of good taste and masculine eloquence but all the rest was sorry stuff to my mind.

Yours sincerely
S. Lobb.

Will you send me a copy of your lecture?

XVI.

April 12. 1868.

My Dear Greesh,

I send you some of my perhaps crude ideas on woman. It strikes me *entre nons* that the Hon. Justice Fhear and Co. talk a great deal of nonsense, and exercise very bad taste in preaching sermons when they are merely called upon to amuse. I don't interfere myself in these matters, because I think where I understand so little it would be an impertinence to give advice, and I am certain that in the present disordered state of things in Europe we Englishmen are not in a position to give much advice to others till we have set our own house in order. Perhaps you will say I belie myself then by writing as I do in my letter, well it may [be] I do to a certain extent for we are few of us thoroughly consistent; but what I want to bring out is the danger of tampering with a woman's faith till you can put something in its place, and that this something will be better discovered by Hindoos themselves than by Europeans, and that under any circumstances the present is not the time for any such experiment.

I have asked Mr. Tagore to postpone his lecture so kindly omit the advertisement in future. I have not been feeling at all well of late, and am trying what the air of Chandernagore will do for me. The change I think is benefitting me considerably.

I read your paper in the Social Science Transactions: it was interesting and amusing. To me it disclosed quite a new world.

You see I don't make use of the term *lady* which I regard as mean and conventional, whereas *woman* has a noble ring about it and is good for all ages, all climes, all circumstances. When a man is reading a grave ethical lecture upon the other *sex*, and talks all through about the *ladies* the impression produced upon one's mind is partly painful and partly ludicrous. Ladies and gentlemen are very good conventional terms but were never intended to be used when dignity was required. You will think me in a critical mood, but I am inclined to believe that many of your countrymen are led astray as to the exact purport and use of the terms *ladies* and *gentlemen*.

Yours sincerely,
S. Lobb.

XVII.

Chinsurah April 23. 1868.

My Dear Greesh,

Mr. Harrison is very anxious that I should write an article in the Calcutta Review on the " Training of Women " from the point of view I took in the article you so kindly published last Saturday. I have told him I know nothing about the subject in its details, but he will insist on my making the attempt and I do not altogether like to refuse him.

Now could you give me some facts which might serve as a basis for an Essay, and could you indicate the best sources whence I may draw information on the subject considered generally ?

I am glad you think there is some force in the view which I take and if you would assist me in working it out a little more elaborately I should feel infinitely obliged. If I cannot get reliable materials to work upon I shall decline to write the article.

Yours sincerely
S. Lobb.

XVIII.

July 24. 1868.

Dear Greesh,

This batch completes the view of Positivism. I have here given Comte's social doctrine at tolerable length—it is taken almost wholly from the Catechism.

I may add a table or two to the pamphlet when it is ready.

Your speech reads very well in the Daily News of today (Friday). The whole proceedings of that evening really make a very interesting little episode in the history of positivism. You certainly go in very strong for the details, stronger I think than I as yet feel inclined to go in. The principal point to keep before the public mind is the contradictory nature of all the theological and metaphysical solutions of the social problem. Once convinced of the sandy nature of the old foundations and they must have recourse to a human basis.

There are several points in Mr. Macdonald's lecture I should like to notice, and may perlaps trouble you with a letter on the subject.

Yours sincerely,
S. Lobb.

I have sent a copy of your life of Ram Doolal to Mr. Congreve, who, as I suppose you are aware, is an eminent Positivist. He will be interested to read such a faithful picture of Hindoo life. Do you feel inclined to give us another lecture here before October.

Mr. Cantopher has desired me to send you a copy of his poems. He is very anxious to get them reviewed. I can't say they are by any means first rate, but he is a tender-hearted man, so if you review them don't be too hard.

XIX.

October 10, 1868.

Dear Greesh,

Thanks for the number of that National. I think the article admits of a very good answer, but I am too busy just now to enter the lists. The critic has not properly interpreted me on several points, and he uses against me language of my own which was only intended as an *adhominem* appeal to the Edinburgh Review.

I send you the corrected proofs and shall be obliged if you can let me have some more sheets. I shall have to add several foot notes.

The P. and O. Steamer I find is not expected before the 15th or 16th so I shall probably be here till next Friday or Saturday.

I am glad Professor Krishna Kamal is going to write an article from a Comtean point of view. I am very anxious to see Positivism discussed from a purely Hindu point of view, a task to which of course I am myself inadequate. You give us at times a Positive Hindu appreciation of things and this is what is required if you gentlemen are anxious to form a school of Indian thought.

I am not sanguine as to the effect of proof against theologians and metaphysicians. Kant has shown us that insoluble problems may be proved in two ways—thus it is equally possible *in foro rationis* to shew that the world had a beginning, or that it could not have had a beginning. proof cannot decide either way. The great argument against Theology and Metaphysics is that they have failed to perform the task to which they aspired, and that they give no one consistent solution of the problems which they attempt to solve. They were useful provisionally but are not adapted for the mature intellect of mankind.

The article in the National is temperately written, and I hope we may continue to carry on the discussion upon its own merits without indulging in personalities or useless recrimination.

Tell me candidly if you ever find my arguments unintelligible. The National seems to think them heavy and confused—if they are so to the generality of minds, then I must confess them weak and untrustworthy, for I always regard confusion as a sure sign of irrationality.

Yours sincerely
S. Lobb.

CPSIA information can be obtained at www.ICGtesting.com
Printed in the USA
BVOW06s1132020916

460972BV00023B/340/P